VIOLENCE, CRIME AND MENTALLY DISORDERED OFFENDERS

WILEY SERIES IN
FORENSIC CLINICAL PSYCHOLOGY

Edited by

Clive R. Hollin

Centre for Applied Psychology, The University of Leicester, UK

and

Mary McMurran

Centre for Applied Psychology, The University of Leicester, UK

COGNITIVE BEHAVIOURAL TREATMENT OF SEXUAL
OFFENDERS
William L. Marshall, Dana Anderson and Yolanda Fernandez

VIOLENCE, CRIME AND MENTALLY DISORDERED
OFFENDERS: Concepts and methods for effective treatment
and prevention
Sheilagh Hodgins and Rüdiger Müller-Isberner (*Editors*)

VIOLENCE, CRIME AND MENTALLY DISORDERED OFFENDERS

Concepts and Methods for Effective Treatment and Prevention

Edited by

Sheilagh Hodgins

University of Montreal, Quebec, Canada, and
The Karolinska Institute, Stockholm, Sweden

Rüdiger Müller-Isberner

Haina Forensic Psychiatric Hospital, Haina, Germany

JOHN WILEY & SONS, LTD
Chichester · New York · Weinheim · Brisbane · Singapore · Toronto

Other Wiley Editorial Offices

John Wiley & Sons Inc., 111 River Street, Hoboken, NJ 07030, USA

Jossey-Bass, 989 Market Street, San Francisco, CA 94103-1741, USA

Wiley-VCH Verlag GmbH, Boschstr. 12, D-69469 Weinheim, Germany

John Wiley & Sons Australia Ltd, 33 Park Road, Milton, Queensland 4064, Australia

John Wiley & Sons (Asia) Pte Ltd, 2 Clementi Loop #02-01, Jin Xing Distripark, Singapore 129809

John Wiley & Sons Canada Ltd, 22 Worcester Road, Etobicoke, Ontario, Canada M9W 1L1

Library of Congress Cataloging-in-Publication Data

Violence, crime, and mentally disordered offenders : concepts and methods in effective
treatment and prevention / edited by Sheilagh Hodgins, Rüdiger Müller-Isberner.
        p. cm. — (Wiley series in forensic clinical psychology)
     Includes bibliographical references and index.
     ISBN 0-471-97727-6 (paper)
       1.   Criminals—Mental health.   2. Prisoners—Mental health.   3. Criminals—Mental
health services.   4. Prisoners—Mental health services.   I. Hodgins, Sheilagh.   II. Müller-
Isberner, Rüdiger. III. Series

RC451.4.P68 V56 2000
616.89'0086'927—dc21

                                                              99–053687

British Library Cataloguing in Publication Data

A catalogue record for this book is available from the British Library

ISBN 0-471-97727-6

Typeset in 10/12pt Palatino by Dorwyn Ltd, Rowlands Castle, Hants
Printed and bound in Great Britain by Antony Rowe Ltd, Chippenham, Wiltshire.
This book is printed on acid-free paper responsibly manufactured from sustainable forestry
in which at least two trees are planted for each one used for paper production.

We would like to dedicate this book to our children, Nora Isberner and Sean Raboy. They inspire us to always remember that things can and do change for the better.

CONTENTS

ABOUT THE EDITORS

Sheilagh Hodgins

Sheilagh Hodgins completed her PhD in clinical psychology at McGill University, where she spent many hours in courses and informal discussions with D. O. Hebb. Inspired and motivated by this insightful teacher, she embarked on a career studying the relationship between psychopathology and violence with a view to a more fundamental understanding of how biological, psychological and social factors interact to determine behaviour. Her work has focused on aetiological factors (genetic factors, perinatal factors, parenting, early childhood functioning) and the development of persons with schizophrenia and the major affective disorders who display antisocial behaviour from an early age.

Rüdiger Müller-Isberner

Rüdiger Müller-Isberner, having completed his specialist training in psychiatry, was appointed as Director of the forensic hospital for the German state of Hessen, with inpatient and outpatient treatments for persons with major mental disorders, antisocial personality disorders, sex offenders, and offender rehabilitation. He and his collaborators have developed specific programmes designed to address the needs of the various categories of mentally disordered offenders and also a structured, multi-component, intensive after-care programme. In addition to directing the hospital, Dr Müller-Isberner initiated and participates in the translation and validation of the PCL-R, the PCL-SV, the HCR-20 and the SVR-20 and is the author of numerous publications on the treatment of mentally disordered offenders and on risk assessment.

LIST OF CONTRIBUTORS

Joseph Bloom, MD

School of Medicine, Oregon Health Sciences University, Mail code: L 102, 3181 S.W. Sam Jackson Park Road, Portland, OR 97201–3098, USA

Heather Burke, MA

Department of Psychology, Simon Fraser University, Burnaby, British Columbia, Canada V5A 1S6

Leslie Citrome, MD, MPH

Director, Clinical Research and Evaluation Facility, Nathan S. Kline Institute for Psychiatric Research, 140 Old Orangeburg Road, Orangeburg, NY 10962, USA

Derek Eaves, MD

Forensic Psychiatric Services Commission, Forensic Psychiatric Institute, 70 Colony Farm Road, Port Coquitlam, British Columbia, Canada V3C 5X9

Stephen D. Hart, PhD

Department of Psychology, Simon Fraser University, Burnaby, British Columbia, Canada V5A 1S6

Kirk Heilbrun, PhD

Department of Clinical and Health Psychology, MCP Hahnemann University, Mail Stop 626, 245 North 15th Street, Philadelphia, Pennsylvania 19102–1192, USA

Sheilagh Hodgins, PhD

Department of Psychology, University of Montreal, C.P. 6128, Succursale Centre-Ville, Montreal, Quebec, Canada H3C 3J7

Rüdiger Müller-Isberner, MD

Haina Forensic Psychiatric Hospital, Hohe-Lohr-Weg 10, D-35114 Haina, Germany

Norbert Nedopil, MD

Abteilung fur Forensische Psychiatrie, Nervenklinik der Universität München, Nussbaumstrasse 7, D-80336 München, Germany

Lori Peters

Department of Clinical and Health Psychology, MCP Hahnemann University, Mail Stop 626, 245 North 15th Street, Philadelphia, Pennsylvania 19102–1192, USA

George Tien, PhD

6061 Chancellor Boulevard, Vancouver, British Columbia, Canada V6T 1E8

Jari Tiihonen, MD, PhD

Department of Forensic Psychiatry, University of Kuopio, Niuvanniemi Hospital, FIN-70240 Kuopio, Finland

Jan Volavka, MD, PhD

Chief, Clinical Research Division, Nathan S. Kline Institute for Psychiatric Research, 140 Old Orangeburg Road, Building 37, Orangeburg, NY 10962, USA

Derek Wilson, MA

Forensic Psychiatric Services Commission, Forensic Psychiatric Institute, 70 Colony Farm Road, Port Coquitlam, British Columbia, Canada V3C 5X9

William H. Wilson, MD

Associate Professor of Psychiatry, Oregon Health Sciences University, Mail Code UHN-79, 3181 S.W. Sam Jackson Park Road, Portland, OR 97068, USA

Steve Wong, PhD

Regional Psychiatric Center, PO Box 9243, 2520 Central Avenue, Saskatoon, Saskatchewan, Canada S7K 3X5

SERIES EDITORS' PREFACE

ABOUT THE SERIES

At the time of writing it is clear that we live in a time, certainly in the UK and other parts of Europe, if perhaps less so in other parts of the world, when there is renewed enthusiasm for constructive approaches to working with offenders to prevent crime. What do we mean by this statement and what basis do we have for making it?

First, by "constructive approaches to working with offenders" we mean bringing the use of effective methods and techniques of behaviour change into work with offenders. Indeed, this might pass as a definition of forensic clinical psychology. Thus, our focus is application of theory and research in order to develop practice aimed at bringing about a change in the offender's functioning. The word *constructive* is important and can be set against approaches to behaviour change that seek to operate by destructive means. Such destructive approaches are typically based on the principles of deterrence and punishment, seeking to suppress the offender's actions through fear and intimidation. A constructive approach, on the other hand, seeks to bring about changes in an offender's functioning that will produce, say, enhanced possibilities of employment, greater levels of self-control, better family functioning, or increased awareness of the pain of victims.

A constructive approach faces the criticism of being a "soft" response to damage caused by offenders, neither inflicting pain and punishment nor delivering retribution. This point raises a serious question for those involved in working with offenders. Should advocates of constructive approaches oppose retribution as a goal of the criminal justice system as incompatible with treatment and rehabilitation? Alternatively, should constructive work with offenders take place within a system given to retribution? We believe that this issue merits serious debate.

However, to return to our starting point, history shows that criminal justice systems are littered with many attempts at constructive work with offenders, not all of which have been successful. In raising the spectre of success, the second part of our opening sentence now merits attention: that is, "constructive approaches to working with offenders *to prevent crime*". In order to achieve the goal of preventing crime, interventions must focus on the right targets for behaviour change. In addressing this crucial point, Andrews and Bonta (1994) have formulated the *need principle*:

> Many offenders, especially high-risk offenders, have a variety of needs. They need places to live and work and/or they need to stop taking drugs. Some have poor self-esteem, chronic headaches or cavities in their teeth. These are all "needs". The need principle draws our attention to the distinction between *criminogenic* and *noncriminogenic* needs. Criminogenic needs are a subset of an offender's risk level. They are dynamic attributes of an offender that, when changed, are associated with changes in the probability of recidivism. Non-criminogenic needs are also dynamic and changeable, but these changes are not necessarily associated with the probability of recidivism. (p. 176)

Thus, successful work with offenders can be judged in terms of bringing about change in noncriminogenic need *or* in terms of bringing about change in criminogenic need. While the former is important and, indeed, may be a necessary precursor to offence-focused work, it is changing criminogenic need that, we argue, should be the touchstone of working with offenders.

While, as noted above, the history of work with offenders is not replete with success, the research base developed since the early 1990s, particularly the meta-analyses (e.g. Lösel, 1995), now strongly supports the position that effective work with offenders to prevent further offending is possible. The parameters of such evidence-based practice have become well established and widely disseminated under the banner of "What Works" (McGuire, 1995).

It is important to state that we are not advocating that there is only one approach to preventing crime. Clearly there are many approaches, with different theoretical underpinnings, that can be applied. Nonetheless, a tangible momentum has grown in the wake of the "What Works" movement as academics, practitioners, and policy makers seek to capitalise on the possibilities that this research raises for preventing crime. The task now facing many service agencies lies in turning the research into effective practice.

Our aim in developing this Series in Forensic Clinical Psychology is to produce texts that review research and draw on clinical expertise to advance effective work with offenders. We are both committed to the ideal of evidence-based practice and we will encourage contributors to the Series to follow this approach. Thus, the books published in the Series will not be practice manuals or "cook books": they will offer readers authoritative and critical information through which forensic clinical practice can develop. We are both enthusiastic about the contribution to effective practice that this Series can make and look forward to it developing in the years to come.

ABOUT THIS BOOK

Those of us working with mentally disordered offenders need to understand the complexities of aetiology, assessment, treatment, and management of our patients. Keeping abreast of the academic and professional literature is a daunting task for many busy practitioners. We are delighted to see these major issues described and explained so eruditely for us in this book and in respect of a range of mental disorders. It is laudable too that the Editors, Sheilagh Hodgins a clinical psychologist and Rüdiger Müller-Isberner a psychiatrist, have drawn together contributions from the academic–professional disciplines of clinical psychology and psychiatry, both of which have so much to offer in respect of understanding and treating mentally disordered offenders.

Crimes committed by mentally disordered offenders excite much public interest and professionals involved in risk assessment and risk reduction through treatment are seemingly expected to be infallible with this particular group. The material presented here is firmly based upon evidence of "what works" and as such is consistent with the ethos of this Series. Evidence-based practice will never equal error-free perfection, but to practise in any other way is to court disaster and invite justifiable criticism. We are pleased, therefore, to be instrumental in presenting this excellent text to a professional readership who we are sure will make good practical use of the material.

February 2000   Clive Hollin and Mary McMurran

PREFACE

We wrote this book for clinicians and administrators who in their daily work struggle to identify, implement and conduct effective treatment programmes for mentally disordered offenders. We wanted to present to them the most up-to-date information about what works and what doesn't work. Our aim was to present this information in a manner that it could be readily adapted to different clinical settings and used to improve existing programmes or to establish new ones. This is necessary because clinicians and administrators who are responsible for the care of mentally disordered offenders simply do not have the time to find, read and integrate the relevant scientific literature which is dispersed throughout many sub-fields. Unfortunately, the forensic psychiatric and psychological journals include few articles on effective treatment. They are filled with research on assessing the risk of violent behaviour, which as we note is essential for effective treatment, and on laws and regulations, while ignoring, in large part, how to treat different types of mentally disordered offenders. This may be due, at least to some extent, to the large investment of so many academics and so much money in assessing mentally disordered offenders when they commit a criminal offence as compared to the small investment in long-term treatment.

The authors are all clinician–researchers who brought to their task many years of clinical training and experience with mentally disordered offenders. They have skillfully used their experience to evaluate and filter the relevant scientific evidence. Their understanding of the scientific literature and their ability to draw practical conclusions from the published research and to make concrete recommendations is evident in each chapter.

In our experience, the problems confronted by clinicians and administrators who care for mentally disordered offenders in many different countries are remarkably similar. While the laws, regulations and administrative structures vary quite considerably from one jurisdiction to another, staff, politicians and the public share similar fears and reject mentally disordered offenders. The knowledge reviewed in this volume provides an empirical basis for the development of effective treatment for different types of mentally disordered offenders. This knowledge is applicable and useful virtually everywhere.

Throughout this volume we try to incite clinicians and administrators responsible for the care of mentally disordered offenders to participate in building an empirical basis for the treatment of these patients. By breaking out of their isolation and exchanging information with colleagues who, daily, face similar challenges and responsibilities, clinicians and administrators may well find that their burden feels less heavy. By evaluating their treatment programmes, as we advocate, clinicians and researchers begin to contribute not only to improving the programmes for which they are personally responsible, but also to building an empirical base for the effective treatment of mentally disordered offenders everywhere.

We welcome feedback from readers about the extent to which we have achieved our objectives. We recognize that "knowing how something should be done" and "doing it" is not always easy. The research reviewed demonstrates, however, that "it can be done" with a lot of effort and perseverance. Hopefully, this volume will be a useful tool and a source of encouragement to those who wish to try.

We have learned a lot in writing this book, both from each other and from the authors. Rüdiger Müller-Isberner, the director of a large security hospital for the state of Hessen in Germany, ensured that the scientific literature was reviewed in a manner that was useful to clinicians and administrators. Sheilagh Hodgins, a university-based researcher, attempted to ensure that the literature reviews were complete and that empirical proof was available for all the conclusions that were drawn. We hope that, if nothing else, our collaboration demonstrates the benefits of collaboration between clinicians and researchers.

We want to thank the contributors to this volume. Despite their heavy workloads, they spent many, many hours studying the scientific literature relevant to their topics, writing and re-writing their chapters. Their professionalism, seriousness and sense of humour in the face of our requests for re-writes, knowledge and clinical expertise made collaborating with them a very pleasant learning experience. As we hope the reader will agree, they have done an exceptional job! We express our gratitude to each of them.

There are also many other persons that we would like to thank. Sheilagh would like to acknowledge and thank the numerous clinicians from around the world who have so patiently responded to her incessant questions about what they do and how they do it. Rüdiger would like to thank all of his colleagues at the Haina Forensic Psychiatric Hospital, in particular Sara Gonzalez Cabeza, Sabine Eucker, Petra Born, Dieter Jöckel, and Roland Freese. During these past years, these colleagues helped to conceive and develop the idea that there is an urgent need to build an evidence-based approach to the treatment of mentally disordered offenders by providing constructive criticism of the day-to-day treatment practices.

SHEILAGH HODGINS
RÜDIGER MÜLLER-ISBERNER

INTRODUCTION

Sheilagh Hodgins
AND
Rüdiger Müller-Isberner

This book is addressed to mental health professionals and administrators who, on a daily basis, are called upon to provide care to persons who present both mental disorders and a history of criminal offending and/or repetitive aggressive behaviour towards others. The book provides a practical, feasible guide to the treatment of individuals with five types of mental disorders—brain damage, personality disorders, psychopathy, schizophrenia and major affective disorders—who have a history of offending and/or violence. The authors are all clinician/researchers with many years of experience. They have critically reviewed the scientific literature relevant to their subject in order to identify treatments with proven efficacy. They analyse these findings not only to establish their scientific validity, but also in an effort to assess their feasibility and applicability in clinical settings. The authors use their clinical experience to temper the results of the empirical studies. Based on the scientific evidence and the clinical reality, the authors make specific treatment recommendations for each population.

The book does not deal with the laws and regulations affecting the disposition of mentally disordered individuals who offend. These laws and the resulting practices differ in many ways from one country to another. Rather, this book deals with what is similar to so many countries in the Western industrialized world since mental health care was deinstitutionalized. There is now a large population of chronically mentally disordered offenders who are rejected not only by the public but also by general mental health services. This book attempts to provide the most up-to-date, empirically-based evidence on the treatment and management of this population in a manner that is accessible and practical for those who are in a position to apply it.

Clinicians and administrators who are responsible for the treatment of mentally disordered offenders and other violent patients, often feel as marginalized from general mental health services as their patients are from society. General psychiatric services are reluctant to accept, and in many cases openly resist, the transfer of patients from forensics services and social services hesitate to integrate forensic patients into community housing designated for the mentally disordered. This situation is due, in part, to the characteristics of mentally disordered offenders who typically present several chronic co-morbid mental disorders, poor psychosocial functioning and a long history of antisocial behaviour. Often, general psychiatric and social services, especially those offered in the community, demand life and social skills that most mentally disordered offenders do not have. While the rejection of forensic psychiatric patients by general psychiatric and social services is due, in part, to the inappropriateness and inadequacy of these services to meet their needs, it is also due to general mental health professionals' lack of knowledge about mentally disordered offenders, about the conditions in which they present risks, and lack of confidence in forensic clinicians who treat and assess risk in this population. By implementing treatment programmes that are based on empirical proof of efficacy, and evaluating and gradually refining them and thereby increasing their efficacy, not only will the rejection of forensic patients be reduced, but so will the spurning of forensic clinicians.

Mentally disordered offenders, as all clinicians and administrators who attempt to care for them know, present multiple problems, each requiring treatment and management. The primary mental disorder has to be treated and managed, as do the secondary and tertiary ones, and in addition the offending and/or aggressive behaviour needs to be eliminated. This necessitates, in turn, knowledge about the effective treatment of each of the various problems. Concretely, it means keeping up with the ever-growing literature on the most effective treatment for each mental disorder (and of course, each sub-type), on treatments that have been shown to be effective in reducing antisocial and aggressive behaviours, on ways to combine and co-ordinate these various treatments, and on strategies that have proved effective to ensure patient compliance. This is an impossible task, given the explosion of knowledge about mental disorders, violence and offending. This task is further complicated by the almost complete separation between the literature on the effective treatment of the various disorders and forensic treatment, and consequently of knowledge indicating whether treatments that have been shown to be effective with non-offender patients are also effective with a patient with the same primary disorder and a long history of antiso-cial behaviour.

Not only is knowledge of a vast and ever-growing scientific literature necessary, so are human and financial resources. Explaining to politicians, civil servants, and the public the need for funds for services for mentally disordered offenders is an additional and onerous task that many forensic clinicians and administrators must attend to. It requires much time and patience that could be well used otherwise. However, requesting funds in order to implement treatment programmes that have been proved to be effective, and then insisting that the funding continue by empirically dem-onstrating the positive impact of the programme, keeps the discussion calm and rational, avoids ideological debates, and increases the likelihood of a favourable response. This book is an effort to provide clinicians and admin-istrators with ammunition to use to convince those who fund their services of the importance and usefulness of treatment and management.

The book has 10 chapters. The first chapter describes a series of principles for the effective treatment of mentally disordered offenders. It lays out a framework in which readers can readily incorporate the material presented in subsequent chapters, including (a) an overview of the common features of effective treatments for the mentally disordered and effective rehabilitation strategies for offenders; (b) a discussion of the institutional framework necessary for service delivery (organization, staffing requirements, staff se-lection, training and supervision); (c) security problems during treatment; (d) evaluating treatment efficacy; and (e) special issues (dealing with politi-cians, the media and ethical dilemmas).

Chapters 2 to 7 all follow the same format. Each chapter begins with a clear and precise definition of the disorder in question. Next, a review of the outcome studies on treatments aimed at preventing criminality and violence among persons with this disorder are presented. In this review, an effort is made to distinguish pure and co-morbid forms of the disorder and their responses to treatment, and to take account of other individual factors that affect the response to a particular treatment. Next, contradictions in the outcome literature that has been reviewed are discussed and, hopefully, explained. In conclusion, the authors offer their opinions as to the best treatment for preventing criminality and violence among persons with the disorder in question.

Chapter 2 describes effective treatments for a population not often discussed, especially by forensic experts—persons with brain damage who behave aggressively. Only in a small proportion of cases does the aggression lead to charges in criminal court. However, the aggressive behaviour is the principal target of treatment, as it is this aspect of the disorder which often necessitates long-term inpatient care and limits the possibility of re-integration into the community. The chapter distinguishes between disorders of the elderly, particularly dementias, and traumatic damage to younger persons as the treatment goals and effective strategies for these two sub-populations differ. The similarity of the effective treatments with this population and with both psychotic and personality-disordered offenders is to be noted.

Chapter 3 describes the very limited empirical base of knowledge for the treatment of individuals with personality disorders. The chapter begins with a description of the development of the concept of personality disorders and of the diagnostic criteria for each disorder. Acknowledging the lack of empirical evidence for these categories, and for the categorical approach to personality in general, the chapter recommends the use of a dimensional approach for documenting traits and behaviours. This approach, it is suggested, produces specific targets for treatment. The effect of the treatment on the target behaviour can then be measured empirically. This alternative to the traditional way of diagnosing and treating personality disorders is less overwhelming for both the patient and the clinician, and is more likely to lead to the development of treatments that are effective in preventing crime and violence.

Chapter 4 takes on the challenge of the effective treatment of psychopathy. As a result of many failures to successfully modify the behaviour of individuals with psychopathy who had a long history of offending, most countries currently provide no treatment, only incarceration, for this population. However, in some countries the law requires that treatment be provided, at least to the small number of offenders who meet the diagnostic criteria for psychopathy. Psychopaths are the most active of all offenders. Their criminal careers span four, five, even six decades. In addition, these individuals leave in their wake numerous victims who are never heard from in the criminal court. Despite their limited numbers, the costs, both human and financial, related directly to these behaviours, to their offending, to their prosecution and to their incarceration are enormous. In addition, there are all the costs associated with psychopaths' manipulation of the legal and mental health systems. A few courageous clinicians and administrators have accepted the challenge of treating incarcerated psychopaths. While there is as yet no empirical evidence of efficacy for such programmes, a wealth of clinical experience with this population and knowledge of effective interventions with other types of offenders are being used to develop new programmes. The rationale and description of such a programme is described.

Chapter 5 describes the treatment of persons with schizophrenia who commit crimes. This is a problem that has emerged since mental health care was deinstitutionalized. It requires the identification of strategies for providing consistent, rather than intensive care over many decades, addressing each of the multiple behavioural, emotional and cognitive difficulties presented by the offender afflicted with the schizophrenia. In addition, it requires finding ways to get the patient to comply with all the various interventions that are needed. The chapter reviews the efficacy of various medications and psychosocial interventions for preventing recidivism.

Chapter 6 addresses the treatment of individuals with major affective disorders who offend. This is a neglected area of study and the chapter makes a valuable contribution to filling what is rightly described as a void. It provides a conceptual framework and practical guidelines for the treatment of offenders with recurrent major affective disorders.

Chapters 7 and 8 review the evidence on the effectiveness of various medications for preventing violent behaviour among persons with psychoses, and among those who present both a personality disorder and substance abuse. The authors, experts in psychopharmacology, provide practical guidelines for the use of various medications, highlighting the advantages and the disadvantageous of each.

Because of the chronicity of both the mental disorders and the offending and/or aggressive behaviour, treatment for mentally disordered offenders must be long-term and continuous. In reality, this means that while some time is spent in hospitals or other types of institutions, most time is spent in the community. Chapter 9 reviews the evidence on the effectiveness of community treatment programmes for mentally disordered offenders, which is far more positive and encouraging than is generally realized. Based on what has been learned from the evaluation studies of specialized forensic community treatment programmes, the authors provide practical advice on how such programmes should be structured and implemented in order to prevent recidivism.

The concluding chapter presents an overview of what is known about effective treatment for mentally disordered offenders and how to structure and organize such treatment. It argues for the necessity of implementing evidence-based treatment programmes and for the continual improvement and modification of treatment programmes through the use of empirical evaluation.

Chapter 1

EVIDENCE-BASED TREATMENT FOR MENTALLY DISORDERED OFFENDERS

Rüdiger Müller-Isberner and Sheilagh Hodgins*

Haina Forensic Psychiatric Hospital, Haina, Germany
*Université de Montréal, Quebec, Canada, and The Karolinska Institute, Stockholm, Sweden

INTRODUCTION

Mentally disordered offenders, by definition, are mentally disordered individuals who commit crimes. However, the nature of the relationships between the various mental disorders and criminal behaviour are unclear. The term "mentally disordered offender" has been used to refer to many different types of offenders, for example, mentally ill inmates of correctional facilities, offenders who have been judged incompetent to stand trial, mentally disordered sex offenders, and offenders found guilty but not responsible or only partially responsible due to a mental disorder. The legal terms and definitions vary from one country to another. Even within one jurisdiction, the definitions of particular terms often change over time. Whether or not an offender is judged to be "mentally disordered" depends upon the particular practices of police, prosecutors and the courts on the insanity standards in the jurisdiction where the crime is committed, and on clinical assessments, more than on his/her psychopathology. Whether mentally

Violence, Crime and Mentally Disordered Offenders. Edited by S. Hodgins and R. Müller-Isberner.
© 2000 John Wiley & Sons, Ltd.

disordered offenders are transferred to a psychiatric or a correctional setting, and whether they are treated in the community or in a secure hospital,
depends far more on the laws, regulations, policies, practices and ideologies
of public safety that are particular to each jurisdiction than on the psychopathology or history of criminality of the particular offender. It has been
suggested that the kind of disposal, psychiatric or penal, rests as much upon
chance as upon any more clearly discernible factors (Prins, 1993). The diversity of laws, regulations and organizations for the treatment of mentally
disordered offenders is perplexing and beyond the scope of this book (for an
overview, see a special issue of the *International Journal of Law and Psychiatry*,
16, 1993, which describes some of these national differences).

Regardless of their legal status and how they are labelled, and regardless
of where they are treated, in the mental health or the correctional system,
mentally disordered offenders present multiple challenges to the administrators and clinicians who are charged with their care. Morality, professional ethics and public accountability demand that treatment be based on
empirical evidence of effectiveness. No such basis currently exists for the
treatment of mentally disordered offenders. However, scientific evidence
and a wealth of clinical experience can be used to begin the long process of
developing this necessary empirical base.

This chapter begins with brief descriptions of the principal types of mentally disordered offenders. Next, the procedures for assessing mentally disordered offenders are described, as they differ from those used to assess
patients with no criminal record. Assessment is an integral part of treatment;
the initial assessment provides the information which is used to develop an
individualized treatment programme and subsequent assessments, conducted
during treatment, measure progress. The chapter then examines three bodies
of empirical findings that are relevant to the development of effective treatment programmes for mentally disordered offenders. These findings provide
a solid basis on which to begin developing comprehensive and effective treatment programmes. However, many of the components of treatment that have
been shown to be effective with other clienteles and in other situations have to
be modified for use with mentally disordered offenders. These modifications
involve taking account of the particularities of treatment within security hospitals, of organizational requirements, and of the ethical dilemmas encountered in treating mentally disordered offenders.

MENTALLY DISORDERED OFFENDERS

Persons with brain damage

Brain injury or disease is only rarely directly related to offending. Very
rarely, disease or injury to particular cerebral structures leads to violent

outbursts. Somewhat more common, but still rare, are victims of brain injury who in the years following the trauma gradually undergo changes in personality and become more and more irritable and aggressive. Some commit violent offences and are subsequently institutionalized for long periods. Much more common among persons who have suffered a brain injury is persistent aggressive behaviour which does not lead to criminal charges. Similarly, among the elderly, various degenerative diseases are often characterized by aggressive behaviour. These behaviours are not usually prosecuted. However, they dominate the organization of institutional care for this population and seriously limit the possibilities for living with family or in other types of housing in the community. The expertise and treatments used in reducing aggressive behaviour among persons with brain damage, even when they are treated outside of a forensic system, are similar to those used with formally designated mentally disordered offenders.

Offenders with personality disorders

Most offenders present a pattern of symptoms that have been stable since early adolescence that are sufficient for a diagnosis of at least one personality disorder (see, for example, Hodgins & Côté, 1995). A perusal of the symptoms which constitute personality disorders (in either the DSM or ICD classifications) suggests strongly that several of the symptoms, or traits, constitute a vulnerability for behaviours that would lead to criminal charges. For example, in the DSM-IV, among the general criteria for personality disorders is the lack of impulse control. Among the Cluster A disorders, the two that are genetically related to schizophrenia—paranoid personality disorder and schizotypal personality disorder—include symptoms of suspiciousness, inability to trust others and paranoia. Given the defining characteristics of these disorders, it is not surprising how little is known about them. Persons with these disorders rarely consent to participate in research projects, and usually can only be intensely studied when they commit violent offences. Schizoid personality disorder, like the disorders which constitute what is referred to as the Cluster C disorders—avoidant, dependent, obsessive-compulsive personality disorder—may lower the risk of offending. Cluster B disorders—antisocial, borderline, histrionic and narcissistic—are clearly and directly associated with behaviour patterns that are likely to lead to prosecution in criminal court.

Personality disorders are often complicated by the presence of a long history of substance abuse and the consequent damage to the central nervous system. Less than average verbal intelligence, difficulties in concentration, less than the average level of formal education and little or no history of stable employment provide no base for the development of a non-criminal life-style.

How to conceptualize these constellations of behaviour patterns and characteristics and how to describe them in a way that is useful for treatment remain major obstacles to the development of effective interventions. Further, it is generally assumed that personality traits that emerge gradually through childhood and solidify in adulthood are resistant to change. The question is whether or not it is necessary to modify the personality traits in order to reduce recidivism. Can specific behavioural and cognitive training programmes produce sufficient change in the patterns of behaviour, attitudes, morality and ways of problem solving that are sufficient to alter a lifestyle? That is the challenge and it remains to be seen whether such programmes will produce changes that can support a new, legal life-styles.

These programmes will, for the majority of the individuals concerned, have to include intensive and rather long-term interventions aimed first at reducing and eliminating substance abuse and then at preventing the recurrence of the abuse when life gets tough. While clinicians have long known the difficulty of this task, recent evidence demonstrating hereditary vulnerabilities for abuse of various substances and the neurobiological bases of these dependencies explain, in part, the resistance to change (Bierut et al., 1998; Lappaleinen et al., 1998; Merikangas et al., 1998). These findings clearly indicate the necessity of intensive, highly structured, long-term programmes that help the individual to develop over time, behavioural and cognitive patterns that are inconsistent with abuse of alcohol and/or drugs.

Psychopathy

Psychopaths are a special category of offenders with personality disorders. They are special because they commit the most crimes, the most violent crimes, and because they are thought to be the least changeable of all offenders. This diagnosis does not appear in either the DSM-IV or ICD-10. It has been developed over the past 20 years in studies of incarcerated male offenders, and then used with female offenders, and a modified version with adolescents. The diagnosis is made using Hare's Psychopathy Checklist (PCL-R) (Hare, 1991). Clinicians trained to use the PCL-R obtain high inter-rater agreement and stable ratings over time. The validity of the diagnosis has been established by numerous studies showing that offenders diagnosed as psychopaths (using the PCL-R) have patterns of behaviour, cognition, emotional reactions and central and peripheral nervous system activity that are distinctive, even from offenders who meet criteria for antisocial personality disorder (Cooke, Forth & Hare, 1998).

The prevalence of psychopathy has never been studied in a general population sample. However, a rough estimate can be made from available statistics on antisocial personality disorder. All those who meet the criteria for psychopathy also meet the diagnostic criteria for antisocial personality disorder (DSM-III, DSM-III-R, DSM-IV), but less than one-third of those who meet the criteria for antisocial personality disorder also meet the criteria for psychopathy. Since the prevalence of antisocial personality disorder has been documented at less than 7% in males and 2% in females, the prevalence of psychopathy would be considerably less (Robins, Tipp & Przybeck, 1991). In the justice system, however, psychopaths are numerous. For example, in Canada one in five men who are sentenced to two years or more of incarceration meet the criteria for psychopathy (Hare, 1991), as do between 11% and 20% of women (Côté, Hodgins & Toupin, in press). Whether or not the prevalence of psychopathy varies from one culture to another is still in question (see e.g. Cooke, 1997).

In treatment settings, whether inside or out of the prison system, psychopaths are disruptive. They do not simply refuse to comply with treatment, they often undermine the treatment of other offenders. When and if they do comply with treatment, they have been shown in the past to be able to manipulate it in order to use what they learn to perfect their antisocial skills. In treating psychopaths, therefore, clinicians and administrators not only have to be concerned with achieving efficacy but also with not making them worse than they are already.

Offenders with major mental disorders

The major mental disorders include schizophrenia, major depression, bipolar disorders and atypical (but non-toxic) psychoses. Schizophrenia and bipolar disorder afflict equal numbers of men and women and their prevalence rates are estimated to be approximately 0.85% and 1.6%, respectively (Hodgins, 1996) These rates are similar in all Western industrialized countries, except for the rate of bipolar disorder, which may be lower in Finland than elsewhere (Veijola et al., 1996). The prevalence of major depression is difficult to establish. It appears to be increasing and it varies, somewhat, from one country to another. While one US study estimated the prevalence to be 21.3% among women and 12.7% among men (Kessler et al., 1994) a cross-cultural comparative study which used a less sensitive diagnostic instrument obtained rates varying from 12–22% in women and 6–11% in men (Weissman et al., 1996) The major mental disorders onset in late adolescence or early adulthood and are characterized by recurring acute episodes and poor psychosocial functioning between the episodes (Hodgins, 1996). Among those born since the mid-1940s who developed their disorders in countries that have deinstitutionalized mental health services, the risk of criminality, and especially of violent criminality, is increased as compared to non-disordered persons in the same country (Hodgins, 1998). Recent evidence suggests that while the risk of offending among persons who develop schizophrenia is higher, persons who develop major affective disorders are also at increased risk for violent offences (Brennan, Mednick & Hodgins, submitted). Other evidence suggests that those with an affective disorder, who are generally more compliant with treatment than those with schizophrenia, may recidivate more often because of inadequate and/or inappropriate community care (Hodgins, Lapalme & Toupin, in press). Epidemiological findings indicate that some of these persons display a stable pattern of antisocial behaviour from a young age and are often convicted for crimes before the major mental disorder is manifest (Hodgins, Côté, & Toupin, 1998). Among the others, the first offence occurs after the onset of the disorder. This risk of offending among persons with major mental disorders continues to grow even into the fourth decade of life (Hodgins et al., 1996).

Patients with major mental disorders who offend present multiple difficulties (positive symptoms, negative symptoms, impoverished life skills and social skills) associated with the major mental disorder, each of which requires a specific type of intervention. Those with a history of offending dating from adolescence present a well-entrenched antisocial life-style, which includes substance abuse. Consequently, they require a programme of treatment that includes multiple components designed to address the various aspects of the major mental disorder and to reduce antisocial behaviour and substance abuse. All of these various treatment components have to be coordinated and compliance ensured. Supervision and compulsory inpatient and outpatient care are often required. Special consideration needs to be given to schizophrenic patients with low intelligence who are unable to cope with and to learn in traditional psychoeducational treatment programmes.

Mentally retarded offenders

One large-scale epidemiological study and several studies of incarcerated offenders indicate that the prevalence of offending among both males and females who are mentally retarded is elevated in comparison with the general population (Crocker & Hodgins, 1997). Prosecution and conviction of such offenders often leads to tragedies because within correctional facilities they are targets for abuse by other inmates. Since policies of "normalization" of the retarded were implemented, and they go to school, live and work in the community, the issue of crimes by mentally retarded persons is considered taboo, politically incorrect, and consequently there is almost no research on the subject. This perpetuates the current situation and limits advances in knowledge that would contribute to identifying a solution to the problem. For example, behaviour problems in early adolescence have been shown to characterize the majority of those who go on to offend as adults (Crocker & Hodgins, 1997). This finding, albeit from only one study, suggests that early intervention programmes that target the behaviour problems in childhood and teach prosocial skills might have a positive long-term impact in preventing crime. Yet, almost no research of this type goes on, primarily for ideological reasons. Other research has shown that mentally retarded adults who are arrested have difficulty in responding appropriately to police interrogations and may confess to offences that they did not commit (Clare & Gudjonsson, 1993, 1995).

There is a serious lack of specialized services for mentally retarded offenders. Psychiatrists and psychologists who do pre-trial assessments in order to advise the court on culpability seldom have any specific training in either assessing or treating such patients. Similarly, in forensic hospitals and in the community there are seldom specific programmes for such offenders. Not surprisingly, then, when we set out to edit this book we identified few experts in the world on this issue. In many cases their experience and knowledge was limited to the treatment of aggressive behaviour and behaviour problems of the severely retarded who lived in institutions.

Conclusion

As can be seen from these brief descriptions, mentally disordered offenders are a heterogeneous group. There are important differences both between and within diagnostic groups that are relevant to treatment. A general pattern of characteristics common to mentally disordered offenders can be identified. Most present a long history of difficulties, relating to both the primary mental disorder and antisocial behaviour. As adults seen in forensic settings, they present multiple problems, which include rather severe affective and cognitive deficits and poor life skills and social skills. Many of them, in addition, present a long history of substance abuse, a life-style conducive to deviant behaviour and a high risk of re-offending. Because of the severity and number of problems that they present, mentally disordered offenders tend to be difficult to assess. Often, if not usually, they are not interested in treatment and non-compliant. In general, they are difficult to manage, and both their mental health problems and their antisocial behaviour tend to be chronic (Eaves, Tien & Wilson, 1997). Treatment must include multiple components which target the different problems presented by the mentally disordered offender, it must be planned and organized in a long-term perspective, it must be intense and involve outreach (that is, clinicians must take responsibility for developing and ensuring compliance with treatment), and include close supervision.

ASSESSMENT OF RISK AND NEEDS

Those who undertake the task of treating mentally disordered offenders begin with an intensive two-part assessment of the patient. The first part involves assessing the risk of criminal and/or violent behaviours in the future. In the psychiatric literature this is referred to as "predicting dangerousness". As well as assessing the risk of future offending, the behaviours, cognitions and lack of skills that contribute to the offending are identified. This is necessary in order to design interventions that specifically and directly address the various problems. During the course of treatment, changes in the degree of risk and in the targets of treatment require periodic re-evaluation.

Repeated assessments during treatment measure progress. In contrast to the lack of empirical knowledge about effective interventions for reducing risk among mentally disordered offenders, there is a large and ever-growing body of literature on how to assess risk in this population.

The second component of the assessment focuses on the mental disorder and the associated problems, both acute and chronic, and also on characteristics of the patient that promote offending and/or violent behaviour.

At this stage all the information necessary for developing an individualized treatment programme is gathered. Multiple sources are tapped to gather the information, including interviews with the mentally disordered offender, tests that assess cognitive, behavioural and affective functioning, interviews with family and friends, and both mental health and criminal justice file information. Observation of the individual on an inpatient unit provides invaluable information.

Risk assessment

Clinicians treating mentally disordered offenders need to be familiar with procedures developed for the assessment of the risks of offending and/or violent behaviour. Such an assessment is necessary to determine whether or not treatment efforts designed to reduce recidivism are necessary at all. Further, the assessment of the risk of recidivism, which includes identifying situations which increase risk and those that decrease risk, is critical to determining the setting in which effective treatment can be provided and public safety protected. It has been demonstrated empirically that in order to assess accurately the risk of future criminal and/or violent behaviour, it is necessary to take account of actuarial data (historical information). Consequently, accurately documenting the history of antisocial behaviour is essential. The risk estimate based on actuarial data, it is thought, is modified only slightly by the addition of clinical information (Webster et al., 1994).

Instruments such as the Level of Service Inventory–Revised (LSI-R) (Andrews & Bonta, 1995), the Violence Prediction Scheme (Webster et al., 1994) and the HCR-20 (Douglas, 1999; Grann, Belfrage & Tengström, in press; Webster et al., 1997) have been shown to produce the most accurate predictions, and to be readily learned and applied by mental health professionals. The risk assessment has to be re-done whenever new information on the mentally disordered offender becomes available. Estimating the risk of re-offending and/or violent behaviour is often a time-consuming task because so much information is required from so many different sources. However, it has been clearly demonstrated that only by using multiple sources to reconstruct the history of the antisocial behaviour can valid estimates of risk be made. When assessing risk of potentially dangerous offender–patients, it is important to adopt an attitude of disbelief and scepticism: nothing should be taken at face value, all interview and file information must be cross-checked. While risk assessment is not the topic of this book, it is an integral part of effective treatment. Knowledge of the research in this area and the use of standardized, validated risk assessment instruments are essential for successful treatment of mentally disordered offenders.

Assessment of treatment needs

In order that the assessment provides all the information necessary for designing an individualized treatment programme, it focuses on symptoms and psychosocial problems, rather than on diagnoses. In addition, individual characteristics and/or situations that have been empirically related to criminal recidivism are identified. Treatment planning also requires an evaluation of individual characteristics that influence compliance and response to treatment (Andrews et al., 1990).

Two general categories of treatment needs are presented by mentally disordered offenders: (a) needs resulting from the specific deficits associated with a mental disorder; and (b) needs that have been identified as criminogenic (factors which promote or are associated with criminal behaviour). Once identified, these needs become treatment targets. Among mentally disordered persons, offending may be associated with a variety of psychological problems, neuropsychological deficits, dysfunctional cognitive processing and deviant interpersonal beliefs (Blackburn, 1997). Depending on the specific disorder, treatment needs can result from skill deficits, low intelligence and active symptoms, such as hallucinations, delusions, irritability and hyperactivity. In addition, the need for eliminating co-occurring substance abuse must be given a high priority, regardless of the other mental disorders that are present. Substance abuse not only increases the risk of offending and of violent behaviour, it decreases compliance with all components of a treatment programme and in some disorders, for example the psychoses, it exacerbates symptoms (Swartz et al., 1998).

The assessment of risk and needs among mentally disordered offenders is not easy, as these patients are often uncooperative. Their motivation to complete assessments is usually rather low. When adequate time is available for observation and interviewing, most patients with major mental disorders, as well as those with severe intellectual deficits, usually present no serious problems for assessment. By contrast, those with personality disorders and delusional disorder can be difficult to assess accurately. This may be due to the presence of co-morbid disorders, and/or the reluctance of the patient to acknowledge symptoms, and/or the refusal of the patient to talk about his/her history and psychosocial functioning.

Mentally disordered offenders usually present multiple difficulties (Abram, 1989; Hodgins & Côté, 1995). Consequently, it is necessary to identify all the disorders that they have. Co-occurring disorders, especially substance use disorders and antisocial personality disorder, undermine treatment and increase the risk of recidivism (Borum et al., 1997; Swartz et al., 1998). These co-morbid disorders complicate treatment considerably, as they often interact negatively with the primary disorder. For example, while substance abuse exacerbates the symptoms of schizophrenia, schizophrenia makes placement in a drug rehabilitation programme impossible.

It must be noted that comprehensive assessments are not possible during an acute episode of a mental disorder. Best results are obtained when diagnoses are made by experienced clinicians using structured instruments during periods when there are no, or few, acute active symptoms. Thus, a period of treatment for the acute symptoms on an inpatient unit where there is no access to alcohol and drugs is usually essential.

Assessing criminogenic needs

It appears likely that the individual characteristics associated with antisocial behaviour among non-disordered offenders also play a role in the offending of those afflicted with mental disorders. Among non-disordered offenders, research has demonstrated that the most important risk factors include: pro-criminal attitudes, values, and beliefs; personal cognitive supports of crime (e.g. pro-criminal values, not considering the consequences of one's behaviour); pro-criminal friends and associates; inadequate socialization; impulsivity and/or a lack of self-control; restless aggressive energy; egocentrism; below-average verbal intelligence; a pattern of, and liking for, sensation seeking or novelty seeking; poor problem-solving skills; a history of antisocial behaviour from a young age, in a variety of settings and involving many different types of behaviour; criminality, mental disorder and substance abuse in the family of origin; poor parenting, including little affection, caring and family cohesiveness, inadequate supervision, harsh and inconsistent discipline, neglect and abuse; and low levels of education and career success (Andrews & Bonta, 1994; Andrews, 1995). In order to design a treatment programme that is likely to succeed in modifying offending and/or violent behaviour and in providing the skills necessary to live in the community without offending, all of these characteristics have to be assessed.

Conclusion

Assessment is an integral part of treatment. The initial assessment provides the information necessary for the development of an individualized treatment programme. Repeated assessments provide measures of progress. The assessment of mentally disordered offenders involves gathering and verifying a great deal of historical information from multiple sources, as well as observation, testing and discussions with the patient. The first part of the assessment involves estimating the risk of future offending and/or violent behaviour. This part of the assessment is best conducted using standardized, validated instruments. In addition to providing a great deal of information on the patient's history, this part of the assessment determines in large part the setting in which treatment will be provided. The second part of the assessment focuses on identifying the numerous targets of treatment, as well as the limitations and strengths of the individual that need to be taken into account when developing and conducting treatment. The assessment is complicated not only because of the many different types of problems presented by mentally disordered offenders, but also by their lack of cooperation.

TREATMENT COMPONENTS THAT MAY PROVIDE A BASE FOR DEVELOPING EFFECTIVE TREATMENT PROGRAMMES

There is not much agreement among clinicians about what constitutes appropriate treatment for mentally disordered offenders. The problem is conceptualized in two distinct ways: the medical model identifies symptoms to be treated, while the psychological model identifies skill deficits and interventions designed to teach skills for avoiding difficulties in the future (Blackburn, 1997). There is currently little, or no, scientific literature on the effectiveness of comprehensive, multi-component treatment programmes for mentally disordered offenders. There are, however, three areas of study that provide an empirical basis for the development of such programmes.

These rather diverse, but highly relevant, areas of study provide know-ledge about the initial ingredients for "state-of-the-art" treatment pro-grammes (Harris & Rice, 1997; Müller-Isberner, 1998). The three areas of study are: (a) treatments and services for persons with major mental disor-ders that have been shown to be effective in reducing symptoms and increasing the level of psychosocial functioning; (b) rehabilitation pro-grammes that have been shown to effectively reduce recidivism among non-disordered offenders; and (c) specialized forensic psychiatric com-munity treatment programmes. Knowledge extracted from these different sources will be briefly reviewed.

The effective treatment of the major mental disorders

Effective services for persons with major mental disorders are comprehen-sive, with an emphasis on teaching and learning and enforcing compliance with medication. Comprehensive treatment programmes have been shown to reduce the number and severity of symptoms, improve the level of psy-chosocial functioning, and increase the patient's happiness and the public's safety. These important changes result from three components of treatment: medication, psychoeducation and case management.

Medication

There has been considerable progress in research on the pharmacological treatment of the primary symptoms of the major mental disorders and of aggressive behaviour, as described in Chapters 7 and 8. Appropriate medi-cation taken on a long-term basis is one of the essential components of effective treatment for persons suffering from these disorders. The develop-ment of new medications has significantly improved the treatment of these patients. However, it is critical to remember that medication only improves one aspect of the problems presented by offenders with major mental disor-ders. Many patients resist taking medication, especially on a long-term basis, and therefore additional components of treatment designed to ensure com-pliance are required. A few of those afflicted with major mental disorders are unimproved by available medication. This usually leads to long-term hospitalization.

Life and social skills training and psychoeducation

The use of behavioural–psychoeducational methods to improve patients' skills has been an important development in the treatment of the major mental disorders (for review, see Mueser, Drake & Bond, 1997). Many offenders with major mental disorders lack life skills (basic skills for personal hygiene, nutrition, looking after their living environment, using public transportation) and social skills (interacting in an appropriate manner with others, resolving conflicts without resorting to physical aggression, being sufficiently assertive to resist abuse by others). Psychoeducational interventions target social isolation and attempt to limit it through active interaction between the patient and the clinician. Opportunities for patients to share responsibility are offered. Specific contingency management techniques are used to teach patients with low levels of psychosocial functioning the behaviours necessary to allow them to leave the hospital and live in the community (Paul & Lentz 1977). Together with appropriately delivered medication, a combination of life skills, social skills and vocational training can lead to profound improvements (Benton & Schroeder, 1990; Liberman, 1988, 1992; Lukoff, Liberman & Nuechterlein, 1986; Payne & Halford, 1990; Wallace, 1993; Wallace & Liberman, 1985). All of these behavioural programmes focus on systematically providing positive consequences for independent, prosocial behaviours, while decreasing or eliminating reinforcements, generally attention, for dependent, symptomatic behaviour.

Skills training for patients' families provides information about major mental disorders, teaches them how to recognize and lessen stressors that may induce relapse, encourages acceptance of the patient, teaches effective communication and problem-solving skills, trains family members in the use of reward and encouragement as means to effect behaviour change, and teaches family members how to encourage compliance with medication and other components of treatment (Glick et al., 1990; Hogarty et al., 1991; Liberman, Falloon & Aitchison, 1984; Tarrier et al., 1989). Family skills training seems especially effective when implemented with families high in over-involvement and criticism, and when provided continuously over a long period of time with refresher and consultation sessions (Liberman, 1988). The feasibility and effectiveness of intervening with the families of mentally disordered offenders remains to be demonstrated. However, the recent studies of Sue Estroff and her colleagues in the USA suggest that, in that country, mentally disordered persons often live with their families of origin and this environment contributes to both aggressive behaviour and victimization (Estroff et al., 1998).

Case management

Case management refers to the coordination, by a case manager, of the various components of a community treatment programme. Case managers help to ensure that patients comply with all the components of their individualized treatment programmes, and facilitate contacts with social service agencies to ensure adequate housing and income and, when possible, appropriate employment. It is essentially an "advocate and service broker" model. Case management can also be provided by a team of individuals with sufficient expertise among them to provide all the necessary services. This is referred to as a "full service and support" model.

In order to be effective, case managers have to accept and respect patients' limitations. Putting too much pressure on them to get involved in interpersonal activities may trigger aggressive behaviour. Case management has been shown to be more cost-effective than traditional community support services and hospitalization (Bond et al., 1988; Hammaker, 1983; Rubin, 1992; Solomon, 1992; Solomon, Draine & Meyerson, 1994) These studies also suggest, however, that some case management services or styles have little, no, or even a negative impact on quality of life, symptoms, social adjustment and antisocial behaviour, compared to allowing patients to organize their own treatment. Most studies demonstrate that case management can reduce the frequency and duration of hospitalization (for review, see Mueser et al., 1997). Certain factors have been shown to be associated with case management that is effective. First, case management must be assertive. That is, effective case managers seek out their clients wherever they are in order to ensure compliance with all the components of the treatment programmes. Second, effective case management depends on the quality of the relationship between the case manager and the patient. Effective case managers tailor the intensity of the patients' social interactions to their fluctuating capacity to tolerate social stimulation. They give patients responsibility and permission to make some mistakes. They employ praise, reward, reinforcement and encouragement, rather than withdrawal, punishment and sanctions, in order to effect changes in behaviour. Third, effective case managers maintain long-term relationships with patients, either as individual clinicians or as small cohesive teams.

Conclusion

Thus, evaluation studies which demonstrate what are and what are not, effective treatments for persons with major mental disorders constitute the first domain of knowledge that is useful for developing treatment programmes for mentally disordered offenders in general. This literature highlights the importance of identifying the different types of problems presented by patients—cognitive symptoms, lack of emotional control, few life and social skills, the necessity of ensuring compliance with pharmacological treatments for reducing psychotic symptoms and for keeping them to a minimum over the long term, and for providing supervision and coordination of all the treatments and services deemed necessary for the patient. This is the first of the three sources of knowledge relevant to the development of effective treatment programmes for mentally disordered offenders.

The treatment of offenders

The second source of knowledge relevant to the development of effective treatment programmes for offenders with mental disorders is the large body of research on the rehabilitation of offenders (for review, see Andrews & Bonta, 1994; Gendreau, 1996; McGuire, 1995). The results of several meta-analyses are quite consistent in identifying positive crime prevention effects resulting from these interventions (for review, see Lösel, 1995). These analyses indicate that rehabilitation programmes lead to anywhere from a "mild" to a "moderate" reduction in recidivism. Taking account of the clinical appropriateness of the particular rehabilitation programme, the average correlation between the intervention and reduced recidivism reached 0.30. This indicates that psychologically appropriate treatment, as compared to control conditions, leads to a reduction of up to 50% in recidivism (Andrews et al., 1990; Lipsey, 1995).

The results of these meta-analyses demonstrate that the effective programmes were conducted in the community and that they were characterized by a high degree of structure and a behavioural or cognitive-behavioural orientation. In addition, treatment integrity was maintained. The staff were enthusiastic and the clients were at high risk to recidivate. Further, the effective programmes were multi-modal, targeting the many skill deficits presented by the offenders, and intensive, in terms of both the number of hours per day that clients were engaged in treatment-related activities and the overall length of programme. By contrast, punishment-based programmes, as well as client-centred casework and traditional psychotherapy, were shown to be considerably less effective. Some of these latter programmes were even shown to be harmful for certain offenders (McCord, 1978; Rice, Harris & Cormier, 1992) Finally, the meta-analyses provide little evidence to indicate that factors such as age, sex or race of the offender made a difference to treatment outcome.

Andrews and Bonta (1994) have developed a psychology of criminal conduct, which provides a conceptual basis for understanding, predicting and modifying criminal behaviour. They hypothesize that the factors which determine criminal conduct are not unlike those that determine all socially valued human behaviour (Andrews, 1995). The planning and delivery of effective offender rehabilitation involves taking account of individual differences in *risk*, *need* and *responsivity*. The *risk* principle suggests that intensive rehabilitation is best reserved for individuals at the highest risk for criminal conduct. This once more underlines the necessity of a comprehensive and valid risk assessment as a basis for designing any treatment programme. The *crimogenic need* principle suggests that the appropriate targets of treatment are those changeable characteristics of individuals and of their circumstances that have been demonstrated to be related to criminal conduct. Andrews and his colleagues (1990) have identified the following intermediate targets for rehabilitation programmes: (a) *reducing* antisocial attitudes, antisocial feelings, antisocial friends and associates, chemical dependencies; (b) *increasing* affection for and communication with family members, monitoring and supervision by family members, identification with anti-criminal role models, self-control, self-management and problem-solving skills; (c) *replacing* the skills of lying, stealing and aggressive behaviour with more pro-social alternatives; (d) *modifying* the rewards and costs of criminal and non-criminal activities, so that non-criminal activities are preferred. In addition, it is necessary to provide some offenders with an undemanding, sheltered, supportive living arrangement. It is also necessary to change other attributes of offenders and their circumstances that individualized assessments of risk and need suggest are associated with criminal conduct. Finally, it is essential to teach the offender to recognize risky situations and to devise and rehearse with him/her a concrete plan for dealing with those situations (Andrews, 1995).

The *responsivity* principle suggests that approaches to treatment be matched to the intermediate targets (those targets listed above) and to the learning style of the individual offender. The most effective types of rehabilitation are based on learning theory, and they employ cognitive-behavioural and social learning techniques such as modelling, graduated practice, role playing, reinforcement, extinction, resource provision, concrete verbal suggestions and cognitive restructuring (Andrews, 1995). In order that these treatments are effective with offenders, establishing and maintaining the authority of staff is critical. Staff have to clearly and fairly distinguish between rules and requests and relate in open, enthusiastic and caring ways with the offenders. Staff must reinforce compliance with the various aspects of the rehabilitation programme, model and consistently reinforce anti-criminal thinking and behaviour and prosocial behaviours. Staff must design and implement the programme so that anti-criminal behaviour in settings such as home, school and work is increasingly rewarded (Andrews, 1995).

Conclusion

Knowledge of rehabilitation programmes that have been shown to be effective in reducing recidivism among offenders is the second source to be tapped in developing treatment programmes for mentally disordered offenders. Targeting individual characteristics—behaviours, cognitions, feelings—and situations that promote offending, and using behavioural and cognitive strategies to modify them, have proven to be effective. Not surprisingly, since the treatment is based on learning, individual capacities must be taken into account in planning the programme. Staff behaviour and attitudes contribute to the success of these programmes. Notably, the pro- grammes that were most effective were carried out in the community.

Evidence from specialized forensic psychiatric community treatment programmes

The third body of evidence that is relevant for developing effective treat- ment programmes for mentally disordered offenders is made up of a small number of evaluations of specialized community programmes for mentally disordered offenders. There are studies from Canada (Wilson, Tien & Eaves, 1995), Germany (Müller-Isberner, 1996) and the USA (Bloom, Williams & Bigelow, 1991; Heilbrun & Griffin, 1993; Wiederanders, 1992; Wiederanders, Bromley & Choate, 1997) which show that violence and crime can be pre- vented by assertive forensic psychiatric community programmes, even among mentally disordered offenders who are at high risk for re-offending.

Given the different legal and institutional frameworks in which these com- munity programmes have been developed, it is surprising, but very encourag- ing, that they share a number of common features. The principal features common to the effective programmes include: (a) compulsory participation (ordered by a court or tribunal); (b) a recognition and acceptance by the mental health professionals who carry out the programme that they have a double mandate, which includes treating the mental disorder and preventing offending and/or violent behaviour; (c) legal powers for the mental health professionals to rapidly rehospitalize patients against their will if they think that they may offend and/or behave violently; (d) structure, intensity, and diversity to address the multiple problems presented by mentally disordered offenders; and (e) staff responsibility for ensuring compliance with all aspects of the programme.

As well as being more effective than residential programmes, community programmes offer another advantage. The close monitoring and intensive case management that are integral parts of these programmes provide oppor- tunities for ongoing and frequent assessments of the patients' functioning, compliance with all of the components of treatment, and potential problems. In addition, such programmes have been demonstrated to be cost-effective (Bigelow, Bloom & Williams, 1990) and to have positive effects, not only in reducing offending and violent behaviour but also on the other problems presented by mentally disordered offenders (Wiederanders & Choate, 1994).

Conclusion

While there are currently few studies of comprehensive treatment programmes for mentally disordered offenders, there are three bodies of knowledge that provide information relevant for developing such programmes.

The first identifies three components of treatment that have been shown to be effective for the treatment of persons with major mental disorders—pharmacotherapy, psychoeducational training programmes and assertive case management. The second body of knowledge relevant to the development of treatment programmes for mentally disordered offenders includes the studies which have identified rehabilitation strategies that succeed in reducing recidivism among non-disordered offenders. The third relevant knowledge base includes the small number of specialized forensic community treatment programmes that have proved to be effective in limiting offending and/or violent behaviour. In order to develop comprehensive multi-component treatment programmes for mentally disordered offenders, it is necessary to modify and adapt knowledge from these three areas by taking account of the particularities of the provision of treatment for mentally disordered offenders. These include long-term compulsory treatment in high-security hospitals which may or may not be clinically indicated, an organizational structure that takes account of the characteristics and needs of the patients as well as the public's and the politicians' attitudes to mentally disordered offenders, and the difficulty of empirically demonstrating the effectiveness of treatment.

TREATMENT IN SECURE SETTINGS

The inpatient treatment of severely mentally disordered offenders is organized in some countries as part of the prison system (e.g. in Austria), in others as part of the mental health system (e.g. in Sweden), and in others in a government agency that is distinct from both the correctional and health systems (e.g. in Germany). Regardless of the system to which security hospitals belong, they all have a similar patient population and many common problems related to service delivery. Generally, the majority of the patients suffer from chronic disorders, and for many, finding a cure is an unrealistic goal. These patients present special problems related to their lack of motivation for treatment and multiple psychosocial deficits. Often, it is their offending and/or violent behaviour which makes transition to less restrictive environments hard to achieve. The goals of treatment in secure settings focus on symptom reduction, stabilization, and the development of life skills, social skills and skills to cope with stress, in an effort to enable these patients to move to less restrictive environments.

The delivery of service in security hospitals is plagued by several types of problems:

1. These institutions usually have no control over admissions and discharges. Consequently, overcrowding is frequent and leads to serious problems in maintaining the integrity of multi-modal treatment

programmes (Kerr & Roth, 1987). Unlike in general psychiatric hospitals, decisions about admission and discharge to security hospitals are influenced, at least to some extent, by concerns for public safety.

2. Secure hospitals admit and keep patients for whom no treatment can be provided.

3. Security hospitals are often disconnected from mainstream knowledge and clinical practice, and they have a tendency to develop a life of their own, in isolation from general mental health services. Consequently, they are often immune to external influence (e.g. to new evidence about an effective treatment that is published in the general psychiatric literature), expend too little effort in determining what needs to be done at the initial assessment stage, and fail to match patients to programmes adequately (Webster, Hucker & Grossman, 1993). A decade ago, Quinsey (1988) concluded that: "Today, treatment programmes in secure psychiatric institutions are noteworthy primarily by their absence, poor implementation, unevaluated status, lack of conceptual sophistication, and incomplete description and documentation" (p. 444). There is no evidence that fundamental and widespread changes have occurred since Quinsey evaluated the situation.

4. Security hospitals are often located in rural areas. Such a location facilitates the initial steps of programmes which gradually re-integrate patients into the community, but limits the final stages, which may include finding a job, appropriate housing and leisure activities. Further, the location of security hospitals often makes it difficult to integrate patients' families into the treatment programme. On the other hand, rural settings provide distinct advantages for the re-integration of patients. In rural settings patients are supervised informally, like it or not, by the local inhabitants. This informal supervision can be used positively, and in some cases it permits the patients more access to the community than would be possible in urban centres. Encouraging the patients to live in such rural areas after discharge, rather than returning to their old neighbourhoods, may help reduce both relapse and recidivism.

5. Secure hospitals have a tendency to block treatment efforts because staff consider security and order to be their priorities.

6. Security hospitals are places where the rejection and exploitation of severely ill patients occurs at the hands of patients with higher levels of psychosocial functioning. Therefore, secure hospital treatment should be reserved for those cases in which any less restrictive alternative presents a serious risk to public safety.

Despite all of these problems, large security hospitals, if organized properly, may be advantageous in that they can provide a variety of specialized treatment programmes. As described earlier, mentally disordered offenders are a highly heterogeneous group. Consequently, this diversity must be reflected in the way security hospitals are organized. In order to provide different ward milieux adapted to the specific needs of particular types of patients, wards have to be specialized, admitting only patients of a certain type who present similar levels of risk and a similar needs profile. Both empirical and clinical strategies have been used to try and identify the sub-types of patients that are relevant to treatment in security hospitals. Quinsey, Cyr and Lavallé (1988) used cluster analyses of patient characteristics and identified seven types of patients in a security hospital in Ontario: good citizens, social isolates, personality disorders, institutional management problems, institutionalized psychotics, psychotics, and the mentally retarded. These same types were identified in a sample from a security hospital in Quebec. The practical implications and use of this typology for treatment planning and organization have been described (Harris & Rice, 1990; Rice et al., 1990). A clinically derived model of specialization in a secure hospital has also been described (Müller-Isberner & Jöckel, 1994). The implementation of specialized wards has been found to lead to remarkable changes inside a security hospital, including increased calmness on the wards, more structured treatment components, a reduction in the number of incidents, a reduction in the number of complaints by patients against staff, an increase in ward staff's identification with their work, and an improvement in long-term outcome (Müller-Isberner, 1993).

Maximum security hospitals are required to keep their patients for lengthy periods of time. While patients today usually stay in general psychiatric hospitals less then one month, patients admitted to secure hospitals may stay for a number of years. Although often hard to achieve over this long period of time, patient management must stay linked to individualized treatment programmes aimed at reintegration into the community.

Tensions and violence on wards result both from confinement in a close community of disordered persons and from symptoms of mental disorders. In some cases, seclusion and enforced medication are required. However, interventions by staff that are based on an understanding of the antecedents of disruptive behaviour can often prevent aggressive behaviours and thereby avoid the use of these rather drastic methods (Harris & Rice, 1992).

Institutional programmes have traditionally emphasized occupational and educational training in a highly structured environment. Interventions in security hospitals include group and individual psychotherapy, therapeutic communities, social skills training, anger management, problem-solving training, token economies and behavioural procedures for teaching life and social skills. In institutional settings, contingency management systems have proved to be effective for extinguishing cognitive symptoms and aggressive behaviour, for promoting pro-social, non-symptomatic behaviour, and for encouraging participation in behavioural and cognitive-behavioural training sessions.

As institutions tend to take responsibility away from patients, a structured concerted effort is necessary to allow patients gradually to assume more and more responsibility for themselves and their care.

During residential stays, risks and needs must be reassessed continuously. Gradually, the patient can be allowed more and more privileges. As patients are seen frequently, the assessment of the risk of future offending and violent behaviour is made for short periods. These predictions for limited periods of time and in clearly defined situations tend to be quite valid (Gretenkord & Müller-Isberner, 1991).

Treatment is by no means finished when symptoms are under control and life skills have been learned. The task is then to identify an environment into which the patient can be safely discharged. Careful evaluation of the patient before and during treatment will enable staff to define the sorts of environment in which he/she will likely comply with treatment and refrain from antisocial behaviour. However, sometimes it is hard to convince the patient that not any place is a good place for him/her, that long-term medication is essential, and that treatment and supervision while living in the community is both necessary and inevitable.

As patients who have been treated in high-security hospitals are highly unpopular in general psychiatric services, attempts to transfer them to less secure facilities often fail. This is usually due to a reluctance by general psychiatric staff and administrators to accept patients with criminal records of severe violence. Even when transfers are made, patients are often returned to the security hospital because of aggressive behaviour, hostility or a low level of functioning. For example, one study found that a history of long-term care and assaultiveness in hospital were negatively related to successful referral from a security hospital to general psychiatric services, and that other clinical variables and the history of offending played no role (Brown, Shubsachs & Larkin, 1992). As noted above, conditional release with court-ordered participation in a community treatment programme has been shown to be effective and less costly than prolonged detention for many chronically disordered offenders. It is likely that such programmes will grow in number and provide the follow-up to inpatient care in a security hospital. However, the evaluations of the effective community programmes suggest that rapid access to inpatient wards for short periods is necessary to prevent both relapse and recidivism. The security hospital may be the most appropriate setting for such re-admissions.

Conclusion

In adapting what has been learned about the effective treatment of persons with major mental disorders, the successful rehabilitation of offenders and specialized community programmes that reduce recidivism, to developing comprehensive multi-modal treatment programmes for mentally disordered offenders, it is necessary to take account of the fact that many of these patients are treated in security hospitals. The decision to send the patient to a security hospital is usually not made by mental health professionals, neither is the determination of the length of stay. In addition to the fact that treatment staff in these institutions cannot make decisions about either admission or discharge, many other problems have historically plagued these institutions. However, large security hospitals provide the advantage of being able to provide a variety of specialized programmes adapted to the needs of the different types of mentally disordered offenders.

ORGANIZATION OF SERVICES FOR MENTALLY DISORDERED OFFENDERS

Staff

The importance of the "human factor" cannot be over-estimated in the treatment of mentally disordered offenders. In selecting staff, regardless of their specific role, important selection criteria include the ability to keep a distance from the patients and not to get over-involved in their problems, while being caring, empathic and enthusiastic about the prospects of recovery. The education and training of front-line staff who actually do most of the treatment is essential for success. They must be specifically trained for the tasks that they will carry out, for example, in understanding, setting up and managing behavioural and cognitive-behavioural interventions, psycho-educational training techniques, and strategies to anticipate, prevent and manage aggressive behaviour. Those involved with the patient need a clear understanding of the patient's problems and limitations, and how these may affect behaviour and functioning. Staff members should interact frequently with patients and model pro-social values and non-aggressive ways of resolving conflicts. They must try to be empathetic, while at the same time firmly but fairly enforcing the rules. Staff must understand that a patient's antisocial behaviour is not necessarily deliberately rebellious but simply uncontrolled. Those who appear to contradict rules without regard for the consequences, and in spite of repeated warnings, may simply be unable to inhibit certain behaviours. Stability of staff and clarity of their roles and purpose are other factors which are critical for success. Staff shortages and frequent changes in staff threaten the integrity of the treatment programme. It has been shown that a disciplined ward regime leads to more positive change in cognitive and social functioning and less offending than do therapeutic communities or programmes which focus on education and counselling (Craft & Craft, 1984). In sum, front-line staff have to be sufficiently stable and strong themselves to cope with mentally disordered offenders, they have to be adequately and appropriately trained for the jobs they are required to do, they have to be supervised, and they have to be supported. Acknowledging their competencies and successes and providing support is especially important for those who work with antisocial offenders. These patients frequently make complaints about staff and make appeals to the courts and various government agencies complaining about their treatment. While the accusations all have to be thoroughly investigated, staff must be actively supported by their superiors when the accusations are shown not to be true.

The specialists, in most cases psychiatrists and psychologists, assess the patient and then design and direct the individualized treatment programme. They provide the leadership for the multidisciplinary treatment team and this requires intelligence, enthusiasm, clarity of purpose, communication skills, sincerity, emotional stability and courage (Harris & Rice, 1997). These specialists also work individually with each patient in an effort to explain the nature of their disorders, symptoms, deficits and behaviour patterns. In order for treatment to be successful, it is necessary that patients accept the conclusions drawn by staff after the initial assessment and also the individualized treatment programme that has been developed on the basis of these conclusions. Helping patients to understand is a challenge requiring considerable clinical skill and a sympathetic acceptance of patients' limitations. It has been shown to be an essential ingredient of successful treatment (Sellars, Hollin & Howells, 1993).

Funding, support and protection

Those who conduct treatment for mentally disordered offenders have to take care of the bureaucratic and political environment. It is their task to care for those who provide the resources. Administrators must ensure coordination between mental health services, correctional services, social services who provide housing and income, educational services, and all of the other agencies who may be involved with the patients. The idea of treating mentally disordered offenders does not sell itself! Both residential and community programmes need administrators who are supportive and knowledgeable in dealing with the legislature and governmental agencies who provide funding. As treatment programmes for mentally disordered offenders need to be intensive and long-lasting, adequate long-term funding must be assured. Consequently, programme directors and administrators must provide information to senior bureaucrats, agencies and law makers that will ensure continuous adequate financing. To ensure this stable funding, they must establish good contacts with the public, disseminating the idea that treatment leads to a reduction in crime.

The notion that mentally disordered offenders should and can be treated requires advocacy. This means that those working in the field need to spend some of their time educating policy makers and those who make decisions about funding. The returns on the investment need to be stressed. Convincing the political decision makers that the treatment of mentally disordered offenders is cost-effective is probably the best way to ensure long-term, adequate funding. It is important not to oversell treatment. Offender treatment is not a cure for criminality. Rather, the accumulated evidence suggests that treatment can lead to small or moderate reductions in recidivism rates. These are significant, however, as even small reductions in the number and severity of crimes that are committed have important human and financial implications.

Recidivism discredits treatment. When offences are committed by patients, it is important to deal adequately with the media in order to limit the damage that the event can do in undermining treatment for all mentally disordered offenders. Madness, violence, sex and crime is a mixture that inevitably attracts attention. Mentally disordered offenders combine characteristics that provoke fears and fantasies of mystery, magic and demons. This public reaction results in a serious threat to the provision of services for all mentally disordered offenders. Therefore, when a patient re-offends, an organized, structured and strongly worded public response must be made rapidly. The best strategy may be to contact editors and journalists who have a sense of responsibility and an understanding of the enormous powers that the media have to influence public opinion and decision makers, and to provide them with the information necessary to put the offence in a larger context. It is important to provide them with statistics on recidivism of similar types of offenders, comparing treated and untreated cases. Additionally, it is essential to make clear that treatment staff always consider public safety in making decisions regarding their patients and that they do not ally with patients against the public. Hopefully, providing such information will encourage journalists to report and discuss the incident in a way that is supportive of on-going treatment programmes.

Outcomes

In order to improve the effectiveness of treatment and to ensure accountability and continued funding, a four-step programme of evaluation is required. The first step involves systematizing, structuring and making usable all the information that is collected during the initial assessment of the patient. The second step involves measuring the impact of each component of the treatment programme. For example, nurses rate symptoms on standardized, validated scales before and while the patient takes a particular medication or a particular combination of medications, the number of incidents of aggressive behaviour is documented in the week preceding and during the time a patient takes a medication which is supposed to reduce his/her aggressive behaviour, life skills are measured before, at the end and several months after a life skills training programme. The third step involves identifying how the various treatment components should be organized in order to maximize their effectiveness. The fourth step in the evaluation measures the impact of the treatment programme as a whole by following patients in the community and documenting relapse and recidivism. This is the only way that the programmes can be improved and that accountability is assured. Such information is seldom tabulated as a matter of routine. This means that clinicians and administrators of treatment programmes for mentally disordered offenders rarely receive accurate feedback about the impact of their work. Consequently, they have no empirical basis for modifying treatment programmes.

Although many mentally disordered offenders do achieve adequate levels of recovery, as measured by lower levels of offending and/or violent behaviour, this clinical fact is not reflected in the scientific literature. As the subsequent chapters in this book document, there are remarkably few studies demonstrating a positive effect of either a treatment programme or a specific component of a treatment programme. In 1993, Webster and his colleagues asked:

> . . . whether it is the clinicians who cannot do the job or the researchers who cannot or will not amass disinterested evidence to show what in fact clinicians can and cannot do for schizophrenic, mood-disordered, and organically impaired forensic patients and offenders (p. 88).

ETHICAL ISSUES

Mental health treatment services provided to mentally disordered offenders must be designed, directed and carried out by sensitive and psychologically informed clinicians. All aspects of treatment, and their application to individual cases, must be legal, ethical, decent and cost-effective. Although mental health professionals and their organizations cannot shoulder responsibility either for the inevitable ethical dilemmas in which they find themselves, or for the establishment of questionable policies, they need to be sensitive to and concerned about some problematic implications of their roles and functions. Some special ethical and policy dilemmas associated with the handling of mentally disordered offenders can be identified (for a broader discussion, see Shah, 1993).

Mental health professionals do not function as agents of the patients when they provide services in coercive contexts and for purposes other than the well-being of the patient. In these situations, other parties (the mental health and criminal justice systems) and interests (public safety) are also involved. It is seldom clear, in such situations, precisely where health professionals' allegiances and obligations lie and to what extent patients have been informed about these matters. Ethical principles require that mental health professionals provide such information to patients before initiating assessment and treatment. Another conflict arises from the combination of the roles of therapist and evaluator, for example in assessing a patient's readiness for discharge.

When mental health professionals are not functioning primarily as agents of their patients, the usual assumptions and understandings about confidentiality do not apply. The mental health professionals are required, for example, to submit progress reports to courts and/or legal tribunals. Again, considerations of fundamental fairness require that patients be informed about the nature and limits of confidentiality in each particular context.

When mental health professionals work with forensic patients, they have a professional and ethical obligation to educate themselves about the relevant legal issues and their implications for service provision. A related concern is when mental health professionals go beyond providing information about the patient's status, and draw conclusions about issues that are the domain of the courts or of a particular legal tribunal. In so doing, they take over the roles and responsibilities that belong to those who are designated to make decisions.

While certain decisions about the patients are made by persons other than the treating clinicians, in many jurisdictions treatment providers have considerable powers to decide about levels of security. For example, the lowest security level which can be decided by staff may differ little from actual discharge. While public safety is a dominant concern, the rights of patients must also be recognized.

Some ethical dilemmas result from the fact that some interventions (e.g. medication) may increase the likelihood of the most desired outcome (no criminal recidivism), while at the same time worsening others (decrease in happiness and quality of life). Again, this issue has to be discussed openly with the patient.

A mental disorder combined with a high risk of recidivism can lead to extended, and in some cases even indeterminate, periods of institutionalization. Being sent by the criminal court to the mental health system for treatment often involves longer periods of confinement in security hospitals than if the offender had been convicted and sentenced to prison. This situation poses problems for administrators and clinicians who work within these institutions because the length of time the patient is detained cannot be justified on clinical grounds. The ethical dilemma is further complicated when adequate treatment resources are not available and/or when treatment has never been shown to have a positive effect or has been shown to have a negative impact, for example, in the case of psychopaths (Rice, Harris & Cormier, 1992). In these cases, diversion to the mental health system often means incapacitation or preventive detention in which containment rather than treatment is the primary goal.

CONCLUDING REMARKS

While there is currently no empirical base for the treatment of mentally disordered offenders, components of treatment that have been shown to be effective for a number of the problems presented by mentally disordered offenders have been identified. Modifying and adapting these interventions, organizing them as parts of long-term treatment and management programmes and evaluating the impact, is the challenge of the next decade. This challenge requires the collaboration of policy makers, administrators, clinicians and researchers. As Lipsey (1995) has shown, collaboration between clinicians and researchers leads to increased efficacy of treatment. Furthermore, collaboration ensures that service providers are not marginalized from new developments and that scientists become more aware of the practical problems of establishing treatment programmes and of maintaining their integrity.

REFERENCES

Abram, K. M. (1989).   The effect of co-occurring disorders on criminal careers: interaction of antisocial personality, alcoholism, and drug disorders. *International Journal of Law and Psychiatry*, **12**, 133–148.

Andrews, D. (1995).   The psychology of criminal conduct and clinical criminology. In L. Stewart L. Stermac & C. Webster (Eds), *Clinical Criminology: Toward Effective Correctional Treatment* (pp. 130–150). Toronto: Correctional Service of Canada.

Andrews, D. A. & Bonta, J. L. (1994).   *The Psychology of Criminal Conduct*. Cincinnati, OH: Anderson.

Andrews, D. A. & Bonta, J. L. (1995).   *The Level of Service Inventory Revised*. Toronto: Multi-Health Systems.

Andrews, D. A., Zinger I., Hoge R. D., Bonta J., Gendreau, P. & Cullen, F. T. (1990).   Does correctional treatment work? a clinically relevant and psychologically informed meta-analysis. *Criminology*, **28**, 369–404.

Benton, M. K. & Schroeder, H. E. (1990).   Social skills training with schizophrenics: a meta-analytic evaluation. *Journal of Consulting and Clinical Psychology*, **58**, 741–747.

Bierut, L. J., Dinwiddie, S. H. Begleiter, H., Crowe R. R., Hesselbrock, V., Nurnberger, J. I., Porjesz, B., Schuckit, M. A. & Reich, T. (1998).   Familial transmission of substance dependence: alcohol, marijuana, cocaine, and habitual smoking. *Archives of General Psychiatry*, **55**, 982–988.

Bigelow, D. A., Bloom, J. D. & Williams, M. H. (1990).   Costs of managing insanity acquittees under a psychiatric security review board system. *Hospital and Community Psychiatry*, **41**, 613–614.

Blackburn, R. (1997).   Mentally disordered offenders. In C. Hollin (Ed.), *Working with Offenders. Psychological Practice in Offender Rehabilitation* (pp. 119–149) Chichester: Wiley.

Bloom, J. D., Williams, M. H. & Bigelow, D. A. (1991).   Monitored conditional release of persons found not guilty by reason of insanity. *American Journal of Psychiatry*, **148**, 444–448.

Bond, G. R., Miller, L. D., Krumwied, R. D. & Ward, R. (1988).   Assertive case management in three CMHCs: a controlled study. *Hospital and Community Psychiatry*, **39**, 411–418.

Borum, R., Swanson, J., Swartz, M. & Hiday, V. (1997).   Substance abuse, violent behavior, and police encounters among persons with severe mental disorders. *Journal of Contemporary Criminal Justice*, **13**, 236–250.

Brennan, P. A., Mednick, S. A. & Hodgins, S. (1998).   Psychotic disorders and criminal violence in a total birth cohort (manuscript submitted for publication).

Brown, S., Shubsachs, A. & Larkin, E. (1992).   Outcome of referrals from Rampton Hospital to local mental health services, 1988–1990. *Journal of Forensic Psychiatry*, **3**, 463–475.

Clare, I. H. C. & Gudjonsson, G. H. (1993).   Interrogative suggestibility, confabulation and acquiescence in people with mild learning disabilities (mental handicap): implications for reliability during police interrogations. *British Journal of Clinical Psychology*, **32**, 295–301.

Clare, I. H. C. & Gudjonsson, G. H. (1995).   The vulnerability of suspects with intellectual disabilities during police interviews: a review and experimental study of decision-making. *Mental Handicap Research*, **8**, 110–128.

Cooke, D. J. (1997).   Psychopaths: oversexed, overplayed but not over here? *Criminal Behaviour and Mental Health*, **7**(3), 3–11.

Cooke, D., Forth, A. & Hare, R. D. (Eds) (1998).   *Psychopathy: Theory, Research and Implications for Society.* Dordrecht: Kluwer Academic.

Côté, G., Hodgins, S. & Toupin, J. (in press).   Psychopathie: prévalence et spécificité clinique. In T. H. Pham (Ed.), *Psychopathie Théorie et Recherche.* Lille Presses Universitaires du Septentrion.

Craft, M. & Craft, A. (Eds) (1984).   *Mentally Abnormal Offenders.* London: Baillière Tindall.

Crocker, A. G. & Hodgins, S. (1997).   The criminality of non-institutionalized mentally retarded persons: evidence from a birth cohort followed to age 30. *Criminal Justice and Behavior*, **24**, 432–454.

Douglas, K. (1999).   HCR-20 Violence risk assessment scheme: Overview, and annotated bibliography. Unpublished manuscript, Simon Fraser University.

Eaves, D., Tien, G. & Wilson, D. (1997).   A systems approach to the management of impulsive behaviour. In C. Webster & M. Jackson (Eds). *Impulsivity* (pp. 409–433). New York: Guilford.

Estroff, S. E., Swanson, J. W., Lachicotte, W. S., Swartz, M. & Bolduc, M. (1998).   Risk reconsidered: targets of violence in the social networks of people with serious psychiatric disorders. *Social Psychiatry and Epidemiology*, **33**(1), 95–101.

Gendreau, P. (1996).   Offender rehabilitation: what we know and what needs to be done. *Criminal Justice and Behavior*, **23**, 144–161.

Glick, I. D., Spender, J. H., Clarkin, J. F., Haas, G. L., Lewis, A. B., Peyser, J., DeMane, Good-Ellis, M., Harris, E. & Lestelle, V. (1990).   A randomized clinical trial of inpatient family intervention. IV. Follow-up results for subjects with schizophrenia. *Schizophrenia Research*, **3**, 187–200.

Grann, M., Belfrage, H. & Tengström, A. (in press).   Actuarial assessment of risk for violence: predictive validity of the VRAG and the historical part of the HCR-20. *Criminal Justice and Behavior*.

Gretenkord, L. & Müller-Isberner, R. (1991).   Entweichungen aus dem Maßregelvollzug—Analyse eines Symptoms. *Monatsschrift für Kriminologie und Strafrechtsreform*, **74**, 305–315.

Hammaker, R. (1983).   A client outcome evaluation of the statewide implementation of community support services. *Psychosocial Rehabilitation Journal*, **7**, 1–10.

Hare, R. D. (1991).   *Manual for the Hare Psychopathy Checklist-Revised*. Toronto: Multi-Health Systems.

Harris, G. T. & Rice, M. E. (1990).   An empirical approach to classification and treatment planning for psychiatric inpatients. *Journal of Clinical Psychology*, **46**, 3–14.

Harris, G. T. & Rice, M. E. (1992).   Reducing violence in institutions: maintaining behavior change. In R. Peters, R. J. McMahon & V. L. Quinsey (Eds), *Aggression and Violence Throughout the Life Span* (pp. 261–282). Newbury Park, CA: Sage.

Harris, G. & Rice, M. (1997).   Mentally disordered offenders: what treatment research says about effective service. In C. Webster & M. Jackson (Eds), *Impulsivity* (pp. 361–393). New York: Guilford.

Heilbrun, K. & Griffin, P. (1993).   Community-based forensic treatment of insanity aquittees. *International Journal of Law and Psychiatry*, **16**, 133–150.

Hodgins, S. (1996).   The major mental disorders: new evidence requires new policy and practice. *Canadian Psychology*, **37**, 95–111.

Hodgins, S. (1998).   Epidemiological investigations of the associations between major mental disorders and crime: methodological limitations and validity of the conclusions. *Social Psychiatry and Epidemiology*, **33**(1), 29–37.

Hodgins, S. & Côté, G. (1995).   Major mental disorder among Canadian penitentiary inmates. In L. Stewart, L. Stermac & C. Webster (Eds), *Clinical Criminology: Toward Effective Correctional Treatment* (pp. 6–20). Toronto: Solliciteur Général et Service Correctionnel du Canada.

Hodgins, S., Côté, G. & Toupin, J. (1998).   Major mental disorders and crime: an etiological hypothesis. In D. Cooke, A. Forth & R. D. Hare (Eds), *Psychopathy: Theory, Research and Implications for Society.* (pp. 231–256). Dordrecht: Kluwer Academic.

Hodgins. S., Lapalme. M. & Toupin, J. (in press).   Criminal activities and substance use of patients with major affective disorders and schizophrenia: a two year follow-up. *Journal of Affective Disorders*.

Hodgins, S., Mednick, S. A., Brennan, P., Schulsinger, F. & Engberg, M. (1996).   Mental disorder and crime: evidence from a Danish birth cohort. *Archives of General Psychiatry*, **53**, 489–496.

Hogarty. G. E., Anderson, C. M., Reiss, D. J., Kornblith, S. J., Greenwald, D. P., Ulrich, F. & Carter, M. (1991).   Family psychoeducation, social skills training, and maintenance chemotherapy in the aftercare treatment of schizophrenia. *Archives of General Psychiatry*, **48**, 340–347.

Kerr, C. A. & Roth. J. A. (1987).   *Survey of Facilities and Programs for Mentally Disordered Offenders* (DHHS Publication No. (Adm) 86–1493). Washington, DC: National Institute of Mental Health, US Department of Health and Human Services.

Kessler et al. (1994).   Lifetime and 12-month prevalence of DSM-III-R psychiatric disorders in the United States. *Archives of General Psychiatry*, **51**, 8–19.

Lappalainen, J., Long, J. C., Eggert. M., Ozake, N., Tobin, R. W., Brown, G. L., Naukkarinen, H., Virkkunen, M., Linnoila, M. & Goldman, D. (1998).   Linkage of antisocial alcoholism to the serotonin 5-HT$_{1B}$ receptor gene in two populations. *Archives of General Psychiatry*, **55**, 989–995.

Liberman, R. P. (1988).   Behavioral family management. In R. P. Liberman (Ed.), *Psychiatric Rehabilitation of Chronic Mental Patients* (pp. 200–244). Washington, DC: American Psychiatric Press.

Liberman, R. P. (1992).   Future prospects for psychiatric rehabilitation. In R. P. Liberman (Ed.), *Handbook of Psychiatric Rehabilitation* (pp. 317–325). New York: Macmillan.

Liberman, R. P., Falloon I. R. & Aitchison, R. A. (1984).   Multiple family therapy for schizophrenia: a behavioral, problem-solving approach. *Psychosocial Rehabilitation Journal*, **7**, 60–77.

Lipsey, M. W. (1995).   What do we learn from 400 research studies on the effectiveness of treatment with juvenile delinquents? In J. McGuire (Ed.), *What Works: Reducing Reoffending* (pp. 63–78). Chichester: Wiley.

Lösel, F. (1995).   The efficacy of correctional treatment: a review and synthesis of meta-evaluations. In J. McGuire (Ed.), *What Works: Reducing Reoffending* (pp. 79–111). Chichester: Wiley.

Lukoff, D., Liberman, R. P. & Nuechterlein, K. (1986).   Symptom monitoring in the rehabilitation of schizophrenic patients. *Schizophrenia Bulletin*, **12**, 578–602.

McCord, J. (1978).   A thirty-year follow-up of treatment effects. *American Psychologist*, **33**, 284–289.

McGuire, J. (1995).   *What Works: Reducing Reoffending*. Chichester: Wiley.

Merikangas, K. R., Stolar M., Stevens D. E., Goulet J., Preisig M. A., Fenton B., Zhang H., O'Maley, S. S. & Rounsaville, B. J. (1998).   Familial transmission of substance use disorders. *Archives of General Psychiatry*, **55**, 973–979.

Müller-Isberner, R. (1993).   Managing insane offenders. *International Bulletin of Law & Mental Health*, **4**, 28–30.

Müller-Isberner, R. (1996).   Forensic psychiatric aftercare following hospital order treatment. *International Journal of Law and Psychiatry*, **19**, 81–86.

Müller-Isberner, R. (1998).   Ein differenziertes Behandlungskonzept für den psychiatrischen Massregelvollzug. Organisationsfragen und methodische Aspekte. In E. Wagner & W. Werdenich (Eds), *Forensische Psychotherapie* (pp. 197–209). Vienna: Facultas Universitätsverlag.

Müller-Isberner, R. & Jöckel, D. (1994).   Differenzierte Kriminaltherapie. *Krankenhauspsychiatrie*, **5**, 170–172.

Mueser, K. T., Drake, R. E. & Bond, G. R. (1997).   Recent advances in psychiatric rehabilitation for patients with severe mental illness. *Harvard Review Psychiatry*, **5**, 123–137.

Paul, G. L. & Lentz R. J. (1977).   *Psychosocial Treatment of Chronic Mental Patients: Milieu versus Social Learning Programs*. Cambridge, MA: Harvard University Press.

Payne, P. V. & Halford, W. K. (1990).   Clinical section: social skills training with chronic schizophrenic patients living in community settings. *Behavioural Psychotherapy*, **18**, 49–64.

Prins, H. (1993). Service provision and facilities for the mentally disordered offender. In K. Howells & C. R. Hollins (Eds), *Clinical Approaches to the Mentally Disordered Offender* (pp. 35–67). Chichester: Wiley.

Quinsey, V. L. (1988). Assessment of the treatability of forensic patients. *Behavioural Sciences and the Law*, **6**, 443–452.

Quinsey, V. L., Cyr, M. & Lavallé, Y. J. (1988). Treatment opportunities in a maximum security psychiatric hospital: a problem survey. *International Journal of Law and Psychiatry*, **11**, 179-194.

Rice, M. E., Harris, G. T. & Cormier C. (1992). Evaluation of a maximum security therapeutic community for psychopaths and other mentally disordered of fenders. *Law and Human Behavior*, **16**, 399–412.

Rice, M. E., Harris, G. T., Quinsey, V. L. & Cyr, M. (1990). Planning treatment programs in secure psychiatric facilities. In D. Weisstub (Ed.), *Law and Mental Health: International Perspectives*, Vol. 51 (pp. 162–230). Elmsford, NY: Pergamon.

Robins, L. N., Tipp, J. & Przybeck, T. (1991). Antisocial personality: the diagnosis. In L. N. Robins & D. A. Regier (Eds), *Psychiatric Disorders in America: The Epidemiologic Catchment Area Study* (pp. 258–290). New York: Free Press.

Rubin, A. (1992). Is case management effective for people with serious mental illness? A research review. *Health and Social Work*, **17**, 138–150.

Sellars, C., Hollin, C. & Howells, K. (1993). Mental illness neurological and organic disorder, and criminal behaviour. In K. Howells & C. R. Hollins (Eds), *Clinical Approaches to the Mentally Disordered Offender* (pp. 71–86). Chichester: Wiley.

Shah, S. A. (1993). A clinical approach to the mentally disordered offender: an overview and some major issues. In K. Howells & C. R. Hollin (Eds), *Clinical Approaches to the Mentally Disordered Offender* (pp. 211–236). Chichester: Wiley.

Solomon, P. (1992). The efficacy of case management services for severely mentally disabled clients. *Community Mental Health Journal*, **28**, 163–180.

Solomon, P., Draine, J. & Meyerson, A. (1994). Jail recidivism and receipt of community mental health services. *Hospital and Community Psychiatry*, **45**, 793–797.

Swartz, M. S., Swanson, J. W., Hiday, V. A., Borum, R., Wagnes, R. & Burns, B. J. (1998). Taking the wrong drugs: the role of substance abuse and medication non-compliance and violence among severely mentally ill individuals. *Social Psychiatry & Psychiatric Epidemiology*, **33**(1), S75–80.

Tarrier, N., Barrowclough, C., Vaughn, C., Bamrah, J., Porceddu, K., Watts, S., & Freeman, H. (1989). Community management of schizophrenia: a two year follow-up of a behavioural intervention with families. *British Journal of Psychiatry*, **154**. 625–628.

Veijola, J., Räsänen, P., Isohanni, M. & Tiihonen, J. (1996). Low incidence of mania in Northern Finland. *The British Journal of Psychiatry*, **168**, 520–521.

Wallace C. J. (1993). Psychiatric rehabilitation. *Psychopharmacology Bulletin*, **29**, 537–548.

Wallace, C. J. & Liberman, R. P. (1985). Social skills training for patients with schizophrenia: a controlled clinical trial. *Psychiatry Research*, **15**, 239–247.

Webster, C. D., Hucker, S. J. & Grossman, M. G. (1993). Clinical programmes for mentally ill offenders. In K. Howells C. R. Hollins (Eds), *Clinical Approaches to the Mentally Disordered Offender* (pp. 87–109). Chichester: Wiley

Webster, C. D., Harris, G. T., Rice, M. E., Cormier, C. & Quinsey, V. L. (1994). *The Violence Prediction Scheme: Assessing Dangerousness in High Risk Men*. Toronto: University of Toronto, Centre of Criminology.

Webster, C. D., Douglas, K. S., Eaves, D. & Hart, S. D. (1997). *HCR-20. Assessing the Risk of Violence, Version 2.* Burnaby: Simon Fraser University and British Columbia Forensic Services Commission.

Weissman, M. M., Bland, R. C., Canino G. J., Faravelli, C., Greenwald, S., Hwu, H.-G. Joyce, P. R., Karam, E. G., Lee, C. K., Lellouch, J., Lépine J.-P., Newman, S. C., Rubio-Stipec, M., Wells, J. E., Wickramaratne, P. J., Wittchen, H.-U. & Yeh, E.-K. (1996). Cross-national epidemiology of major depression and bipolar disorder. *Journal of the American Medical Association,* **276**(4), 293–299.

Wiederanders, M. (1992). Recidivism of disordered offenders who were conditionally vs. unconditionally released. *Behavioral Sciences and the Law,* **10**, 141–148.

Wiederanders, M. R. & Choate P. A. (1994). Beyond recidivism: measuring community adjustments of conditionally released insanity acquittees. *Psychological Assessment,* **6**, 61–66.

Wiederanders, M., Bromley, D. & Choate, P. (1997). Forensic conditional release programs and outcomes in three states. *International Journal of Law and Psychiatry,* **20**, 249–257.

Wilson, D., Tien G. & Eaves, D. (1995). Increasing the community tenure of mentally disordered offenders: an assertive case management program. *International Journal of Law and Psychiatry,* **18**, 61–69.

Chapter 2

OFFENDERS WITH BRAIN DAMAGE

Norbert Nedopil

*Abteilung für Forensische Psychiatrie, Psychiatrische Klinik der Universität München,
Germany*

INTRODUCTION

This chapter describes the treatment of the most common forms of brain
damage associated with violent and/or criminal behaviour. For practical
reasons, brain damage occurring in the elderly and brain damage among
younger people are discussed separately. Although pharmacological treatments in young and in elderly patients make use of similar substances, they
do not follow the same principles. Therefore, they are also dealt with separately in this chapter. The other types of therapy used to prevent violent and
disruptive behaviour in brain-damaged patients are very similar for younger and older patients and are discussed together at the.end of the chapter.
These therapies must take into consideration the impaired cognitive functioning of the clients and therefore differ somewhat from treatment programmes designed for other violent offenders.

"Brain damage" appears to be a very broad and heterogeneous diagnostic
category, which includes different disorders, each with a distinct aetiology,
which differentially affect individuals depending on their age. The term may
be applied to a child who has experienced perinatal trauma, as well as to an

Violence, Crime and Mentally Disordered Offenders. Edited by S. Hodgins and R. Müller-Isberner.
© 2000 John Wiley & Sons, Ltd.

older person with dementia of the Alzheimer type. Most authors do not systematically differentiate between the diagnostic subcategories and tend to use broad terms, such as "organic disorder", "organic psychosis", "organic brain syndrome", "neuropsychological deficit", "dementia", "mental handicap", "mental retardation", to include a number of different disorders in their studies. The lack of differentiation in studies conducted in forensic settings results, primarily, for two reasons.

First, the number of patients with any kind of brain damage in forensic hospitals and institutions is relatively small, ranging from 3.1% (Athen, 1985) to 17% (Schumann, 1987). The prevalence rates obtained in larger surveys conducted in Germany range from 6% to 10% (Dessecker, 1997; Leygraf, 1988). These figures correspond well with findings from other countries. For example, Gunn (1991) and his colleagues found only 1% of organic brain disorder when they looked at a much wider variety of delinquency in England, whereas Grant (1997) reported that 9.3% of forensic patients presented to a Review Board in British Columbia suffered from organic brain disorder. Subcategories of organic brain disorder are often not distinguished in epidemiological research for statistical reasons and also in order to include enough subjects for treatment studies. The second reason for the lack of differentiation of diagnostic sub-categories in studies conducted in forensic settings is the fact that although different aetiological factors may lead to brain damage, the treatment of the disorders and of the associated psychopathological symptoms and behavioural disturbances are similar.

Practitioners in both general and forensic psychiatry, however, have to be aware that brain damage is not a uniform disorder and that the different syndromes affect different age groups, follow different courses, have different outcomes, and require different treatment goals. Whereas the treatment goal for an elderly patient suffering from Alzheimer's disease may be to enable him/her to spend the rest of his/her days in a nursing home, the rehabilitation of a young person suffering from traumatic brain injury would aim at social reintegration at the highest level possible.

When studying the forensic literature, we find very few papers dealing with these disorders. This fact and the above-mentioned relatively small number of forensic patients suffering from brain damage is surprising, since a number of organic brain disorders are associated with aggression. The DSM-IV (American Psychiatric Association, 1994) cites several disorders in which aggression is either a diagnostic or an associated feature, and among them are four with an organic aetiology:

- Dementia of the Alzheimer type (DAT).
- Dementia caused by head trauma.
- Personality change due to general medical condition (aggressive type).
- Post-concussional disorder.

The psychiatric and general medical literature lists several other organic brain disorders that are either believed to be, or in fact are, associated with violence, although their link is not as well proved (Fava, 1997).

- Epilepsy.
- Huntington's chorea.
- Korsakow psychosis.
- Brain tumours.
- Mental retardation.

Since the time of Lombroso (1894), violent crime has repeatedly been associated with organic brain dysfunction. Several studies have examined abnormalities and other markers of brain damage, such as performance on neuropsychological tests that may be correlated with aggressive and violent behaviours (for review, see d'Orban et al., 1993). This research, although often criticized, has continued, including biochemical analyses (Virkunnen et al., 1994), and has led to some of today's treatment recommendations for aggressive patients suffering from brain damage. Most of these recommendations are, however, not found in the forensic-psychiatric literature. Systematic analyses of epidemiological data and of other research findings show that patients with clinically relevant brain damage do not commit violent crimes more often than would be expected according to their proportion in the general population (d'Orban et al., 1993; Häfner & Böker, 1982; Toone, 1990). Even the former assumption, that some disorders, such as epilepsy, are associated with violent crime, is not confirmed by the scientific literature (Gunn, 1977; Treiman, 1986). In reviewing the epidemiological studies of the impact of head injury on criminal behaviour, Rivara and Farrington (1994) concluded that the results are somewhat confusing and not consistent. Looking at delinquency in general, head injury may be a relatively unimportant factor, but it may be important among a minority of persistent and serious offenders. Perinatal complications and early brain injury appear to be most important in children at high risk for criminality also because of their association with other risk factors, such as parental delinquency and/or substance abuse, poverty or broken homes. Acquired brain injury in later life has been found to increase the risk of violent behaviour but not of other types of criminal behaviour.

These inconsistent findings do not contradict the knowledge we have about aggressive and disruptive behaviour of *certain* patients with brain damage. The estimates of the frequency of such behaviours range from 18% in demented patients (Eastley & Wilcock, 1997) to 60% in patients with frontal lobe injuries (Grafman et al., 1996). The term "aggression" is, however, used very broadly in these studies, and most of these patients are not seen by forensic psychiatrists but are treated in special institutions or in outpatient settings. Apparently, the violent behaviour of patients with brain damage does not lead to interventions by the criminal justice system as often as could be expected from the above-mentioned numbers. Research about the treatment of aggression in these patients is, therefore, more often found in neurological and rehabilitation journals than in psychiatric or even forensic-psychiatric journals.

ORGANIC BRAIN DISORDER IN THE ELDERLY

Most dementias, for example dementia of the Alzheimer type, vascular dementia, dementia due to Pick's disease or dementia associated with Huntington's chorea, are progressive and curing or arresting the progression is not possible. Treatment is intended to slow down deterioration, to avoid complications and to organize the social support which will be needed throughout the duration of the illness. Aggression and violence constitute only two of the many complications of dementia, but only a few demented patients commit crimes of violence and reports of such crimes are mostly anecdotal. The few studies of crime by older people have not documented high rates of dementia in such samples (Hucker & Ben Aron, 1984, Weber, 1992). The risk for violent crime is higher if delusions complicate the dementia; frequently, in such cases, close relatives or neighbours are the victims of these crimes. Also, the violent act is often preceded by a conflict of long duration between the perpetrator and the victim, sometimes over a very trivial matter (Nedopil, 1996). Although it does not appear in criminal court files, aggression and agitation of demented patients is a major problem in nursing homes and for caregivers of the elderly in outpatient settings. Again, exact definitions and robust data on how much violence really occurs are lacking, but estimates range from 18% (Eastley & Wilcock, 1997) to 48% (Chandler & Chandler, 1988; Reisberg, Borenstein & Salob, 1987). Rabins, Mace and Lucas (1982) reported that 75% of caregivers considered aggression to be the most serious problem in agitated demented patients.

Pharmacological treatment

When opting for pharmacological treatment of elderly brain-disordered patients, several aspects of their functioning have to be considered. The first problem is that of the multiple disorders which often afflict such patients. Diabetes mellitus, elevated blood pressure and cardiovascular diseases are the most common, but not the only, co-morbid diseases occurring among older demented patients. The majority of such patients require several different types of medication, which may interact, or anti-aggressive treatment, which may interfere with some underlying disease, for example, β-blocking agents may lower blood pressure and decrease heart rate to intolerable levels.

The second issue to consider is the sensitivity of such patients to psychotropic medication. Older persons are much more sensitive to psychotropic (and other) medications. Paradoxical reactions are more common than among younger persons. Thus, drug treatment must be carefully monitored in order to avoid adverse effects, which may be harmful and outweigh the benefits of treatment (e.g. akathisia after neuroleptic treatment may increase irritation and lead to disruptive behaviour).

The third aspect of the functioning of elderly demented patients to consider is the influence of medication on cognitive impairment. Most demented individuals suffer from gross cognitive impairment. Medication that further impairs cognition, either by sedation or other intrinsic activity, should not be administered to demented patients except for short periods of crisis intervention. This is especially true if programmes addressing cognitive functioning are planned to help the patients to maintain some of their mental capacities.

A number of medications have been and are used to treat the agitation, disruptive and aggressive behaviour of demented patients, but there are few controlled studies of the effects.

Neuroleptics

Outside of institutions, most agitated people with dementia are prescribed neuroleptics, although their effect is only modest (Schneider, Pollock & Lyness, 1990). No neuroleptic has been found to be more effective than another for the treatment of agitation. The selection of the particular type of neuroleptic should take into account the adverse effects and possibly the previous response of the patient to the same or a similar medication. Sedation, cognitive impairment and the high risk of older individuals to develop dyskinesia and parkinsonism limit the use of neuroleptics for older non-psychotic patients.

Benzodiazepines

Benzodiazepines may be effective in treating acute agitation and aggression, but special attention has to be paid to their influence on cognition, memory and motor coordination. The impairment of motor coordination can lead especially to falls and fractures in this population (Granek, Baker & Abbey, 1987). Both neuroleptics and benzodiazepines should be restricted to short-term treatment of acute agitation, threatening or otherwise aggressive behaviour (Yudofsky, Silver & Hales, 1990).

Anti-epileptics

Several case reports and open studies suggest that carbamazepine is effective in the treatment of agitation and irritability of demented patients (Levibovici & Tariot, 1988; Patterson, 1987). One controlled study did not confirm these results (Kunik et al., 1994); consequently, the efficacy of carbamazepine in treating the aggression of demented patients is yet to be established. Lott, McElroy and Keys (1995) found valproate effective in reducing agitated behaviour among eight of 10 elderly patients. Again, there is no controlled study to confirm these findings.

β-Adrenergic blockers

Although propranolol and pindolol have been used successfully in the treatment of agitation of elderly patients (Greendyke & Kanter, 1986; Weiler, Mungras & Bernick, 1988), their usefulness in the treatment of demented patients is limited because of side effects such as hypotension, bradycardia, heart failure and the exacerbation of asthma.

Serotonergic agents

Selective serotonin re-uptake inhibitors (SSRIs) are better tolerated by elderly persons than are neuroleptics, benzodiazepines or carbamazepine. In a placebo-controlled study, Nyth and Gottfries (1990) found that 65 patients with dementia due to Alzheimer's disease profited from citalopram. Among other symptoms, agitation, irritability and restlessness were reduced. Twenty-four patients suffering from vascular dementia did not improve on the same medication. Sertraline, another SSRI, has been reported to be effective in reducing aggressive behaviour in two patients with Huntington's chorea (Ranen et al., 1996). Case reports have shown buspirone, a serotonergic anxiolytic, to be effective in reducing aggression in patients with dementia due to Alzheimer's disease and in those with vascular dementia (Colenda, 1988; Holzer, Gittelman & Price, 1995; Jeanblanc & Davis, 1995). These serotonergic agents result in few sedative or cognitive effects and may therefore be more useful in the long-term treatment of agitated, aggressive patients with dementia. Although another serotonergic antidepressant, trazodone, has been demonstrated to be effective in treating disruptive behaviour of demented patients (Greenwald et al., 1986), its use is limited by side effects, such as sedation and hypotension.

Summary

Current knowledge about the pharmacological treatment of aggression in demented patients suggests that neuroleptics are useful for rapid intervention and for dementias that are complicated by delusions or other psychotic symptoms. Benzodiazepines may also be effective in acute situations, but their use is limited to interventions of short duration. SSRIs, such as buspirone or sertraline, may be useful for long-term treatment, although further studies are necessary in order to confirm the efficacy that has been observed clinically. β-Adrenergic blockers and carbamazepine are of limited use in the long term treatment of aggression in demented patients.

ORGANIC BRAIN DISORDER IN YOUNGER PATIENTS

Whereas aggression in elderly people is rare and aggressive impulses cease relatively quickly, younger individuals behave aggressively much more frequently and more vigorously. This fact is also true for patients with brain damage. Thus, violence is much more prominent in younger patients with organic brain disorder than in those patients with Alzheimer's disease or other dementias of old age. Indeed, the frequency of violence is estimated at 18% in demented patients (Eastley & Wilcock, 1997) and at 60% in younger patients with frontal lobe injuries (Grafman et al., 1996). The variations in the prevalence of violence are therefore not only attributable to the different disorders but also to the age of the afflicted individual. Besides age, other factors contribute to the extent to which aggression may be expected, namely whether the brain damage is diffuse or localized. The location and extent of the damage and the possible concomitant misuse of alcohol and drugs are other major influences. The most common organic brain disorders among young adults are epilepsy and traumatic brain injury.

Epilepsy

Contrary to the common belief of lay people and even medical professionals, that epilepsy and violence are linked (Fenwick, 1989), epidemiological studies show that epileptics are not over-represented among prisoners who have committed violent offences (Gunn, 1977; Treiman, 1986). Yet in several investigations, they were found to be over-represented among other prisoners (Gunn, 1977; King & Young, 1978). Some authors suggest that the social deterioration and the underprivileged background of the epileptics, rather than the disorder itself, are the causes of the higher than expected number of epileptics in the prison system (Toone, 1990). For example, Mendez et al. (1993) compared 44 aggressive epileptic patients to 88 patients with epilepsy who had no prior history of violent behaviour. They found that interictal violence was more often associated with mental disorders and retardation than with epileptiform activity or other seizure variables.

Violence during seizures (ictal violence) is extremely rare, but does occur (Fenwick, 1989; Treiman, 1986). Sometimes aggressive behaviour is also reported during the prodromal phase of a seizure, when mood changes, irritability, and physical sensations dominate the psychopathological syndrome (prodromal aggression). Aggressive behaviour may also occur during a post-ictal confusional state or during post-ictal automatism.

In prodromal and in post-ictal aggression, it is important to recognize the patient's situation and to avoid provocations that may lead to violent outbursts. Benevolent physical restraint can trigger post-ictal aggression (Fenwick, 1989). Most of the violent crimes committed by persons with epilepsy occur between seizures and several studies show a higher prevalence of violent behaviour among patients with temporal lobe epilepsy than in the general population (Kligman & Goldbert, 1975; Lindsay, Dunstead & Richards, 1979; Mende, 1960). Again, however, these studies have not used adequate control groups, and a correction for social and psychopathological factors could reduce the significance of the association that has been found between violence and epilepsy (Fenwick, 1989).

There is no question that optimal medical treatment of epilepsy reduces the risk of violent outbreaks in such patients. It is beyond the scope of this chapter to review different treatments for epilepsy, but it should be stressed that successful treatment requires the cooperation of the patient and careful monitoring of several parameters (plasma levels of the medications, blood cell count, liver functioning). Some patients and some prisoners require less medication while in an institution; others develop a higher risk of seizures due to increased stress in closed situations and require higher doses of antiepileptics (D'Orban et al., 1993). Adjusting dosages and monitoring other health parameters should be carried out with particular care after patients with epilepsy enter or leave secure institutions. Cooperation does not only mean compliance with medication, but also abstinence from alcohol and other psychotropic substances. Cooperation must be considered a goal during treatment of epileptic patients, especially in forensic institutions and in the prison system, where patient autonomy and responsibility for their own well-being are not easily established. Educational programmes and information on how to recognize symptoms and to take responsibility for one's own disease and its treatment are important factors to consider in attempting to reduce the risk of recidivism after release from a secure institution. Before release, a consistent and reliable aftercare programme should be organized. If possible, the organization of the outpatient treatment should be carried out by the patient, with assistance and guidance from staff. Continuous medical treatment and social support are the most important factors in avoiding future violence by these patients.

Brain injury

The number of patients with traumatic brain injury is relatively high in industrialized countries. Vogenthaler (1987) gave estimates of 440,000 head injuries in the USA each year, 20% of which are serious enough to alter the victim's life. Traumatic brain injury is one of the disorders most frequently associated with aggressive behaviour. Brooks et al. (1986) reported that 15% of 42 patients with severe brain injury were judged to be violent by their relatives during the first year after the trauma; the proportion of patients who were violent increased to 54% at five years. Hall et al. (1994) found that 35% of caretakers regarded aggressiveness as a moderate to severe problem two years after head injury and that outbursts of temper increased over time. The Vietnam Head Injury Study indicated that frontal lobe involvement was most frequently associated with all types of aggression, including physical violence. In this investigation, over 60% of the patients showed some sort of aggression and 11% were physically assaultive (Grafman et al., 1996). Measures of aggression were not correlated to the size of the brain lesion or to the other organic symptoms, such as neurological signs or seizures, but to the location of the lesion and to social factors, such as disruption of family activities. Ventromedial frontal lobe lesions were linked to the risk of violence.

Frontal lobe syndrome

Frontal lobe syndrome is characterized by changes in personality with little or no impairment of cognitive and intellectual functioning. Originally authors differentiated the syndrome according to the localization of the lesion, which was found to be associated with different psychopathological features (Kleist, 1934; Luria, 1966). These distinctions remain valid today (Kaplan & Sadock, 1995).

Orbitofrontal lesions may simulate the characteristics of antisocial personality disorder, with the exception of being manipulative. Lack of concern for others, irritability and inappropriate and socially unacceptable behaviours (e.g. exhibitionism) are the most common symptoms. Patients may behave violently, especially under the influence of even small amounts of alcohol or in situations which are mildly irritating. This is due to their lack of control, to their inability to reflect on the consequences of their behaviour, and to their lack of concern for others. Prefrontal lesions lead to apathy and inactivity. Loss of initiative, lack of spontaneity or unawareness of social necessities may cause conflicts with other persons. Irritability can lead to violent outbursts, although these are rarer in persons with prefrontal lesions than in those with orbitofrontal lesions.

Concomitant factors increasing the risk of violence in persons with brain injury

Kreutzer, Marwitz & Witol (1995) pointed out that young adult males have the highest rate of traumatic brain injury. They also belong to the age group with the highest rate of criminality and especially of violent criminality. This same age and sex group also has the highest rate of substance abuse (Miller & Cisin, 1983). Given the high prevalence of brain injury among young men and their propensity to use alcohol and drugs, it is surprising how few are seen by forensic psychiatrists or sentenced to prison. The actual numbers of such patients found in forensic hospitals and in prisons do not reflect the high risk of violent crime by persons with brain injury. Hodgins (1995) found that only 0.4% of male penitentiary inmates warranted a diagnosis of "organic brain syndrome" (which is a much broader term than "traumatic brain injury"). Similarly the proportions of patients with organic brain syndrome in forensic hospitals is below 10% and is not greater than that in general psychiatric hospitals (Häfner & Böker, 1982, in Germany; Grant, 1997, in Canada).

Several studies suggest that the criminality of individuals with brain injury may be attributed to a large extent to premorbid personality traits, to the social disintegration which follows the injury, and not only to the injury itself (Bond, 1984; Brooks et al., 1986; Prigatano, 1987). Kreutzer et al. (1995) studied a sample of 327 patients with varying severities of traumatic brain injury. Those arrested after the brain injury were more likely to have had a history of police contacts before the brain injury than those who were not arrested. Patients who had been arrested before the head injury for criminal behaviour also had a history of heavy drinking, and were more often in psychiatric treatment than were patients with no criminal record.

These observations and considerations do not rule out the fact that some very violent crimes are associated with brain lesions due to trauma or tumours. For example, Hadfield, who attempted to murder George III, was acquitted by reason of insanity in 1800; he had a penetrating head injury from a gunshot (Walker, 1968). Charles Whitman, who in 1966 climbed to the top of the clock tower at the University of Texas at Austin and opened fire, killing 16 people, one day after having killed his wife and his mother, had a glioblastome multiform tumour, probably in one medial frontal lobe (Sweet, Ervin & Mark, 1969).

Several indicators are associated with a high risk of violence and criminality among patients with brain injury: lesion of the ventromedial frontal cortex; history of criminality before the head injury; history of substance abuse before (and after) head injury; disintegration of family structures; and disorientation, impairment of cognitive functioning, and increased irritability (Fugate et al., 1997a).

The treatment of aggression in patients with brain injury requires special skills, since neither specific guidelines for therapy nor convincing studies on how to do this exist. Pharmacotherapy, as well as behavioural treatment, have to be individualized and social support provided, in order to avoid social disintegration.

Pharmacotherapy of persons with brain injuries

Anti-epileptics   Anti-epileptics were first used as anti-aggressive agents because of the old notion that temporal lobe epilepsy causes violent behaviour. Although this assumption has been shown to be wrong, the efficacy of these drugs in the treatment of aggressive individuals has been demonstrated in many cases.

Carbamazepine is the drug most frequently used by specialists and general practitioners in the treatment of agitation and aggression following traumatic brain injury (Fugate, 1997b). A number of case reports (de Vogelaer, 1981; Hakola & Laulaumaa, 1982; Mattes, 1984; Neppe, 1983) have shown the efficacy of carbamazepine in reducing aggression in psychotic patients. Patterson (1987) studied eight aggressive men with known organic pathology who responded to 8–12 mg/l carbamazepine with a rapid and sustained decrease in violent behaviour. Foster, Hillbrand and Chi (1989) showed that their four patients returned to their previous aggressiveness after carbamazepine was discontinued. Larger controlled studies of carbamazepine as an anti-aggressive agent are unavailable. Dosages reported in different studies as being effective vary from 200 to 1000 mg/day. There seems to be agreement that carbamazepine is effective as an anti-aggressive agent in psychotic patients and patients with brain injury, and that the dosage has to be adjusted individually according to its clinical effect, adverse effects and plasma levels (Young & Hillbrand, 1994). The initial dose in adults is recommended to be 400 mg/day for five to seven days. If tolerated and if symptoms are not reduced sufficiently, the dosage can be increased by increments of 100 mg every five to seven days (Pabis & Stanislav, 1996). The plasma levels of carbamazepine and cell blood counts (CBC) should be monitored every two weeks for the first two months and then every three to six months, to avoid intoxication and serious side effects (Hart & Easton, 1982). Plasma levels should not exceed 12 mg/l.

Valproic acid has been successfully used to treat mood disorders following brain injury (Jorge et al., 1993) and also in a case of repetitive explosive behaviour following brain injury (Geracioti, 1994). It has also been used to treat the aggressive behaviour of mentally retarded persons (Mattes, 1992) and older patients with organic psychosis (Mazure, Druss & Cellar, 1992). Wroblewski et al. (1997) documented very rapid reduction of destructive and aggressive behaviour in five patients with brain injury at doses between

750 and 2250 mg/day (plasma levels 60–101 mg/l). These patients had unsuccessfully been treated with other medications, including β-adrenergic blockers, antidepressants and neuroleptics. Besides the positive effects it had on maladaptive behaviour, the advantage of valproic acid was that it caused little cognitive impairment. Although these reports appear promising, the number of patients studied so far is too small to recommend the medication as a first or second choice for the treatment of aggression in patients with brain injury.

Neuroleptics   Neuroleptics were formerly advocated in the treatment of aggression in patients with brain injury and are still widely used by practitioners (Fugate et al., 1997b; Langer & Heimann, 1883; Riederer, Laux & Pöldinger, 1995). Available evidence suggests that their use should be limited to acute interventions. Even clozapine, which has been used successfully to treat aggressive behaviour of mentally retarded and psychotic persons who had been refractory to other drugs (Cohen & Underwood, 1994; Volavka et al., 1993), is only of limited effectiveness in patients with brain injury. Side effects such as sedation and seizures, which affected two of the nine patients in the study of Michals et al. (1993), further reduce the usefulness of this drug for patients and brain injury.

Tricyclic antidepressants   Although recent studies are not available and newer review articles (Fava, 1997; Pabis & Stanislav, 1996) fail to even mention them, most specialists use tricyclic antidepressants as the medication of second choice for the treatment of aggressive behaviour in patients with brain injury (Fugate et al., 1997b). Both the tranquillizing and mood-stabilizing properties are useful. Side effects, such as sedation, lowering of blood pressure and cholinergic side effects, appear to be tolerable and most tricyclic antidepressants are well accepted by patients with brain injuries.

Lithium   Lithium was found to be effective in the treatment of aggressive behaviour as early as 1971 (Sheard, 1971), but studies that confirm these findings among patients with brain injuries are rare (Glenn et al., 1989). The positive effects of this medication have been more convincingly shown with mentally retarded patients (Tyrer et al., 1984; Craft et al., 1987) or in impulsive and assaultive individuals with no brain damage (Tupin et al., 1973; Langee, 1990). The limited usefulness of lithium in patients with brain injury may be due to the fact that many of them do not tolerate high plasma concentrations because of increased susceptibility to adverse side effects, such as sedation and ataxia.

β-Adrenergic blockers   Only a few rather unconvincing studies exist on the use of propranolol for treating aggression in patients with brain injury

(Greendyke et al., 1986). Greendyke and Kanter (1986) reported that pindolol was more effective than a placebo in reducing hostility in 11 patients with organic brain syndromes. This finding, however, was not replicated in a later study (Greendyke & Kanter, 1986). β-Adrenergic blockers are the medication of second choice, following carbamazepine for most general practitioners for the treatment of aggressive behaviour in patients with brain damage, while specialists prefer tricyclic antidepressants as second choice (Fugate et al., 1997b).

Serotonergic substances   The usefulness of serotonergic substances in patients with brain injury has been suggested by a number of case reports and by some controlled trials. Buspirone, a 5-HT_{1A} receptor partial agonist, was reported to be effective in reducing aggression in two retrospective studies of hospitalized patients with brain injury (Gualtierie, 1991; Stanislav et al., 1994). Trazodone, a 5-HT_2 receptor agonist, reduced assaultive behaviour in three of seven patients with brain injuries (Pinner & Rich, 1988) and in four elderly patients with organic brain syndromes who did not respond to neuroleptics (Simpson & Foster, 1986).

Other therapies

Psychotherapy, as well as pharmacotherapy, must address symptoms other than aggressive and violent behaviour when treating patients with brain damage. The syndrome presented by such patients may include a number of other symptoms, most often impaired cognitive functioning, diminished insight, lack of motivation and energy, disinhibition and impulsivity. Therapies that require cognitive flexibility, unimpaired memory and initiative on the part of the patient—like group therapy or psychoanalytic therapies—are not useful. Similarly, pure cognitive therapy, which requires initiative and the mental capacities to restructure cognitions and attitudes, is of little value. Both of these forms of therapy may even worsen the clinical picture of patients with brain damage by demanding too much of the patient and thereby provoking frustration and maladaptive behaviour. Behaviour therapy appears to be the most widely used and most successful psychotherapeutic treatment of patients with brain damage, regardless of the aetiology of the brain damage (Ball, 1993; Burgess & Alderman, 1990; Eames & Wood, 1985; Franzen & Lowell, 1987; Manchester et al., 1997; Matson & Gorman-Smith, 1986). Especially in forensic settings, specialized wards employing behavioural treatment strategies for aggressive patients have been advocated (Bullard & Bond, 1988). Behavioural programmes aim to reduce aggressive, disinhibitive and socially inappropriate behaviour and to strengthen adaptive behaviour. At the outset of the treatment, there has to be a careful analysis of the deficits, limitations and strengths of the client. A very useful approach for this analysis is the A–B–C technique (Alpert & Spillmann, 1997; Wong et al., 1988). The "A" stands for the antecedents of the aggressive behaviour, such as provocations, frustrations, ambivalence or attention seeking. The "B" stands for behaviour, such as swearing, threatening, kicking, biting or spitting. The "C" stands for the consequences that maintain aggressive behaviour, such as the status within a group, attaining a goal, avoiding stress or other unwanted feelings or tasks. The analysis should also identify possible positive reinforcers of behaviour, like cigarette smoking, social contact, television, etc.

The basis of a treatment programme can be derived from this analysis. The treatment should aim at extinguishing the positive as well as the negative reinforcers of aggressive behaviour, and at developing alternative behavioural strategies for reaching the patient's goals. The most important step in the treatment is winning the patient's co-operation. In order to do this, it is necessary carefully and patiently to explain treatment goals and procedures to the patients in a language that they can understand. Patients need to learn how to use the feedback that they receive about their behaviour. This can be a very difficult task and often the patients' understanding lasts for only a short time as a result of their cognitive impairment and memory deficits. Consequently, feedback must be immediate and repetitive. Due to the relatively short attention spans of the patients, progress is made in small steps and treatment may take a considerable time. The general methods of a treatment programme for patients with brain damage do not differ substantially from the methods of behavioural treatment programmes for most other patients (Alpert & Spillmann, 1997).

Three behavioural treatment components have been used successfully with patients with brain damage, and often a combination of these methods can be helpful. Strategies of one treatment component often overlap with those of another, and most institutions use several. Although the treatment programme may be inspired by several different theoretical concepts and be tailored to each individual patient, the therapist should have a clear understanding of the concept underlying the treatment programme.

1. Accelerative and decelerative techniques involve strengthening the behaviours that are incompatible with aggression, using humour, social interaction and work (accelerative technique) and decreasing the frequency of aggressive behaviour by ignoring the patient when he/she is aggressive and by sanctioning the aggressive behaviour with time-out—that is, avoiding social contact after aggressive acts (deceleration).
2. Social skills training teaches on particular behaviours, such as recognizing conflict, and making adequate responses to conflict. Behaviours are rehearsed using role playing, correct responses are positively reinforced,

inadequate or undesired responses are corrected and finally skills are required after much practice.

3. Cognitive behavioural therapy is the most frequently used psycho-therapeutic technique for aggressive offenders (Eucker, 1998), although there are certain limitations in using this treatment for patients with impaired cognitive functioning due to brain damage. Some principles of cognitive-behavioural treatment, however, apply also to this patient group, even if the techniques may have to be modified. The treatment includes explaining and understanding the following concepts (Novaco & Welsh, 1989): which emotions are associated with aggression; which situations are likely to produce these emotions; how to avoid these situations; and how to find other solutions that may not inflict anger or fear. These objectives can be achieved with many patients suffering from brain damage.

The same reinforcers used with other patients in behavioural programmes can be used with brain-damaged patients. Token economies or level systems involve the use of positive reinforcers or a gradual increase in privileges to reward good behaviour, and time-out or ignoring to sanction maladaptive behaviour.

In some patients aggressive behaviour may increase at the beginning of a behavioural programme, when the rules and requirements of the programme provoke frustration.

Behavioural programmes for brain-damaged patients require close and constant cooperation among all treatment staff. Motivating, coaching and supervising the staff are very important in order to avoid sending conflicting signals to the patients. Staff members have to be aware of the patients' deficits and limitations and the strategies used in the programme. They should be able to establish a friendly, trusting climate, so that eventually the attention of, and time spent with, the staff become the principal positive reinforcers of adaptive behaviour. The important task for supervisors is to establish collaboration among all of the staff members in order to ensure friendly, clear and uniform handling of the patients and to avoid ambivalence and ambiguity towards them. Violence on psychiatric wards occurs most often after some sort of provocation by the staff, in situations where the climate on the ward is tense, when the activities on the ward are unstructured, or when restraint is imposed on patients (Edwards, 1988). Previous violence predicts future violence in patients with brain damage as well as in others. Antecedents of violent acts include a sudden refusal to cooperate, changes of vigilance, agitation, suspiciousness, threatening behaviour and withdrawal (Kidd & Stark, 1995). The most important factor in avoiding violence in these situations is to refrain from all provocation, to employ a non-confrontational approach to the patient, and to lead the patient out of the "field" of aggressive tension, that is to lead him away from potential adversaries or other aggression-prone stimuli. The same principles should guide the caregivers in outpatient settings in order to avoid aggressive outbursts by their clients.

SOCIAL SUPPORT

Most individuals with brain damage are unable to continue the life they lived prior to the injury or onset of the degenerative disease. For many of them, the brain injury or degeneration disrupts their previous life pattern and destroys social interaction. But for others, the violent behaviour that accompanies the damage changes their lives. Not all of them can return to their homes and some lose the support of their families. For many of these patients, new social networks have to be developed in order to avoid permanent hospitalization. Those who can return to their families need help and support to cope with their deficits and impairments. Support must be also provided to the care-givers. One of the most important tasks in preventing violence by patients with brain damage is to identify a social setting and care-givers who can cope with the patient's symptoms, continue the therapeutic programmes successfully begun during inpatient treatment, use the same reinforcers, and accept the minimal progress these patients are able to achieve (Manchester, Hodgkinson & Casey, 1997). Care-givers have to monitor medication use and observe patients for signs of deterioration that might constitute a warning of an increased risk of violence. Care-givers in rehabilitation centres, nursing homes or outpatient settings who treat patients after discharge from a forensic institution must be educated and coached on the risks and the proper handling of their patients. They also require adequate supervision to avoid frustration—both theirs and the patients'—and to reduce the risk of violent recidivism.

CONCLUSIONS AND RECOMMENDATIONS

Although the term "brain damage" includes a wide variety of disorders of different aetiologies, the strategies for treatment and rehabilitation are very similar. Most patients with brain damage need a combination of medication and behavioural therapy, as well as social support when they are released into the community. In treating individuals with brain damage, it is important to bear in mind that:

1. Behaviour can be modified in most cases and a defeatist attitude is not justified.

2. These patients present multiple deficits and impairments and consequently treatment requirements or social tasks can overwhelm them and lead to frustration and maladaptive behaviours.
3. Inappropriate treatment demands not only provoke acting-out behaviours and limited, if any, improvement in patients, they also lead to resignation on the part of staff.

Care-givers must always take account of the patient's limitations, and as well of his/her potential to use what skills remain to make considerable improvement (Manchester et al., 1997; Sellars, Hollin & Howells, 1993).

Pharmacological treatment of aggressive and disruptive behaviour of patients with brain damage differs somewhat from the treatment of psychotic or other mentally disordered or mentally retarded patients. Among the brain-damaged, side effects such as sedation and cognitive impairment have to be avoided and special attention paid to diminished tolerance to the neurotoxicity of certain medications. Many patients with brain damage also suffer from other diseases, which may limit the use of certain medications. Since aggressive behaviour is only one of many symptoms presented by patients with brain damage, the treatment programme, and especially pharmacological treatment, should address the entire spectrum of symptoms. Lithium and propranolol, both drugs whose anti-aggressive effects have been proved in different patient groups, are not medications of first choice in patients with brain damage. Medications of first choice for patients with brain injury include carbamazepine and serotonergic agents such as sertraline, buspirone and, in elderly patients with dementia, tricyclic antidepressants. β-Adrenergic blockers are also medications of first choice for elderly patients if their use is not contra-indicated by other symptoms. Neuroleptics are indicated for those who also present psychotic symptoms, such as delusions or hallucinations, or who have to be sedated in emergency situations. Benzodiazepines may also be used in acute situations. These medications should be used for as short a period as is possible. Treatment recommendations are summarized in Table 2.1.

All treatments must respect the patients' limitations and avoid overburdening them. Some therapeutic strategies, such as psychoanalysis and group therapy, are not indicated for these disorders. Behavioural therapy begins with a careful analysis of the client's deficits and his/her remaining capacities. Explaining deficits and remaining skills as well as the immediate treatment goals in a language that the patient can understand helps to win his/her trust and cooperation with the treatment. Treatment goals should be defined in small incremental steps that can be attained within a time frame the client can perceive, enabling the patient to perceive his/her own progress. Treatment must be individually tailored to each patient's needs. Close cooperation among the entire treatment staff is essential for success. The

Table 2.1 Pharmacological treatment of aggressive behaviour of patients with brain damage

	Medication	Indications	Recommended dose	Adverse effects	Monitoring
Antiepileptics	Carbamazepine	Chronic treatment, especially in brain injury and epilepsy, first choice	400 to 1200 mg/day (plasma levels 4–12 mg/l)	Leukopenia, rash, headache, drowsiness	Blood cell count, plasma levels, liver function
	Valproic acid	Chronic treatment, especially in brain injury and epilepsy	500 to 3000 mg/day (plasma levels 50–100 mg/l)	Hepatic toxicity, drowsiness	Liver function, blood cell count, plasma levels
SSRIs	Buspirone	Chronic treatment, first choice in the elderly	15–60 mg/day	Headache, nausea, dizziness	Short half-life, 2–4 doses a day
	Sertraline	Chronic treatment, first choice in the elderly	50–200 mg/day	Headache, drowsiness, nausea	
	Trazodone	Chronic treatment	150–500 mg/day	Sedation, hypotension	Electrocardiogram
	Fluoxetine	Chronic treatment	20–80 mg/day	Headache, drowsiness, nausea	
Mood stabilizers	Tricyclic antidepressants	Chronic treatment, especially in dementia and when accompanied by depression	Different agents, therefore no dose range	Sedation, hypotension, anticholinergic side effects	Electrocardiogram
	Lithium	Chronic treatment, limited effects in patients with brain injury	According to plasma level 0.6–1.0 mEq/l in two divided doses	Polyuria, polydipsia, tremor, gastrointestinal intolerance, hypothyreosis	Thyroid function, renal function, pregnancy, plasma levels, blood cell count, ECG
Classical neuroleptics	Neuroleptics	Acute intervention, psychotic aggression	Different agents, therefore no dose range	Sedation, extrapyramidal symptoms, dyskinesia, akathisia, leukopenia	White blood cell count
Atypical neuroleptics	Clozapine	Acute intervention, psychotic aggression, aggression resistant to other treatments	250–700 mg/day	Sedation, orthostasis, fever, leukopenia	White blood cell count (weekly)
β-Blockers	Propranolol	Chronic treatment, first choice in the elderly, if not contraindicated because of other diseases	160–320 mg/day	Hypotension, sedation, depression, masking hypoglycaemia	Blood pressure, pulse rate
	Pindolol	Chronic treatment	40–60 mg/day	Hypotension, sedation, depression, masking hypoglycaemia	Blood pressure, pulse rate
Benzodiazepines	Benzodiazepines	Acute intervention	Different drugs, therefore no dose range	Sedation, disinhibition dependence, ataxia	Increasing dosage

social setting into which the client will be released must not only be prepared to provide adequate housing but also to meet the needs of the client. Caregivers must accept the client's limitations and avoid making demands which are overwhelming and which may lead to frustration. Caregivers in the community must continue the reinforcement strategies which were successfully used during inpatient treatment and provide support and coaching. This is essential in order to avoid critical situations that may lead to disruptive and aggressive behaviour. Caregivers should be trained to recognize signs of deterioration and precursors of possible violence.

REFERENCES

Alpert, J. E. & Spillmann, M. K. (1997).   Psychotherapeutic approaches to aggressive and violent patients. *Psychiatric Clinics of North America*, **20**, 453–472.

American Psychiatric Association (1994).   *Diagnostic and Statistical Manual of Mental Disorders, 4th edn (DSM-IV)*. Washington, DC: APA.

Athen, D. (1985).   Gegenwärtigen Situationen der Behandlung psychisch kranker Rechtsbrecher. *Monatsschrift für Kriminologie und Strafrechtsreform*, **68**, 35–43.

Ball, G. G. (1993).   Modifying the behaviour of the violent patient. *Psychiatric Quarterly*, **64**, 359–369.

Böker, W. & Häfner, H. (1973).   *Gewalttaten Geistesgestörter*. Berlin: Springer.

Bond, M. R. (1984).   The psychiatry of closed head injury. In D. N. Brooks (Ed.), *Closed Head Injury*. Oxford: Oxford University Press.

Brooks, N., Campsie, L., Symington, M., Beattie, A. & McKinlay, W. (1986).   The five year outcome of severe blunt head injury: a relative's view. *Journal of Neurology, Neurosurgery and Psychiatry*, **49**, 764–770.

Bullard, H. & Bond, M. (1988).   Secure units: why they are needed. *Medicine Science and the Law*, **28**, 312–318.

Burgess, P. W. & Alderman, N. (1990).   Rehabilitation of dyscontrol syndromes following frontal lobe damage. A cognitive neuropsychological approach. In R. L. Wood & I. Fussey (Eds), *Cognitive Rehabilitation in Perspective*. London: Taylor & Francis.

Chandler, J. D. & Chandler, J. E. (1988).   The prevalence of neuropsychiatric disorder in a nursing home population. *Journal of Geriatry, Psychiatry and Neurology*, **1**, 71–76.

Cohen, S. A. & Underwood, M. T. (1994).   The use of clozapine in a mentally retarded and aggressive population. *Journal of Clinical Psychiatry*, **55**, 440–444.

Colenda, C. C. (1988).   Buspirone in treatment of an agitated demented patient. *Lancet*, **1**, 1169.

Craft, M., Ismail, I., Krishnamurti, A. D., Mathews, J., Regan, A. & Seth, R. V. (1987).   Lithium in the treatment of aggression in mentally retarded persons. *British Journal of Psychiatry*, **150**, 685–689.

de Vogelaer, J. (1981).   Carbamazepine in the treatment of psychotic and behavioral disorders. *Acta Psychiatrica Belgica*, **81**, 532–541.

Dessecker, A. (Ed.) (1997).   *Straftäter und Psychiatrie*, Vol. 21. Wiesbaden: Kriminologische Zentralstelle e.V.

D'Orban, P., Gunn, J., Holland, A., Kopelman, M. D., Robertson, G. & Taylor, P. J. (1993). Organic disorder, mental handicap and offending. In J. Gunn & P. J. Taylor (Eds), *Forensic Psychiatry* (pp. 286–328). Oxford: Butterworth-Heinemann.

Eames, P. & Wood, R. (1985). Rehabilitation after severe head injury: a follow-up study of a behaviour modification approach. *Journal of Neurology, Neurosurgery and Psychiatry*, **48**, 613–619.

Eastley, R. & Wilcock, G. K. (1997). Prevalence and correlates of aggressive behavior occurring in Alzheimer's disease. *International Journal of Geriatric Psychiatry*, **12**, 484–487.

Edwards, J., Jones, D., Reid, W. & Chu, C. (1988). Physical assaults in a psychiatric unit of a general hospital. *American Journal of Psychiatry*, **12**, 1568–1571.

Eucker, S. (1998). Verhaltenstherapeutische Methoden in der Straftäterbehandlung. In H. L. Kröber & M. Dahle (Eds), *Sexualstraftaten und Gewaltdelinquenz* (pp. 189–210). Heidelberg: Kriminalistik, Wissenschaft und Praxis.

Fava, M. (1997). Psychopharmacologic treatment of pathological aggression. *Psychiatric Clinics of North America*, **20**, 427–451.

Fenwick, P. (1989). The nature and management of aggression in epilepsy. *J. Neuropsychiatry*, **1**, 418–425.

Foster, H. G., Hillbrand, M. & Chi, C. C. (1989). Efficacy of carbamazepine in assaultive patients with frontal lobe dysfunction. *Progress in Neuropsychopharmacology and Biological Psychiatry*, **13**, 865–874.

Franzen, M. D. & Lowell, M. R. (1987). Behavioral treatments of aggressive sequelae of brain injury. *Psychiatric Annals*, **17**, 389–396.

Fugate, L. P., Spacek, L. A., Kresty, L. A., Levy, C. E. & Johnson, J. C. (1997a). Definition of agitation following traumatic brain injury: I. A Survey of the Brain Injury Special Interest Group of the American Academy of Physical Medicine and Rehabilitation. *Archives of Physical and Medical Rehabilitation*, **78**, 917–923.

Fugate, L. P., Spacek, L. A., Kresty, L. A., Levy, C. E. & Johnson, J. C. (1997b). Measurement and treatment of agitation following traumatic brain injury: II. A Survey of the Brain Injury Special Interest Group of the American Academy of Physical Medicine and Rehabilitation. *Archives of Physical and Medical Rehabilitation*, **78**, 924–928.

Geriacioti, T. D. (1994). Valproic acid treatment of explosiveness related to brain injury. *Journal of Clinical Psychiatry*, **55**, 416–417.

Glenn, M. B., Wroblewski, B., Parziale, J., Levine, L., Whytsse, J. & Rosenthal, M. (1989). Lithium carbonate for aggressive behaviour or affective instability in ten brain-injured patients. *American Journal of Physical Medicine and Rehabilitation*, **68**, 221–226.

Grafman, J., Schwab, K., Warden, D., Pridgen, A., Brown, H. R. & Salazar, A. M. (1996). Frontal lobe injuries, violence, and aggression. *Neurology*, **46**, 1231–1238.

Granek, E., Baker, S. P. & Abbey, H. (1987). Medication and diagnoses in relation to falls in a long term care facility. *Journal of the American Geriatric Society*, **35**, 503–511.

Grant, I. (1997). Canada's new mental disorder disposition provisions: a case study of the British Columbia Criminal Code Review Board. *International Journal of Law and Psychiatry*, **20**, 419–443.

Greendyke, R. M. & Kanter, D. R. (1986). Therapeutic effects of pindolol on behavioral disturbances associated with organic brain disease: a double-blind study. *Journal of Clinical Psychiatry*, **47**, 423–426.

Greendyke, R. M., Kanter, D. R., Schuster, D. B. et al. (1986). Propranolol treatment of assaultive patients with organic brain disease. *Journal of Nervous and Mental Disease*, **174**, 290–294.

Greenwald, B. S., Marin, D. B. & Silvermans, M. (1986). Serotonergic treatment of screaming and banging in dementia. *Lancet*, **2**, 1295–1296.

Gualtierie, C. (1991). Buspirone for the behavioral problems of patients with organic brain disorders. *Journal of Clinical Psychopharmacology*, **11**, 280–281.

Gunn, J. (1977). *Epileptics in Prison*. London: Academic Press.

Gunn, J. (1991). Human violence, a biological perspective. *Criminal Behaviour and Mental Health*, **1**, 34–54.

Häfner, H. & Böker, W. (1982). *Crimes of Violence by Mentally Abnormal Offenders. The Psychiatric Epidemiological Study in the Federal German Republic*. (Marshall, H., Trans.). Cambridge, New York: Cambridge University Press.

Hakola, H. P. A. & Laulaumaa, V. A. (1982). Carbamazepine in treatment of violent schizophrenics. *Lancet*, **V** (June 12), 1358.

Hall, K., Karzmark, P., Stevens, M. et al. (1994). Family stressors in traumatic brain injury: a two year follow-up. *Archives of Physical Medicine and Rehabilitation*, **75**, 876–884.

Hart, R. & Easton, J. D. (1982). Carbamazepine and hematologic monitoring. *Annals of Neurology*, **11**, 309–312.

Hodgins, S. (1995). Assessing mental disorder in the criminal justice system. *International Journal of Law and Psychiatry*, **18**(1), 15–28.

Holzer, J. C., Gittelman, D. R. & Price, B. H. (1995). Efficacy of buspirone in the treatment of dementia with aggression. *American Journal of Psychiatry*, **153**, 812.

Hucker, S. J. & Ben-Aron, M. H. (1984). Violent elderly offenders—a comparative study. In W. Wilbanks & P. K. H. Kim (Eds), *Elderly Criminals* (pp. 69–81). New York: Landham.

Jeanblanc, W. & Davis, Y. B. (1995). Risperidone for treating dementia-associated aggression. *American Journal of Psychiatry*, **152**, 1239.

Jorge, R. E., Robinson, R. G., Starkstein, S. E. et al. (1993). Secondary mania following brain injury. *American Journal of Psychiatry*, **150**, 916–921.

Kaplan, H. J. & Sadock, B. J. (1995). *Comprehensive Textbook of Psychiatry*, Vol. V. Baltimore, MD: Williams & Wilkins.

Kidd, B. & Stark, C. (1995). *Management of Violence and Aggression in Health Care*. London: Gaskell.

King, L. M. & Young, Q. D. (1978). Increased prevalence of seizure disorders among prisoners. *Journal of the American Medical Association*, **239**, 2674–2675.

Kleist, K. (1934). *Gehirnpathologie*. Leipzig: Johann Ambrosius Barth.

Kligman, D. & Goldberg, D. T. (1975). Temporal lobe epilepsy and aggression. *Journal of Nervous and Mental Disease*, **160**, 324–341.

Kreutzer, J. S., Marwitz, J. H. & Witol, A. D. (1995). Interrelations between crime, substance abuse, and aggressive behaviours among persons with traumatic brain injury. *Brain Injury*, **9**, 757–768.

Kunik, M. E., Yudofsky, S. C., Silver, J. M. & Hales, R. E. (1994). Pharmacological approach to management of agitation associated with dementia. *Journal of Clinical Psychiatry*, **55** (Suppl), 13–17.

Langee, H. R. (1990). Retrospective study of lithium use for institutionalized mentally retarded individuals with behaviour disorder. *American Journal of Mental Retardation*, **94**, 448–452.

Langer, G. & Heimann, H. (1983). *Psychopharmaka, Grundlagen und Therapie*. New York: Springer.

Levibovici, A. & Tariot, P. N. (1988). Carbamazepine treatment of agitation associated with dementia. *Journal of Geriatrics Psychiatry and Neurology*, **1**, 110–112.

Leygraf, N. (1988). *Psychisch kranke Rechtsbrecher*. Berlin: Springer.

Lindsay, J., Dunstead, C. & Richards, P. (1979). Long-term outcome in children with temporal lobe seizures: III. Psychiatric aspects in childhood and adult life. *Dev. Med. Child. Neurol.*, **21**, 630–636.

Lombroso, C. (1894). *Der Verbrecher. In anthropologischer, ärztlicher und juristischer Beziehung* (original 1876 edn). Hamburg: Verlagsanstalt u. Druckerei AG.

Lott, A. D., McElroy, S. L. & Keys, M. A. (1995). Valproate in the treatment of behavioural agitation in elderly people with dementia. *Journal of Neuropsychiatry*, **7**, 314–319.

Luria, A. R. (1966). *Higher Cortical Functions in Man.* New York: Basic Books.

Manchester, D., Hodgkinson, A. & Casey, T. (1997). Prolonged severe behavioural disturbance following traumatic brain injury: what can be done? *Brain Injury*, **11**, 605–617.

Matson, J. L. & Gorman-Smith, D. (1986). A review of treatment research for aggressive and disruptive behaviour in the mentally retarded. *Appl Res. Mental Retardation*, **7**, 95–103.

Mattes, A. (1992). Valproic acid for nonaffective aggression in the mentally retarded. *Journal of Nervous and Mental Disease*, **180**, 601–602.

Mattes, J. A. (1984). Carbamazepine for uncontrolled rage outbursts. *Lancet*, **V** (Nov. 17), 1164–1165.

Mazure, C. M., Druss, B. G. & Cellar, J. S. (1992). Valproate treatment of older psychotic patients with organic mental syndromes and behavioural dyscontrol. *Journal of the American Geriatric Society*, **40**, 914–916.

Mende, W. (1960). Brandstiftung im Anfallsintervall. *Monatsschrift für Kriminologie und Strafrechtsreform*, **43**, 177–181.

Mendez, M., Doss, R. C. & Taylor, J. L. (1993). Interictal violence in epilepsy: relationship to behavior and seizure variables. *Journal of Nervous and Mental Disease*, **181**, 566–569.

Michals, M. L., Crismon, M. L., Roberts, S. & Childs, A. (1993). Clozapine response and adverse effects in nine brain-injured patients. *Journal of Clinical Psychopharmacology*, **13**, 198–202.

Miller, J. D. & Cisin, I. H. (1983). *Highlights from the National Survey on Drug Abuse 1982.* Washington, DC: US Government Printing Office.

Nedopil, N. (1996). *Forensische Psychiatrie.* Stuttgart: Thieme.

Neppe, V. M. (1983). Carbamazepine as adjunctive treatment in non-epileptic chronic inpatients with EEG temporal lobe abnormalities. *Journal of Clinical Psychiatry*, **44**, 326–331.

Novaco, R. W. & Welsh, W. N. (1989). Anger disturbances: cognitive mediation and clinical prescriptions. In K. Howells & C. R. Hollin (Eds), *Clinical Approaches to Violence* (pp. 39–60). Chichester: Wiley.

Nyth, A. L. & Gottfries, C. G. (1990). The clinical efficacy of citalopram in treatment of emotional disturbances in dementia disorders: a Nordic multicentre study. *British Journal of Psychiatry*, **157**, 894–901.

Pabis, D. J. & Stanislav, S. W. (1996). Pharmacotherapy of aggressive behaviour. *Annals of Pharmacotherapy*, **30**, 278–287.

Patterson, J. F. (1987). Carbamazepine for assaultive patients with organic brain disease. *Psychosomatics*, **28**, 579–581.

Pinner, E. & Rich, C. (1988). Effects of trazodone on aggressive behaviour in seven patients with organic mental disorder. *American Journal of Psychiatry*, **145**, 1295–1296.

Prigatano, G. P. (1987). Psychiatric aspects of head injury: problem areas and suggested guidelines for research. In H. S. Levin, J. Grafman & H. M. Eisenberg (Eds), *Neurobehavioural Recovery of Head Injury*. New York: Oxford University Press.

Rabins, P. V., Mace, N. L. & Lucas, M. J. (1982). The impact of dementia on the family. *JAMA*, **248**, 333–335.

Ranen, N. G., Lipsey, J. R., Treisman, G. & Ross, C. A. (1996). Sertraline in the treatment of severe aggressiveness in Huntington's disease. *Journal of Neuropsychiatry*, **8**, 338–340.

Reisberg, B., Borenstein, J., Salob, S. P. et al. (1987). Behavioural symptoms in Alzheimers disease: phenomenology and treatment. *Journal of Clinical Psychiatry*, **48**, (5 Suppl), 9–15.

Riederer, P., Laux, G. & Pöldinger, W. (1993). *Neuropsychopharmaka*, Vol. 6. New York: Springer.

Rivara, F. P. & Farrington, D. P. (1994). Head injury and criminal behaviour. In D. Johnson, B. Pentland & E. Glasgow (Eds), *Head Injury and Litigation*. London: Sweet and Maxwell.

Schneider, L. S., Pollock, V. E. & Lyness, S. A. (1990). Meta-analysis of controlled trials of neuroleptic treatment in dementia. *Journal of the American Geriatric Society*, **38**, 553–563.

Schumann, V. (1987). *Psychisch kranke Rechtsbrecher*. Stuttgart: Enke.

Sellars, C., Hollin, C. R. & Howells, K. (1993). Mental illness, neurological and organic disorder, and criminal behaviour. In C. R. Hollin & K. Howells (Eds), *Clinical Approaches to the Mentally Abnormal Offender* (pp. 71–86). Chichester: Wiley.

Sheard, M. H. (1971). Effect of lithium on human aggression. *Nature*, **230**, 113–114.

Simpson, D. & Foster, D. (1986). Improvement in organically disturbed behaviour with trazodone treatment. *Journal of Clinical Psychiatry*, **47**, 191–193.

Stanislav, S. W., Fabre, T., Crismon, M. L. & Childs, A. (1994). Buspirone's efficacy in organic-induced aggression. *Journal of Clinical Psychopharmacology*, **14**, 126–130.

Sweet, W. H., Ervin, F. & Mark, V. H. (1969). The relationship of violent behaviour to focal cerebral disease. In S. Garattini & E. B. Sigg (Eds), *Aggressive Behaviour* (pp. 336–352). Amsterdam: Excerpta Medica.

Toone, B. (1990). Organically determined mental illness. In R. Bluglass & P. Bowden (Eds), *Principles and Practice of Forensic Psychiatry* (pp. 385–392). Melbourne: Churchill Livingstone.

Treiman, D. (1986). Epilepsy and violence: medical and legal issues. *Epilepsia*, **27** (Suppl. 2), 77–102.

Tupin, J. P., Smith, D. B., Clanon, T. L., Kim, L. I., Nugent, A. & Groupe, A. (1973). The long-term use of lithium in aggressive prisoners. *Comprehensive Psychiatry*, **14**, 311–317.

Tyrer, S. P., Walsh, A., Edwards, D. E., Berney, T. P. & Stephens, D. A. (1984). Factors associated with a good response to lithium in aggressive mentally handicapped subjects. *Prog. Neuro-psychopharmacology & Biological Psychiatry*, **8**, 751–755.

Virkunnen, M., Rawlings, R., Tokula, R., Poland, R. E., Guidotti, A., Nemeroff, C., Bisette, G., Kalegeras, K., Karonen, S.-L. & Linnoila, M. (1994). CSF Biochemistries, glucose metabolism, and diurnal activity rhythms in alcoholic, violent offenders, fire setters and healthy volunteers. *Archives of General Psychiatry*, **51**, 20–27.

Vogenthaler, D. R. (1987). An overview of head injury: its consequences and rehabilitation. *Brain Injury*, **1**, 113–127.

Volavka, J., Zito, J. M., Vitrai, J. & Czobor, P. (1993). Clozapine effects on hostility and aggression in schizophrenia. *Journal of Clinical Psychopharmacology*, **13**, 287–289.

Walker, N. (1968). *Crime and Insanity in England. I. The Historical Perspective.* Edinburgh: Edinburgh University Press.

Weber, J. (1992). Diagnosen und Prädeliktion der Alterstäter in der psychiatrischen Begutachtungsstatistik. In A. Kreuzer & M. Hürlimann (Eds), *Alte Menschen als Täter und Opfer* (pp. 148–157). Freiburg: Lambertus.

Weiler, P. G., Mungas, D., & Bernick, C. (1988). Propranolol for the control of disruptive behavior in senile dementia. *Journal of Geriatry, Psychiatry and Neurology*, **1**, 226–230.

Wong, S. E., Woolsey, J. E., Innocent, A. J. et al. (1988). Behavioural treatment of violent psychiatric patients. *Psychiatric Clinics of North America*, **11**, 569–580.

Wroblewski, B. A., Joseph, A. B., Kupfer, J. & Kalliel, K. (1997). Effectiveness of valproic acid on destructive and aggressive behaviours in patients with acquired brain injury. *Brain Injury*, **11**, 37–47.

Young, J. L. & Hillbrand, M. (1994). Carbamazepine lowers aggression: a review. *Bulletin of the American Academy of Psychiatry and Law*, **22**, 53–61.

Yudofsky, S. C., Silver, J. M. & Hales, R. E. (1990). Pharmacologic management of aggression in the elderly. *Journal of Clinical Psychiatry*, **51** (10, Suppl), 22–28.

Chapter 3

PERSONALITY DISORDERED OFFENDERS: CONCEPTUALIZATION, ASSESSMENT AND DIAGNOSIS OF PERSONALITY DISORDER

HEATHER BURKE AND STEPHEN D. HART

Department of Psychology, Simon Fraser University, Burnaby, Canada

INTRODUCTION

Personality disorder is a chronic disturbance in one's relations with self, others and the environment that results in distress or failure to fulfil social roles and obligations [e.g. American Psychiatric Association (APA), 1994; World Health Organization (WHO), 1992]. Because it encompasses such a diverse range of psychopathology, it is common to discuss personality disorder in terms of a number of distinct types. One type—known as psychopathic, antisocial or dissocial personality disorder—has such strong associations with crime and violence that it is the focus of a separate chapter in this volume.

Even though their association with criminality is complex and often indirect, non-psychopathic personality disorders can play an important role in forensic decision-making with respect to treatment. In some cases,

Violence, Crime and Mentally Disordered Offenders. Edited by S. Hodgins and R. Müller-Isberner.
© 2000 John Wiley & Sons, Ltd.

personality disorder is a primary target for treatment because it plays a causal role in the person's criminal and violent behavior. For example, the extreme sexual jealousy sometimes associated with borderline or paranoid personality disorder may result in violence directed at a romantic partner. In other cases, personality disorder is a secondary treatment target, because it is co-morbid with, and complicates the treatment of, an acute mental disorder such as substance use, depression or schizophrenia. For example, the extreme discomfort with interpersonal relations associated with schizoid or avoidant personality disorder can lead to non-compliance with group psychotherapy for major depression.

Our focus in this chapter is on the management of risk for criminal and violent behavior among forensic patients and offenders who have a primary diagnosis of personality disorders other than psychopathy. It is common for these patients to suffer from co-morbid mental disorders such as substance use, dysthymia and anxiety disorders, sometimes referred to as "minor" or "low morbidity" disorders. We will not discuss personality disorders in people with a primary diagnosis of a major mental illness.

The first problem faced by clinicians is identifying people who have a primary diagnosis of personality disorder and characterizing the nature and severity of their symptoms. Thus, the chapter begins with the identification of key issues in the conceptualization, assessment and diagnosis of personality disorder. The second problem for clinicians is deciding how best to manage risk in a given case. In the second section, then, we review research on the association between personality disorder, crime and violence. Included here is a discussion of the prevention of crime and violence among people with personality disorder, drawing inferences from the empirical literature on the treatment of personality disorders and on the efficacy of correctional treatment programs, also known as "recidivism reduction" or "rehabilitation" programs. We conclude with a summary of recommendations for assessment and treatment and suggested priorities for future research.

CONCEPTUALIZATION, ASSESSMENT, AND DIAGNOSIS OF PERSONALITY DISORDER

Categorical models

Two major views of personality disorder evolved in the early part of the twentieth century: those of classical psychiatrists, such as Kraepelin, Bleuler, Kretschmer and Schneider, and those of psychoanalytic theorists, like Freud, Abraham and Reich (Millon & Davis, 1995; Millon et al., 1996). Classical psychiatry described personality disorders as precursors or milder forms of more severe mental disorders. Schneider was the exception here, in that he viewed personality disturbances as distinct disorders that may or may not be co-morbid with other mental disorders. In contrast, from a psychoanalytic personality perspective personality disorders were related to "frustrations or indulgences of instinctual or libidinous drives, especially in conjunction with specific psychosexual stages of maturation" (Millon & Davis, 1995; p. 10). Reich expanded on this, hypothesizing that the nature of a personality trait was not important. What was important, according to his view, was the defensive strategies utilized early in life that developed into characteristic ways of coping and reacting.

The lack of consensus among clinicians regarding the nature of personality disorder resulted, unsurprisingly, in a lack of consistency in diagnostic criteria. Despite several attempts at reconciliation, there is only limited correspondence between the two major nosological systems currently in use, the *International Classification of Diseases*, 10th edn (ICD-10; World Health Organization, 1992) and the *Diagnostic and Statistical Manual of Mental Disorders*, 4th edn (DSM-IV; American Psychiatric Association, 1994). The ICD-10 and DSM-IV do not agree on how best to define and diagnose various personality disorders or, as illustrated in Table 3.1, even how many distinct personality disorders exist.

Even within nosological systems, there has been little consistency over time. For example, the DSM, 1st edn (DSM-I; American Psychiatric Association, 1952) included personality pattern disturbances (e.g. inadequate,

Table 3.1 Personality Disorders in the DSM-IV and ICD-10

DSM-IV	ICD-10
Cluster A (odd–eccentric)	
Paranoid	Paranoid
Schizoid	Schizoid
Schizotypal	—
Cluster B (dramatic–erratic–emotional)	
Antisocial	Dissocial
Borderline	Emotionally unstable
	Impulsive type
	Borderline type
Histrionic	Histrionic
Narcissistic	—
Cluster C (anxious–fearful)	
Avoidant	Anxious (avoidant)
Dependent	Dependent
Obsessive-compulsive	Anankastic

DSM-IV = *Diagnostic and Statistical Manual of Mental Disorders*, 4th edn (American Psychiatric Association, 1994); ICD-10 = *International Classification of Diseases and Causes of Death*, 10th edn. (World Health Organization, 1992); — = no corresponding personality disorder.

schizoid, cyclothymic and paranoid), personal trait disturbances (e.g. passive aggressive and compulsive), sociopathic personality disturbance, special symptom reactions, and transient situational personality disorders under the general heading of personality disorder. In DSM-II (American Psychiatric Association, 1967), personality pattern and trait disturbances were merged into a single category of personality disorders. Some distinct forms of personality disorder that had appeared in DSM-I were dropped; some new forms were added. The publication of DSM-III (American Psychiatric Association, 1980) and its revision (DSM-III-R; American Psychiatric Association, 1987) heralded several major changes, including the addition of a new diagnostic axis devoted primarily to personality disorders, in recognition of the fact that personality disorders were frequently co-morbid with each other and with other mental disorders; the development of fixed and explicit criteria for each disorder, to facilitate reliable diagnosis; and the addition, deletion and renaming of several specific forms of personality disorder. The DSM-IV (1994) contained changes in the general definition of personality disorder; added, deleted or re-named several personality disorders; and changed the diagnostic criteria for those disorders that were retained. Similarly, there have been important, albeit less dramatic, changes over time in the way personality disorders were defined and diagnosed in the ICD.

As indicated in Table 3.1, the DSM-IV includes criteria sets for 10 specific personality disorders. Space limitations prevent a full discussion of each disorder. However, note that the disorders are grouped into three clusters on the basis of similarities in symptomatology. The *odd–eccentric* cluster, Cluster A, comprises paranoid, schizoid and schizotypal personality disorder. These disorders are characterized by asociality and unusual thoughts and behavior. Cluster B, labeled *dramatic–erratic–emotional*, comprises antisocial, borderline, narcissistic and histrionic personality disorder, all characterized by impulsive behavior and affect. Finally, Cluster C, the *anxious–fearful* cluster, comprises avoidant, dependent and obsessive-compulsive personality disorder. On the other hand, ICD-10 includes criteria sets for nine specific personality disorders, one of which has two subtypes. The disorders are not grouped into clusters. Most ICD-10 personality disorders correspond to a DSM-IV disorder; however, the correspondence is not complete. The diagnostic criteria for corresponding disorders generally are quite similar, although they cannot be considered parallel.

The assessment of DSM-IV or ICD-10 personality disorders is a long and complex process. Several structured or semi-structured interviews for personality disorders yield diagnoses of adequate inter-rater and test–retest reliability. Examples here are the International Personality Disorder Examination (Loranger et al., 1994); the Structured Clinical Interview for DSM-IV, Axis II (First et al., 1995); and the Personality Disorder Interview—IV

(Widiger et al., 1995). One problem is that such interviews generally take about 2–3 hours to administer. Adding procedures to increase the validity of interviews, such as evaluating the potential impact of co-morbid mental disorders or obtaining collateral information, increases the administration time considerably. Unfortunately, attempts to develop self-report inventories for the assessment of personality disorders have met with only limited success. Self-reports have low agreement with interview-based diagnoses and tend to be highly susceptible to the biasing effects of illiteracy, failure to comply with assessment, poor insight, and emotional state at the time of assessment.

Dimensional models

The advent of the recent editions of the DSM led to increased interest in personality disorders among researchers. Researchers have identified several major problems with clinical approaches to personality disorder (Costa & Widiger, 1994; Widiger & Sanderson, 1995; Zimmerman, 1994). One is that existing nosologies were based on the opinions of practitioners from a multitude of theoretical backgrounds, in the absence of any empirical support. As Schroeder, Wormworth and Livesley (1994) put it:

> Conceptions of personality disorders are largely the consensus of experts who base their decisions on traditional clinical concepts and clinical experience. Consequently, classifications of personality disorders consist of relatively unstructured lists of diagnoses that reflect multiple theoretical perspectives within the clinical tradition. They do not incorporate, to any significant degree, accumulated empirical knowledge . . . The consequence of these developments is that current classifications tend to lack explicit structure and clear conceptual underpinnings (p. 117).

A second problem is that categorical systems based on clinical approaches fail to capture important information about the nature and severity of symptoms present in a given case. For example, there are 93 different ways to fulfill the diagnostic criteria for borderline personality disorder and 149,495,616 different ways to fulfill the criteria for antisocial personality disorder in DSM-IV, even if one ignores the issue of symptom severity (Widiger & Sanderson, 1995).

Third is the problem of co-morbidity. As noted earlier, later editions of the DSM permit, and even encourage, the diagnosis of more than one personality disorder in a given case. Research indicates that most individuals who suffer from a personality disorder appear to fulfill the diagnostic criteria for two or three separate disorders; indeed, only about 15% of patients meet criteria for a single personality disorder (Costa & Widiger, 1994; Stuart et al., 1998). This may be due to flaws in the DSM conceptualization of personality disorders (e.g. inclusion of disorders that do not exist in nature, incorrect assumption of a categorical structural model) or in the DSM criteria for these disorders (e.g. inordinate length or complexity, reliance on symptoms of poor sensitivity or specificity). Regardless, the high degree of co-morbidity seriously complicates research and clinical practice. If a patient meets criteria for more than one personality disorder, should treatment target all of them separately, or those symptoms common to all the disorders, or only the primary disorder? And, if the latter, what criteria should be used to identify primary vs. secondary personality disorders?

One potential solution to these problems, proposed by those familiar with the traditions of personality psychology, is the adoption of an empirically-based dimensional structural model (Widiger & Frances, 1994; Widiger & Sanderson, 1995). Using dimensional models, it is possible to summarize rich symptom-level information efficiently and reliably. Also, co-morbidity is not a concern under dimensional models; there is no assumption that distinct and separate personality disorders ("types") exist.

Although there is general consensus that dimensional models of personality disorder are superior to categorical models in almost every respect, there is no agreement concerning which of the numerous possible dimensional models is preferable. Dimensional models differ with respect to the nature of the personality disorder symptomatology on which they focus (that is, phenotypic or "surface" vs. genotypic or "source" traits); the generality of those traits (that is, a relatively small number of general or "higher-order" vs. a relatively large number of more specific or "lower-order" dimensions); and the assumed relation among the traits (that is, independent or "orthogonal" vs. correlated or "oblique" dimensions). Once a model is selected, a variety of statistical methods can be used to obtain a solution.

Two models will serve to illustrate these differences. The first is the Five-Factor Model (FFM), which originally was developed to describe normal personality but more recently has been applied to personality disorder. The FFM is described in detail elsewhere; for excellent overviews, see Costa and Widiger (1994) and Wiggins (1996). According to the FFM, five broad, bipolar, orthogonal dimensions are necessary and reasonably sufficient to account for the associations among phenotypic or manifest aspects of personality. One particular version of the FFM (Costa & McCrae, 1992) defines these factors as follows: *neuroticism* is a tendency to be emotionally unstable and experience negative affect; *extraversion* is a tendency to be energetic and sociable; *agreeableness* is a tendency to be warm and non-confrontational; *conscientiousness* is a tendency to be responsible and organized; and *openness to experience* is a tendency to value the exploration of new feelings and ideas over traditionalism. Each broad dimension comprises a number of specific lower-level facet traits (this model is summarized in Table 3.2). The dimensions and their facets have been

Table 3.2 A dimensional model of normal personality: the five-factor model (FFM) as measured by the revised NEO Personality Inventory

NEO-PI-R factor and facet scales
Neuroticism   Anxiety, Hostility, depression, self-consciousness, impulsiveness, vulnerability
Extraversion   Warmth, gregariousness, assertiveness, activity, excitement-seeking, positive emotions
Openness   Fantasy, aesthetics, feelings, actions, ideas, values
Aggreeableness   Trust, straightforwardness, altruism, compliance, modesty, tendermindedness
Conscientiousness   Competence, order, dutifulness, achievement striving, self-discipline, deliberation

NEO-PI-R = revised NEO Personality Inventory (Costa & McCrae, 1992).

explicated over the course of decades by numerous investigators via factor analysis of data from tests of normal personality. One notable strength of the FFM is that it subsumes another empirically-based dimensional model, the Interpersonal Circle; another is its cross-cultural generalizability (Wiggins, 1996).

The second model is the Dimensional Assessment of Personality Pathology (DAPP) developed by Livesley and colleagues (e.g. Livesley, Jackson & Schroeder, 1989, 1992; Schroeder et al., 1994). They chose a "bottom-up" approach, which focuses primarily on lower-level traits and only secondarily on broad, general dimensions. In the DAPP model, 18 oblique dimensions are considered necessary and reasonably sufficient to describe the domain of personality pathology (see Table 3.3). The dimensions were identified through the factor analysis of data from comprehensive measures of personality disorder symptomatology. Subsequent analyses have examined the phenotypic and genotypic structure of the 18 dimensions (Livesley, Jang & Vernon, 1998), identifying four broad, orthogonal factors that parallel the FFM in many respects. Working independently, other investigators have developed models similar to the DAPP in many respects (e.g. Clark, Vorhies & McEwen, 1994). However, at present there is little evidence examining the generalizability of the DAPP across cultures.

Numerous assessment procedures based on dimensional models of personality disorder are available for use in research and clinical practice. Within the framework of the FFM, both self-report inventories (Costa & McCrae, 1992) and structured interviews (Trull et al., 1998) have been developed. The same is true for the DAPP (Schroeder et al., 1994) and similar

Table 3.3 A dimensional model of personality disorder: factors and scales of the Dimensional Assessment of Personality Pathology—Basic Questionnaire (DAPP–BQ)

DAPP–BQ: factors and scales
Neuroticism 　Insecure attachment, anxiousness, diffidence, affective lability, narcissism, social 　avoidance, passive-oppositionality
Disagreeableness 　Rejection, Interpersonal dis-esteem, conduct problems, stimulus seeking, 　suspiciousness
Introversion 　Intimacy problems, restricted expression, identity problems
Compulsivity 　Compulsivity

DAPP–BQ = Dimensional Assessment of Personality Pathology–Basic Questionnaire (Schroeder, Wormworth & Livesley, 1994). Scales that were factorially complex appear under the factor on which they loaded highest. Two additional scales, self-harming behaviors and perceptual cognitive distortions, were not included in the factor analysis.

models (Clark, 1993). These assessment procedures have good psychometric properties and yield highly detailed information, which makes them useful both in research and clinical practice. Also, because these procedures ask respondents to report specific behaviors, experiences and attitudes rather than symptoms, they appear to be less susceptible to bias than are measures based on categorical models of personality disorder.

Assessment of personality disorder: summary and recommendations

Although simple categorical models of personality disorder are consistent with current nosologies, there is little or nothing else to support their continued use (Blackburn, 1997). Dimensional models are superior in virtually every respect. Consequently, we recommend that assessment procedures based on dimensional models like the FFM or DAPP be used instead of, or at very least in addition to, procedures based on categorical models. We further recommend the use of interview-based measures of personality disorder instead of, or in addition to, self-report inventories. Self-report measures are particularly problematic in forensic settings, where illiteracy, deceitfulness and lack of insight are common (Hart & Hare, 1997).

The issue here, it seems to us, is that clinicians and researchers are not much interested in personality disorders *per se*; rather, they are interested in specific traits or symptoms of personality disorder. It is fruitless to develop a different treatment for each personality disorder, given the high degree of co-morbidity among them. For example, putative treatments for "borderline personality disorder" actually focus on symptoms such as self-harmful behavior (Linehan, 1987), disturbed reality testing (Soloff et al., 1986), diffuse ego boundaries (Kernberg, 1975) or problematic interpersonal relations (Benjamin, 1993). None of these symptoms have perfect sensitivity or specificity: some people diagnosed with borderline personality disorder will not have these symptoms, and some people not diagnosed with borderline personality disorder will have them. In a similar vein, no theory links a specific personality disorder (other than psychopathy) with criminal or violent behaviour in a systematic manner. There is considerable speculation, however, about the criminogenic role of specific symptoms, such as impulsivity, deficits in empathy, hostility and so forth (Andrews & Bonta, 1998; Webster & Jackson, 1997).

The principal use of categorical diagnoses, then, is the general description or characterization of patient populations in a terminology that is widely understood (that is, primary personality disorder diagnoses according to DSM-IV or ICD-10 criteria). The principal use of dimensional measures is identifying and monitoring target symptoms for treatment in treatment settings, or measuring treatment changes and controlling for the effects of co-morbid symptomatology in research settings.

PERSONALITY DISORDER, CRIME AND VIOLENCE

Is there an association?

It makes intuitive sense that personality disorders—or at least certain symptoms of these disorders—should be associated with crime and violence. For example, a general trait of antagonism or hostility is characteristic of at least eight of the 11 personality disorders in DSM-IV (Widiger & Trull, 1994), and impulsivity is characteristic of many others (Webster & Jackson, 1997). Two lines of evidence support the existence of this association. The first includes studies of the prevalence of personality disorders among offenders and forensic patients. Research in a number of different countries consistent has reported prevalence rates of 10–15% for primary clinical diagnoses of personality disorder (e.g. Aderibigbe, Arboleda-Florez & Crisante, 1996; Andersen et al., 1996; Birmingham, Mason & Grubin, 1996; Brooke et al., 1996; Fido & Al-Jabally, 1993; Fido et al., 1992; Kullgren, Grann & Holmberg, 1996). When the definition of personality disorder is expanded to include secondary diagnoses—for example, personality disorders in individuals who also suffer from acute mental disorders or substance use disorders— reported prevalence rates are much higher, ranging between 50% and 90%

(e.g. Hare, 1983; Hart & Hare, 1989). These prevalence rates are very high in absolute terms and significantly higher than those observed in community residents, although perhaps not much higher than those in civil psychiatric patients. The second line of evidence includes studies that have directly examined the link between personality disorder and past or future criminality. Typically, the association is positive, although small to moderate in magnitude (e.g. Hart & Hare, 1997; Webster et al., 1994; Widiger & Trull, 1994).

Unfortunately, almost all the existing research focuses solely or primarily on psychopathy, or fails to distinguish between psychopathic and non-psychopathic personality disorders, and is therefore of limited relevance to this chapter. Studies of non-psychopathic personality disorders are very few in number and suffer from a number of serious methodological shortcomings. One reason for the lack of high-quality research is that much criminological research is explicitly disinterested in psychopathological variables, choosing to focus instead on demographic, criminal-historical or other psychological factors. Another reason is that it is very difficult, and sometimes even impossible, to collect data concerning personality disorders in a systematic and reliable manner. This is particularly true for research based on file review or brief clinical interviews, where the quality and quantity of information may be severely limited. Finally, it is difficult to evaluate statistically the associations between personality disorder and crime due to the complexity of diagnostic data. In DSM-IV, there are scores of symptoms (imperfectly) nested within 10 disorders, which in turn are nested within three clusters. Should one analyze symptoms, disorders or clusters? How should one control statistically for co-morbid symptomatology?

To illustrate the problems faced by researchers, consider two empirical studies that examined violence among patients with borderline personality disorder (Snyder, Pitts & Pokorny, 1991; Stone, 1990). Both found that borderline personality disorder was a risk marker for (i.e. associated with) violence. But, is violence associated with borderline personality disorder *per se* or with specific borderline symptoms such as antagonism or impulsivity, which are not specific to borderline personality disorder? Is the association still apparent after controlling for antisocial (psychopathic) personality disorder, a condition that is frequently co-morbid with borderline personality disorder? What is the nature of the association between borderline personality disorder and violence—is violence a cause or a consequence of personality disorder, or does some third variable account for their association?

To summarize, there is some evidence that non-psychopathic personality disorder is associated with crime and violence. The evidence is limited and weak, however, and the nature of that association is unclear.

Effective management of risk for crime and violence: general issues

Clinicians responsible for treating offenders and patients with personality disorders need to know if any interventions are effective in managing or reducing risk for crime and violence. Ideally, the relevant research corpus would consist of studies that: (a) examined the efficacy of a well-described somatic or psychological therapy for personality disorder; (b) performed comprehensive assessments of the target personality disorder at pre- and post-treatment; (c) randomly assigned patients to treatment vs. non-treatment, or novel treatment vs. treatment-as-usual, conditions; (d) carefully monitored the frequency of criminal or violent behavior during a follow-up period using observational, record review and interview methods; and (e) controlled for potentially biasing effects of co-morbid mental disorder and other factors. Such studies would allow one to conclude with confidence that personality disorder is a dynamic causal risk factor for crime and violence—that is, treatment leads to reductions in personality disorder symptomatology, which in turn lead to reductions in risk.

To put it bluntly, no research corpus of this sort exists. Instead, the focus has been on personality disorder as a mediating factor in response to more general treatment programs aimed at reducing crime and violence. Based on studies of the latter sort, personality disorder appears to be a marker variable for poor response to treatment: people with personality disorders improve less during the course of treatment and function worse post-treatment than do other offenders and patients (e.g. Dutton et al., 1997a). This is hardly surprising, however: the treatments are not targeted specifically at people with personality disorders, who generally are more symptomatic than others before treatment even starts. It is impossible to determine from this research whether personality disorder is a causal risk factor, let alone a dynamic (that is, changeable) causal factor.

Treatment of personality disorder

In the absence of directly relevant studies, we are forced to draw inferences from other areas of research. One such area is the more general literature concerning the treatment of personality disorder symptomatology. If one assumes that personality disorder symptomatology is pandemic in forensic populations and that it plays a causal role in criminal and violent behaviour, then any treatment that reduces personality disorder symptomatology may reduce or manage risk.

We caution readers that the literature summarized in this section is rather sparse and that there is a lack of systematic, methodologically adequate research. Also, a major problem is that many of the studies targeted symptoms that are associated with, but not specific to, personality disorder; thus, subjects in these studies may have suffered from major mental illnesses rather than or in addition to personality disorder. Finally, we reiterate that none of these studies directly examined reductions in criminal or violence behavior secondary to improvement in personality disorder symptomatology. With these cautions in mind, we will briefly discuss two major types of treatment for personality disorder symptomatology: pharmacological and cognitive-behavioral therapies (a third type of treatment, traditional psychotherapy, will not be discussed because of the lack of research supporting its efficacy.)

Pharmacological treatments have shown some promise in the management of certain personality disorder symptomatology (Siever & Davis, 1991). The intense negative affect that is commonly observed in patients with borderline personality disorder and, to a lesser extent, in many Cluster B and C personality disorders can be managed through the administration of antidepressants and anxiolytics (Soloff et al., 1986). Hostility such as that commonly found in antisocial personality disorder may be managed with anxiolytics and mood stabilizers, such as lithium or carbamazepine (Coccaro et al., 1990; Cowdry & Gardner, 1988). The impulsivity of patients with borderline and antisocial personality disorder may respond favorably to monoamine oxidase inhibitors or selective serotonin reuptake inhibitors. (Hucker, 1997). Finally, the odd speech, thoughts and behavior observed most often in Cluster A personality disorders can be alleviated by low-dose antipsychotics (Schulz, Schulz & Wilson, 1988). We should emphasize here that medication may be used as the primary form of treatment in some cases, but also should be considered as a secondary or adjunctive treatment in other cases. Clinical experience suggests that motivation for and compliance with psychosocial treatments may be facilitated by concurrent pharmacotherapy (Kristiansson, 1995).

Cognitive-behavioral therapies, in comparison to more traditional psychotherapies, are structured and directive. Like medications, they are used for symptomatic relief, although gains are intended to persist long after the discontinuation of treatment. Rice and Harris (1997) recently conducted a thorough review of the relevant treatment literature, concluding that cognitive-behavioral therapies are potentially useful primary or secondary treatments for a variety of problems related to personality disorder. Their major findings of relevance to the present discussion can be summarized as follows. First, social skills training programs may help to remediate the interpersonal communication and assertiveness deficits observed in a wider range of serious personality disorders, especially DSM Cluster A disorders. For people with impulsivity-related problems, such as educational and vocational deficits or chronic hostility and aggression—a trait commonly found among people who meet the criteria for DSM Cluster B personality disorders—life skills programs may be of assistance. Finally, for people with problems related to anxiety, depression and affective lability, who are likely to meet criteria for DSM Cluster C personality disorders, individual or group treatment programs that teach emotion management skills may be useful.

To summarize, there is some evidence to suggest that clinicians may find pharmacological and cognitive-behavioral therapies useful in the management of personality disorder symptomatology. Pharmacological treatments are most likely to be used in forensic psychiatric settings where trained personnel are available to prescribe, administer and monitor medications. Their use in correctional settings frequently is complicated by a relative lack of personnel, which can lead to security breaches, such as hoarding of medications for sale to other offenders or for use in suicide attempts. One attractive feature of cognitive-behavioral therapies is that the treatment procedures can be specified and explained in an easy-to-use manual. This makes it feasible to train a wide range of staff (psychologists, psychiatrists, nurses, social workers and so forth) in the delivery of treatment. Another is that it is possible—and in many cases desirable—to institute group- or ward-based treatment programs. These features lead to a very substantial reduction in treatment-related costs.

Correctional treatment programs

It is possible to draw inferences about risk management in offenders and patients with personality disorder from the more general correctional treatment literature. The primary goal of correctional treatment programs is to reduce criminal and violent behaviour, that is, to "rehabilitate" offenders. The problem, however, is that the treatments are conceptualized in a social-psychological framework that is alien to traditional psychiatry and clinical psychology. Few correctional treatments explicitly target non-psychopathic personality disorder symptomatology. Instead, they discuss treatment targets such as "association with antisocial peers" or "procriminal sentiments". In this section, we introduce the Psychology of Criminal Conduct (PCC), a conceptual model that is used widely to understand correctional treatment (for an introduction, see the excellent text by Andrews & Bonta, 1998). We then summarize the major findings of the correctional treatment literature within the framework of PCC.

The three fundamental assumptions underlying PCC are the risk, needs and responsivity principles (Andrews & Bonta, 1998). According to the *risk principle*, criminal conduct is associated reliably with a set of risk factors that are static or stable (that is, that change little and slowly, if at all, over time).

Thus, the intensity of correctional treatment should be matched to the offender's risk level: moderate- and high-risk offenders should receive intensive treatment, whereas low-risk offenders should receive low-intensity treatment or no treatment at all. This makes sure that scarce and expensive resources are allocated to those offenders who most require them, and maximizes the potential societal benefits of treatment. A summary of the major static risk factors for general criminality identified through meta-analytic research (Gendreau, Little & Goggin, 1996), along with their importance expressed in terms of effect size, is presented in Table 3.4 (the effect size index used in the table is r, the Pearson product–moment correlation. It can range in value from −1, indicating perfect negative association, to +1, a perfect positive association; values around 0 indicate chance-level associations. Typically, rs with an absolute value of .15–.20 are considered small in magnitude, those around .30 are considered moderate, and those around .50 are considered large). The same factors also appear to be associated with violence and sexual violence (Hanson & Bussière, 1998; Bonta, Law & Hanson, 1998).

The *need principle* states that criminal conduct also is associated reliably with risk factors that are dynamic (that is, that can change over time),

Table 3.4 A meta-analysis of the predictors of criminal recidivism: mean effect sizes

Risk factors	Mean r	Number of studies
Static factors		
Criminal history	0.18	164
Age	0.15	56
Family rearing practices	0.15	31
Juvenile antisocial history	0.13	119
Race	0.13	21
Family criminality	0.12	35
Family structure	0.10	41
Gender	0.10	17
Intellectual functioning	0.07	32
Socio-economic status	0.06	23
Dynamic factors		
Antisocial personality	0.18	63
Antisocial companions	0.18	27
Antisocial attitudes	0.18	67
Interpersonal conflict	0.15	28
Social achievement	0.15	168
Substance abuse	0.14	60
Personal distress	0.05	66

Reproduced by permission from Gendreau et al., 1996.

referred to as "criminogenic needs". The criminogenic needs present in a given case should be the primary targets for correctional treatment. Table 3.4 also lists the major needs and associated effect sizes identified in meta-analytic research (Gendreau, Little & Goggin, 1996). Similar needs are associated with risk for violence and sexual violence (Hanson & Bussière, 1998; Bonta, Law & Hanson, 1998). The need principle also helps to rationalize the allocation of treatment resources. For example, an offender who abuses drugs should receive substance abuse counseling, and an offender with a deficit in vocational skills should receive job training; but an offender who doesn't abuse drugs and who has stable employment does not require substance use counseling or job training. It also makes little sense for treatment to target risk factors that are static and therefore unlikely to change (e.g. family rearing practices, gender, intellectual functioning).

The *responsivity principle* states that correctional treatments should be delivered in a manner that matches the learning style of offenders. The PCC literature suggests that specific regime factors and therapeutic techniques appear to increase response to correctional treatments (as discussed later). Furthermore, some personal characteristics of offenders make them poorly suited for certain forms of treatment. Poor reading skills or low intelligence, for example, may contraindicate reliance on written materials; extreme social anxiety may contraindicate group therapy; and extreme empathy deficits may contraindicate process- or emotion-focused therapy.

The effectiveness of correctional treatment

Correctional treatment has been the focus of intensive scrutiny in recent years. The empirical literature is sufficiently large to permit quantitative review, or meta-analysis. Various meta-analyses, despite the inclusion of different studies and the use of different statistical techniques, have reached similar conclusions regarding correctional treatment. Lösel (1995) reviewed 13 meta-analyses of correctional treatment outcome studies. He discussed several problems with the existing literature, including the fact that few studies examined treatment of adult offenders. Nevertheless, Lösel concluded that cognitive-behavioural, skills-orientated, and multi-modal programs were most effective in reducing recidivism. Such treatments teach offenders specific skills and model anticriminal attitudes and behavior, using techniques such as graduated practice, role playing and cognitive restructuring (Lösel, 1993). With respect to the magnitude of treatment effects, Lösel has concluded that the expected reduction in recidivism associated with correctional treatment is about 10–12% (Lösel, 1996, 1998).

Lösel's conclusions about the general effectiveness of correctional treatment may underestimate the effectiveness of treatments that adhere to the PCC principles of risk, need and responsivity. Important meta-analytic work by Andrews and colleagues demonstrated that correctional treatments consistent with the PCC approach achieved substantial reductions in recidivism, yielding a moderate effect size of $r = .30$ (see Andrews, 1995; Andrews & Bonta, 1998). In contrast, "inappropriate treatments" that targeted low-risk individuals or did not adhere to the principles of need and responsivity were associated with a slight increase in recidivism (effect size of $r = -.06$); and "unspecified treatments" that could not be classified due to lack of information had a small positive effect (effect size of $r = .13$). These findings recently were replicated and updated by Gendreau, Little & Goggin (1996), who found an effect size of $r = .25$ for appropriate treatments, $r = -.03$ for inappropriate treatments and $r = .13$ for unspecified treatments. Similar conclusions were reached by Antonowicz and Ross (1994), with the exception that they did not find clear support for the risk principle of PCC. This may be due to the fact that the association between risk and treatment response may be complex and curvilinear, with little or no treatment response in very high-risk cases (Lösel, 1998). Unfortunately, it is these very high-risk cases that are most likely to suffer from serious personality disorders (Cooke & Philip, in press).

Despite the optimistic conclusions of meta-analytic research, Rice and Harris (1997) caution that there are insufficient data from which to draw definitive conclusions about effective treatment with adult offenders. In examining meta-analyses on juvenile offenders, however, they concur with other reviewers that there is "strong evidence of positive treatment effects" (p. 432), and that the most promising programs were behavioural and skills-based treatment of high-risk offenders in the community.

Treatment of personality disorder: summary and recommendations

The weak state of the scientific literature on the treatment of personality disorders does not permit us to make strong recommendations about the effective management or risk for crime and violence. There is a great need for systematic and methodologically sound research on this topic. Ideally, such research would evaluate the effectiveness of a specific treatment relative to that of "treatment as usual" or compare two specific treatments. At this point, however, even carefully designed small-sample and quasi-experimental studies would be a significant contribution to the literature. Of course, research should take into account issues in the assessment of personality disorder discussed earlier.

In the absence of directly relevant research, our admittedly cursory review of the general personality disorder and correctional treatment literatures suggests two possible approaches to risk management. The first is to alleviate symptoms of personality disorder, which may play a causal role in criminal and violent behavior. This approach is based on the (unproven) assumption that symptom reduction will result in risk reduction. When this approach is used, we recommend that clinicians identify the specific symptoms linked most closely to criminal and violent behavior, and then target these symptoms directly with a combination of pharmacotherapy and cognitive-behavioural therapy. There appears to be no support for the use of traditional (that is, individual psychodynamic or process-orientated) psychotherapies at the present time.

The second approach, working within the framework of PCC, is to target criminogenic needs. This approach does not assume that symptom reduction will result in risk reduction, but instead focuses on empirically-identified risk factors for crime and violence. When this approach is used, we recommend that clinicians address criminogenic needs using cognitive-behavioral therapies, which appear to be most effective. Studies of juvenile offenders clearly support the efficacy of structured, directive therapies that teach offenders specific skills and model anti-criminal attitudes and behavior using techniques such as graduated practice, role playing and cognitive restructuring. Research on adult offenders has some significant limitations, but yields results consistent with that on juveniles. It is important to note here that meta-analytic research to date has examined almost exclusively the effectiveness of treatment in reducing general criminality. The literature on reducing risk for violent criminality is weak at present and does not provide unambiguous support for the efficacy of correctional treatment (e.g. Dutton et al., 1997b; Quinsey, Khanna & Malcolm, 1998).

CONCLUSIONS

Assessment and diagnosis

Decisions regarding treatment depend on accurate and meaningful assessments. Categorical approaches to the diagnosis of personality disorder are fraught with problems, whereas dimensional approaches have a number of strengths when evaluating the nature and severity of personality disorder symptomatology. Accordingly, our major recommendations are as follows:

- Assessment procedures based on dimensional models of personality disorder should be used instead of, or at the very least in addition to, procedures based on categorical models.
- Interview-based measures of personality disorder should be used instead of, or in addition to, self-report inventories.

Risk management

The scientific literature provides little guidance concerning how best to manage risk for crime and violence among patients and offenders suffering from non-psychopathic personality disorders. However, research on the treatment of personality disorder suggests that pharmacotherapy and cognitive-behavioral therapies may be effective in reducing symptomatology. Research on correctional treatment programs indicates that cognitive-behavioral treatment programs are moderately effective in juvenile offenders and may also be effective in adult offenders, many of whom apparently suffer from personality disorder. Our major recommendations concerning risk management were as follows:

- Treatment for personal disorder should identify the specific symptoms linked most closely to criminal and violent behavior in a given case, and then target these symptoms directly with a combination of pharmacotherapy and cognitive-behavioral therapy. There appears to be no support for the use of traditional (that is, individual psychodynamic or process-orientated) psychotherapies at the present time.
- Correctional treatments should identify criminogenic needs and then target them using cognitive-behavioral therapies. Such therapies are most likely to be effective when, in a structured and directive manner, they teach offenders specific skills and model anti-criminal attitudes and behavior using techniques such as graduated practice, role playing and cognitive restructuring.

System issues

Treatments for personality disorder are likely to be adopted readily by mental health professionals. However, there may be some resistance to implementing correctional treatment programs in traditional mental health settings. PCC clearly focuses on characteristics of the individual associated with a single aspect of psychosocial adjustment, namely criminal behavior. PCC is disinterested in psychological distress, which is not reliably associated with risk for crime and violence. Although recognized in PCC as a need factor that should be addressed through intervention, psychological distress is not an important criminogenic need, and thus should not be a primary target of correctional treatment. In contrast, one of the primary goals of clinicians is to reduce symptoms related to psychological distress. This sometimes leads clinicians to perceive correctional treatment as inhumane, interested more in social control than relief of personal suffering. The perception is simplistic, of course; it is simply that PCC focuses on improving and maintaining the social adjustment of offenders over the long term, rather than on short-term reductions in symptomatology. The goals of correctional and traditional mental health treatment are complementary, not incompatible.

Another problem is that a PCC-based evaluation requires considerable information about criminal behavior, social attitudes and day-to-day social relations. As a consequence, clinicians may need to change their assessment procedures, including a change in the information gathered during interviews and increased reliance on historical records and collateral informants (although these procedures will likely be very familiar to mental health professionals with specific forensic training and experience).

Accordingly, we recommend the following:

- Forensic mental health facilities should establish professional advisory committees to consider the implementation of correctional treatment programs. These committees should review the relevant research literature, obtain copies of the manuals and materials for candidate treatments, and evaluate the acceptability of the treatments among staff who likely would be responsible for delivering them.

Future research

There are tremendous gaps in the relevant scientific literature at the present time. Basic descriptive research is needed, including epidemiological studies of the prevalence of personality disorder among offenders and forensic psychiatric patients. Also needed are retrospective and prospective studies that examine the association between personality disorder symptomatology and criminal and violent behavior. These studies should use adequate assessment procedures and control for the confounding effects of comorbid mental disorders (both other personality disorders and acute mental disorders).

Another line of research that should be undertaken is treatment outcome studies that focus on reductions in institutional and/or community crime and violence. Studies should attempt to determine whether reductions in crime and violence are contingent upon reductions in personality disorder symptomatology, or whether the effectiveness of treatment is due to some other mechanism.

ACKNOWLEDGEMENTS

Thanks to Sheilagh Hodgins and Rüdiger Müller-Isberner for their helpful comments.

REFERENCES

Aderibigbe, Y. A., Arboelda-Florez, J. & Crisante, J. (1996). Reflections on the sociodemographic and medicolegal profiles of female criminal defendants. *International Journal of Offender Therapy and Comparative Criminology*, **40**, 74–84.

American Psychiatric Association (1952). *Diagnostic and Statistical Manual of Mental Disorders*. Washington, DC: American Psychiatric Association.

American Psychiatric Association (1967). *Diagnostic and Statistical Manual of Mental Disorders*, 2nd edn. Washington, DC: American Psychiatric Association.

American Psychiatric Association (1980). *Diagnostic and Statistical Manual of Mental Disorders*, 3rd edn. Washington, DC: American Psychiatric Association.

American Psychiatric Association (1987). *Diagnostic and Statistical Manual of Mental Disorders*, 3rd edn. (revised). Washington, DC: American Psychiatric Association.

American Psychiatric Association (1994). *Diagnostic and Statistical Manual of Mental Disorders*, 4th edn. Washington, DC: American Psychiatric Association.

Andersen, H. S., Sestoft, D., Lillebaek, T., Gabrielsen, G. & Kramp, P. (1996). Prevalence of ICD-10 psychiatric morbidity in random samples of prisoners on remand. *International Journal of Law and Psychiatry*, **19**, 61–74.

Andrews, D. A. (1995). The psychology of criminal conduct and effective treatment. In J. McGuire (Ed.), *What Works: Reducing Reoffending—Guidelines from Research and Practice* (pp. 35–62). London: Wiley.

Andrews, D. A. & Bonta, J. (1998). *The Psychology of Criminal Conduct*, 2nd edn. Cincinnati, OH: Anderson.

Antonowicz, D. H. & Ross, R. R. (1994). Essential components of successful rehabilitation programs for offenders. *International Journal of Offender Therapy and Comparative Criminology*, **38**, 97–104.

Benjamin, L. S. (1993). *Interpersonal Diagnosis and Treatment of Personality Disorders*. New York: Guilford.

Birmingham, L., Mason, D. & Grubin, D. (1996). Prevalence of mental disorder in remand prisoners: consecutive case study. *British Medical Journal*, **313**, 1521–1524.

Blackburn, R. (1997). Psychopathy and personality disorder: Implications of interpersonal theory. In D. M. Stoff, J. Breiling & J. D. Maser (Eds), *Handbook of Antisocial Behavior* (pp. 269–301). New York: Wiley.

Bonta, J., Law, M. & Hanson, K. (1998). The prediction of criminal and violent recidivism among mentally disordered offenders: a meta-analysis. *Psychological Bulletin*, **123**, 123–142.

Brooke, D., Taylor, C., Gunn, J. & Maden, A. (1996). Point prevalence of mental disorder in unconvicted male prisoners in England and Wales. *British Medical Journal*, **313**, 1524–1527.

Clark, L. A. (1993). *Manual for the Schedule for Non-adaptive and Adaptive Personality (SNAP)*. Minneapolis, MN: University of Minnesota Press.

Clark, L. A., Vorhies, L. & McEwen, J. L. (1994). Personality disorder symptomatology from the Five-Factor Model perspective. In P. T. Costa & T. A. Widiger (Eds), *Personality Disorders and the Five-Factor Model of personality* (pp. 95–116). Washington, DC: American Psychological Association.

Coccaro, E. F., Astill, J. L., Herbert, J. L. & Schut, A. G. (1990). Fluoxetine treatment of impulsive aggression in DSM-III-R personality disorder patients. *Journal of Clinical Psychopharmacology*, **10**, 373–375.

Cooke, D. J. & Philip, L. (in press). To treat or not to treat: an empirical perspective. In C. Hollin (Ed.), *Offender Treatment*. Chichester: Wiley.

Costa, P. T. Jr & McCrae, R. R. (1992). *Revised NEO Personality Inventory (NEO-PI-R) and NEO Five-Factor Inventory (NEO-FFI): Professional Manual.* Odessa, FL: Psychological Assessment Resources.

Costa, P. T. & Widiger, T. A. (1994). Introduction: personality disorders and the Five-Factor Model of Personality. In P. T. Costa & T. A. Widiger (Eds), *Personality Disorders and the Five-Factor Model of Personality* (pp. 1–12). Washington, DC: American Psychological Association.

Cowdry, R. W. & Gardner, D. L. (1988). Pharmacotherapy of borderline personality disorder: alprazolam, carbamazepine, trifluoperazine, and tranylcypromine. *Archives of General Psychiatry*, **45**, 111–119.

Dutton, D. G., Bodnarchuk, M. A., Kropp, P. R., Hart, S. D. & Ogloff, J. R. P. (1997a). Client personality disorders affecting wife assault post-treatment recidivism. *Violence and Victims*, **12**, 37–50.

Dutton, D. G., Bodnarchuk, M., Kropp, R., Hart, S. D. & Ogloff, J. R. P. (1997b). Wife assault treatment and criminal recidivism: an 11-year follow-up. *International Journal of Offender Therapy and Comparative Criminology*, **41**, 9–23.

Fido, A. A. & Al-Jabally, M. (1993). Presence of psychiatric morbidity in prison population in Kuwait. *Annals of Clinical Psychiatry*, **5**, 107–110.

Fido, A. A., Razik, M. A., Mizra, I. & El-Islam, M. F. (1992). Psychiatric disorders in prisoners referred for assessment: a preliminary study. *Canadian Journal of Psychiatry*, **37**, 100–103.

First, M. B., Spitzer, R. L., Gibbon, M., Williams, J. B. W., Davies, M., Borus, J., Howes, M. J., Kane, J., Pope, H. G. & Rounsaville, B. J. (1995). The Structured Clinical Interview for DSM-III-R personality disorders (SCID-II), II: Multi-site test–retest reliability study. *Journal of Personality Disorders*, **9**, 92–104.

Gendreau, P., Little, T. & Goggin, C. (1996). A meta-analysis of the prediction of adult offender recidivism: what works. *Criminology*, **34**, 575–606.

Hanson, R. K. & Bussière, M. T. (1998). Predictors of sexual recidivism: a meta-analysis. *Journal of Consulting and Clinical Psychology*, **66**, 348–362.

Hare, R. D. (1983). Diagnosis of antisocial personality disorder in two prison populations. *American Journal of Psychiatry*, **140**, 887–890.

Hart, S. D. & Hare, R. D. (1989). The discriminant validity of the Psychopathy Checklist in a forensic psychiatric population. *Psychological Assessment: A Journal of Consulting and Clinical Psychology*, **1**, 211–218.

Hart, S. D. & Hare, R. D. (1997). Psychopathy: assessment and association with criminal conduct. In D. M. Stoff, J. Brieling & J. Maser (Eds), *Handbook of Antisocial Behavior* (pp. 22–35). New York: Wiley.

Hucker, S. J. (1997). Impulsivity in DSM-IV impulse control disorders. In C. D. Webster & M. A. Jackson (Eds), *Impulsivity: Theory, Assessment and Treatment* (pp. 195ff). New York: Guilford.

Kernberg, O. F. (1975). *Borderline Conditions and Pathological Narcissism.* New York: Jason Aronson.

Kristiansson, M. (1995). Incurable psychopaths? *Bulletin of the American Academy of Psychiatry and the Law*, **23**, 555–562.

Kullgren, G., Grann, M. & Holmberg, G. (1996). The Swedish forensic concept of Severe Mental Disorder as related to personality disorders: an analysis of forensic psychiatric investigations of 1498 male offenders. *International Journal of Law and Psychiatry*, **19**, 191–200.

Linehan, M. (1987). Dialectical behavior therapy for borderline personality disorder: theory and method. *Bulletin of the Menninger Clinic*, **51**, 261–276.

Livesley, W. J., Jackson, D. & Schroeder, M. L. (1989). A study of the factorial structure of personality pathology. *Journal of Personality Disorders*, **3**, 292–306.

Livesley, W. J., Jackson, D. & Schroeder, M. L. (1992). Factorial structure of traits delineating personality disorders in clinical and general population samples. *Journal of Abnormal Psychology*, **101**, 432–440.

Livesley, J., Jang, K. & Vernon, P. (1998). Phenotypic and genotypic structure of traits delineating personality disorder. *Archives of General Psychiatry*, **55**, 941–948.

Loranger, A. W., Sartorius, N., Andreoli, A., Berger, P., Buchheim, P., Channabasavanna, S. M., Coid, B., Dahl, A., Diekstra, R. F. W., Ferguson, B., Jacobsberg, L. B., Mombour, W., Pull, C., Ono, Y. & Regier, D. (1994). The International Personality Disorder Examination: the World Health Organization/Alcohol, Drug Abuse, and Mental Health Administration international pilot study of personality disorders. *Archives of General Psychiatry*, **51**, 215–224.

Lösel, F. (1993). The effectiveness of treatment in institutional and community settings. *Criminal Behaviour and Mental Health*, **3**, 416–437.

Lösel, F. (1995). The efficacy of correctional treatment: a review and synthesis of meta-evaluations. In J. McGuire (Ed.), *What Works: Reducing Reoffending—Guidelines from Research and Practice* (pp. 79–111). Chichester: Wiley.

Lösel, F. (1996). Effective correctional programming: what empirical research tells us and what it doesn't. *Forum on Corrections Research*, **6**(3), 33–37.

Lösel, F. (1998). Treatment and management of psychopaths. In D. J. Cooke, A. E. Forth & R.D. Hare (Eds), *Psychopathy: Theory, Research and Implications for Society* (pp. 303–354). Dordrecht: Kluwer Academic.

Millon, T. & Davis, R. D. (1995). Conceptions of personality disorders: historical perspectives, the DSMs and future directions. In W. J. Livesley (Ed.), *The DSM-IV Personality Disorders* (pp. 3–28). New York: Guilford.

Millon, T., Davis, R. D., Millon, C. M., Wenger, A., Van Zuilen, M. H., Fuchs, M. & Millon, R. B. (1996). *Disorders of Personality: DSM-IV and Beyond*, 2nd edn. New York: Wiley.

Quinsey, V. L., Khanna, A. & Malcolm, P. B. (1998). A retrospective evaluation of the Regional Treatment Centre sex offender treatment program. *Journal of Interpersonal Violence*, **13**, 621–644.

Rice, M. T. & Harris, G. T. (1997). The treatment of adult offenders. In D. M. Stoff, J. Brieling & J. Maser (Eds), *Handbook of Antisocial Behavior* (pp. 425–435). New York: Wiley.

Schroeder, M. L., Wormworth, J. A. & Livesley, W. J. (1994). Dimensions of personality disorder and the five-factor model of personality. In P. T. Costa & T. A. Widiger (Eds), *Personality Disorders and the Five-Factor Model of Personality* (pp. 1–12). Washington, DC: American Psychological Association.

Schulz, S. C., Schulz, P. M. & Wilson, W. H. (1988). Medication treatment of schizotypal personality disorder. *Journal of Personality Disorders*, **2**, 1–13.

Siever, L. & Davis, L. (1991). A psychobiological perspective on the personality disorders. *American Journal of Psychiatry*, **148**, 1647–1658.

Snyder, S., Pitts, M. & Pokorny, A. (1991). Selected behavioral features of patients with borderline personality traits. *Suicide and Life-Threatening Behavior*, **16**, 28–39.

Soloff, P. H., George, A., Nathan, R. S., Schulz, P. M., Ulrich, R. F. & Perel, J. (1986). Progress in the pharmacotherapy of borderline personality disorder: a double-blind study of amitriptyline, haloperidol, and placebo. *Archives of General Psychiatry*, **143**, 35–39.

Stone, M. (1990).   Abuse and abusiveness in borderline personality disorder. In P. S. Links (Ed.), *Family Environment and Borderline Personality Disorder* (pp. 131–148). Washington, DC: American Psychiatric Press.

Stuart, S., Pfhol, B., Battaglia, M., Bellodi, L., Grove, W. & Cadoret, R. (1998).   The co-occurrence of DSM-III-R personality disorders. *Journal of Personality Disorders*, **12**, 302–315.

Trull, T. J., Widiger, T. A., Useda, J. D., Holcomb, J., Doan, B., Axelrod, S. R., Stern, B. & Gershuny, B. S. (1998).   A structured interview for the assessment of the Five-Factor Model of Personality. *Psychological Assessment*, **10**, 229–240.

Webster, C. D., Harris, G. T., Rice, M. E., Cormier, C. A. & Quinsey, V. A. (1994).   *The Violence Prediction Scheme: Assessing Dangerousness in High Risk Men*. Toronto: Centre for Criminology, University of Toronto.

Webster, C. D. & Jackson, M. A. (Eds) (1997).   *Impulsivity: Theory, Assessment, and Treatment*. New York: Guilford.

Widiger, T. A. & Frances, A. J. (1994).   Toward a dimensional model for the personality disorders. In P. T. Costa & T. A. Widiger (Eds), *Personality Disorders and the Five-Factor Model of Personality* (pp. 19–39). Washington, DC: American Psychological Association.

Widiger, T. A., Mangine, S., Corbitt, E. M., Ellis, C. G. & Thomas, G. V. (1995).   *Personality Disorder Interview-IV: A Semi-structured Interview for the Assessment of Personality Disorders*. Odessa, FL: Psychological Assessment Resources.

Widiger, T. A. & Sanderson, C. J. (1995).   Toward a dimensional model of personality disorders. In W. J. Livesley (Ed.), *The DSM-IV Personality Disorder* (pp. 433–458). New York: Guilford.

Widiger, T. A. & Trull, T. J. (1994).   Personality disorders and violence. In J. Monahan & H. J. Steadman (Eds), *Mental Disorder and Violence: Developments in Risk Assessment*. Chicago, IL: University of Chicago Press.

Wiggins, J. S. (Ed.) (1996).   *The Five-Factor Model of Personality: Theoretical Perspectives*. New York: Guilford.

World Health Organization (1992).   *International Classification of Diseases and Causes of Death*, 10th edn. Geneva: WHO.

Zimmerman, M. (1994).   Diagnosing personality disorders: a review of issues and research methods. *Archives of General Psychiatry*, **51**, 225–245.

Chapter 4

PSYCHOPATHIC OFFENDERS*

STEPHEN WONG

Regional Psychiatric Centre (Prairies) and University of Saskatchewan, Saskatoon, Canada

INTRODUCTION

Psychopathy is a personality disorder, which has very significant social implications. Psychopaths have been described as:

> . . . predators who use charm, manipulation, intimidation and violence to con-
> trol others and to satisfy their own selfish needs. Lacking in conscience and in
> feelings for others, they cold-bloodedly take what they want and do as they
> please, violating social norms and expectations without the slightest sense of
> guilt or regret . . . it is not surprising that . . . they are responsible for a mark-
> edly disproportionate amount of serious crime, violence and social distress in
> society (Hare, 1996).

Not all psychopaths are incarcerated in prisons or detained in forensic psychiatric institutions; they seem to be just as well represented in the business
and corporate world, especially when supervision and accountability are
lax, such as during major business restructuring (see Babiak, 1995). There is

*The views expressed in this chapter are solely the author's and may not reflect the views of the
Correctional Service of Canada. The support of the Correctional Services of Canada in the
preparation of this article is gratefully acknowledged.

Violence, Crime and Mentally Disordered Offenders. Edited by S. Hodgins and R. Müller-Isberner.
© 2000 John Wiley & Sons, Ltd.

an urgent need to develop an effective treatment programme for this group of highly destructive and recalcitrant individuals. In this chapter, I will first review the definition and diagnosis of psychopathy. Then, I will review the empirical literature on the treatment of psychopaths to determine what, if any, effective treatments for psychopaths exist. Using the results of the review in conjunction with the literature on the effective correctional treatment, I will suggest a number of potentially useful approaches in the design and implementation of a treatment programme for institutionalized violent psychopathic offenders.

DEFINITION AND DIAGNOSIS OF PSYCHOPATHY

There is no universally acceptable definition of psychopathy. Cleckley (1976) provided an insightful clinical account of the psychopath in his book, *The Mask of Sanity*, which has had a major influence on the conceptualization of the disorder. He outlined 16 key characteristics (see Table 4.1) of the psychopath that have been used by researchers as a guideline in the definition and assessment of psychopathy (see Hare & Cox, 1978).

Recent history of the diagnosis

The equivalent of psychopathy in the International Classification of Disease, 9th edition (ICD-9, World Health Organization, 1975) is the "personality disorder with predominantly sociopathic or asocial manifestation (301.7)", and the diagnostic criteria are given in Table 4.1.

The description of psychopathy (referred to as persons exhibiting an antisocial personality) in the Diagnostic and Statistical Manual of Mental Disorders, 2nd edn (DSM-II; American Psychiatric Association, 1968) is also listed in Table 4.1. The overall agreement between the Cleckley, ICD-9 and DSM-II characterization of psychopathy is immediately obvious. These three approaches provide broad diagnostic guidelines but do not present clinicians or researchers with an objective or systematic way of assessing psychopathy. Diagnoses made according to these guidelines are often based on "professional" evaluations and are, therefore, subjective. Some researchers have attempted to operationalize the guidelines, for example, by making global seven-point ratings of psychopathy using Cleckley's (1976) criteria (see Hare & Cox, 1978 for review). The global ratings can be made reliably, but this procedure has been criticized as being unclear as to what is being rated and how the ratings are made.

The subsequent editions of the DSM (DSM-III and DSM-III-R; American Psychiatric Association, 1980, 1987) attempted to refine the definition of

Table 4.1 Characteristics of Psychopathy from Cleckley (1976), ICD Ninth Revision and DSM-II

Cleckley's 16 Characteristics	ICD-9	DSM-II
Superficial charm and good intelligence Absences of delusions and other signs of irrational thinking Absence of "nervousness" or psychoneurotic manifestations Unreliability Untruthfulness and insincerity Lack of remorse or shame Inadequately motivated anti-social behaviour Poor judgement and failure to learn from experience Pathological egocentricity and incapacity for love General poverty in major effective reactions Specific loss of insight Unresponsiveness in general interpersonal relations Fantastic and uninviting behaviour, with drink and sometimes without Suicide rarely carried out Sex life impersonal, trivial and poorly integrated Failure to follow any life plan	Personality disorder characterized by disregard for social obligations, lack of feeling for others, and impetuous or callous unconcern There is a gross disparity between behaviour and the prevailing social norms Behaviour is not readily modifiable by experience, including punishment People are often affectively cold and may be abnormally aggressive or irresponsible Their tolerance to frustration is low; they blame others or offer plausible rationalizations for the behaviour which brings them into conflict with society	Unsocialized Impulsive Guiltless Selfish Callous Rationalize behaviour Fail to learn from experience

psychopathy (referred to as antisocial personality disorder, APD) and to increase diagnostic reliability. A set of rules for arriving at the diagnosis of psychopathy was specified. Also, unlike DSM-II, which uses personality characteristics to define psychopathy, DSM-III and DSM-III-R APD criteria include behavioural equivalents (e.g. assaults) for personality traits in order to increase diagnostic reliability. Since the introduction of the DSM-III and III-R criteria for APD, they have been critized for sacrificing construct validity for diagnostic reliability (see Hare, 1996). For example, assaults, one diagnostic criterion, may be more reliably measured (and therefore lead to better diagnostic reliability) than a personality trait. However, different assaults could have a number of different causes, which may or may not be related to psychopathy (thereby reducing construct validity).

Hare's Psychopathy Checklist

Around 1980, Robert Hare, one of the most influential researchers in the area of psychopathy, first introduced an experimental instrument, later refined and published as the Psychopathy Checklist–Revised (PCL-R) (Hare, 1991), to operationalize and assess psychopathy. Psychopathy was defined as a disorder characterized by:

> . . . a constellation of affective, interpersonal, and behavioural characteristics, including egocentricity, impulsivity, irresponsibility, shallow emotions, lack of empathy, guilt or remorse, pathological lying, manipulativeness, and the persistent violation of social norms and expectations (Hare, 1996).

Hare based his definition largely on Cleckley's conceptualization of psychopathy.

The PCL-R is a 20-item clinical rating scale completed using a semi-structured interview and collateral and/or file information. Each item is scored on a three-point scale (0, 1, 2) according to specific criteria given in the scoring manual. The total score, range 0–40, provides an estimate of the extent to which a given individual matches the prototypical psychopath as exemplified by Cleckley (1976). The psychometric properties of the PCL-R have been established in a number of forensic populations. A score of 30 or more on the PCL-R is usually indicative of psychopathy. A screening version of the PCL-R (PCL-SV) (Hart, Cox & Hare, 1995) which has also been developed, is suitable for use with non-incarcerated individuals and can be completed in less time than the PCL-R.

Factor analyses of the PCL-R consistently reveal a two-factor structure (Harpur, Hakistian & Hare, 1988; Harpur, Hare & Hakistian, 1989). Table 4.2 shows the PCL-R items loading on Factor 1 and 2. Factor 1 consists of items that reflect the interpersonal or affective aspect of psychopathy. PCL-R items in Factor 2 reflect an unstable life-style and social deviancy. The correlation between PCL-R scores and APD diagnoses are usually quite high (r = .55–.65). However, the prevalence rate of the disorder among forensic populations using the PCL-R criteria (15–30%) are much lower than DSM APD criteria (50–80%; Hare, 1980, 1985). As such, DSM criteria have been criticized for confounding APD with general criminality (Hart & Hare, 1997).

Other current diagnoses

The equivalent of psychopathy in the International Classification of Disease, 10th edition (ICD-10, World Health Organization, 1992) is the Dissocial Personality Disorder (F60.2). The conditions for diagnosis are similar to the

Table 4.2 Items in the Hare Psychopathy Checklist (PCL-R)

Factor 1: interpersonal or affective	Factor 2: social deviance	Additional items
Glibness or superficial charm	Need for stimulation or proneness to boredom	Promiscuous sexual behaviour
Grandiose sense of self-worth	Parasitic life-style	Many short-term marital relationships
Pathological lying	Poor behavioural controls	Criminal versatility
Conning or manipulative behaviour	Early behavioural problems	
Lack of remorse or guilt	Lack of realistic, long-term goals	
Shallow affect	Impulsivity	
Callousness or lack of empathy	Irresponsibility	
Failure to accept responsibility for own actions	Juvenile delinquency	
	Revocation of conditional release	

Adapted from Hart and Hare (1997).

ICD-9 criteria, with the addition of two attributes, incapacity to maintain enduring relationships and guiltlessness. To receive the diagnosis, the general criteria for personality disorder (F60) must be met in addition to having three of the six conditions listed in the ICD-10. Where needed, culture-specific manifestations of the six criteria should be considered.

DSM-IV (American Psychiatric Association, 1994) continues with the DSM-III and DSM-III-R approaches of using behavioural equivalents for personality traits in diagnosing psychopathy (APD). However, under a separate section entitled "Associated Features and Disorders", DSM-IV also includes many of the personality characteristics (such as lack of empathy, callousness, glibness and superficial charm used in the PCL-R) as salient features in the diagnosis of APD, especially among forensic populations. Hare (1996) criticized the DSM-IV as having:

> . . . established two different sets of diagnostic criteria for APD, one for the general public and one for forensic settings. Individuals diagnosed as APD outside of forensic settings might not be so diagnosed once they find themselves in prisons or forensic hospitals, unless they also exhibit personality traits indicative of psychopathy . . . an unfortunate consequence of the approach adopted in DSM-IV is that, now more than ever, researchers and clinicians will be confused about the relationship between APD and psychopathy, sometimes using them interchangeably and other times treating them as separate clinical constructs (Hare, 1996, pp. 35–36).

A variety of self-report scales also have been used to assess psychopathy, such as the psychopathic deviate (Pd) scale of the MMPI (Dahlstrom &

Welsh, 1960), the socialization scale of the California Psychological Inventory (Gough, 1969) and the Special Hospitals Assessment of Personality and Socialization (see Blackburn, 1993). However, correlations between the various measures are not high (Hare, 1985) and there are problems in using self-report measures for psychopaths, for example, psychopaths not answering the questions truthfully (Lilienfeld, 1994) or that they are in fact, "diagnosing" themselves.

Conclusion

Despite the widely divergent approaches that have been used to measure psychopathy, there appears to be a surprising degree of convergence regarding the underlying clinical construct. A key attribute of psychopathy evident in the various definitions is a significant affective dysfunction in the interpersonal sphere, as evidenced by callousness, lack of empathy and remorse, egocentricity, pathological lying and manipulativeness. McCord and McCord's (1964) description of the psychopath as loveless and guiltless is apt. The psychopath's persistent violations of social norms, particularly the remorseless exploitation of others for personal gain, are the most obvious behavioural characteristics. Among forensic clients who are psychopaths, persistent criminal behaviour and violence are usually evident. Currently, the best validated diagnostic instrument for psychopathy is the PCL-R.

ARE PSYCHOPATHS TREATABLE?

"Are psychopaths treatable?" is not a good scientific question for researchers because it implies that we can prove the null hypothesis. However, it is what most clinicians would like to know. Perhaps a better question to ask is, "How responsive are psychopaths to the treatments we have tried?". Before answering the question, consider first what others say about treating psychopaths. Some of the *diagnostic systems* (ICD-9, ICD-10; World Health Organization, 1975, 1992), no less, and descriptions of psychopathy (Cleckley, 1976), note that psychopaths are unable to benefit from experience. They fall short of saying that psychopaths are untreatable. In any case, a sizable group of clinicians and researchers appear to be pessimistic about the effectiveness of treatment with psychopaths.

   Cleckley (1982), in his book *The Mask of Sanity*, asserts: "The therapeutic failure in all such patients observed leads me to feel that we do not at present have any kind of psychotherapy that can be relied upon to change the psychopath fundamentally" (p. 280). Early review of the treatment of psychopathy concluded that ". . . psychotherapy offers a little hope, but no assurance, of success. Other approaches to the problem seem even less promising . . ." (McCord & McCord, 1956, p. 99). Suedfeld and Landon (1978), after reviewing the treatment literature up to the mid-1970s, provided an equally gloomy outlook on the treatment of psychopathy, although they did suggest some possible avenues to try.

When Canadian psychiatrists were polled regarding the 10 leading characteristics of the psychopathic personality, "Does not learn from experience" was ranked as the most important one (Gray & Hutchison, 1964). Although not being able to learn from experience is not the same as untreatable, it did reflect the level of pessimism among psychiatrists about the ability of the psychopath to change.

The view that psychopaths are highly resistant to treatment has entered the legal arena. In the 1983 amendment of the Mental Health Act for England and Wales, the phrase "which requires or is susceptible to medical treatment" was removed from the original definition of psychopathic disorder, which is defined as "a persistent disorder or disability of mind . . . which results in abnormally aggressive or seriously irresponsible conduct on the part of the person concerned". Although the legal definition of psychopathic disorder is over-inclusive, non-specific and is not intended for diagnostic purposes, the amendment did reflect the pessimistic view of the impact of treatment on a group of high-risk offenders, some of whom are likely to be psychopathic according to Cleckley's criteria.

On the other hand, some optimism was expressed. In a survey of more than 500 forensic experts, more than two-thirds believed that treatment could succeed, although they did not know what the best treatment approach is (Tennent et al., 1993). Others take the position that the optimal treatment for psychopathy has not been attempted (Blackburn, 1993; Lösel, 1998). The validity of various claims that psychopaths are unresponsive to treatment can only be settled by a careful review of the empirical literature on the treatment effectiveness for psychopathy. A brief summary of the results of such a review (Wong, 1998) are given in the next section.

A REVIEW OF EMPIRICAL TREATMENT OUTCOME STUDIES OF PSYCHOPATHS

Method

The objective of the review (Wong, 1998) is to determine the treatment outcomes of psychopathy based on well-designed empirical studies. Only well-designed and well-implemented studies can give us valid and reliable information on the "treatability" of psychopathy. The review excluded studies in which subjects were under 18 years old, suffering from a psychotic illness, or intellectually subnormal (IQ less than 70). It is generally accepted that the term "psychopathy" should not be applied to anyone younger than 18 years of age (e.g. DSM-IV; cf. Forth, Hart & Hare, 1990). All studies published in English language journals that reported the treatment of psychopathy, sociopathy, antisocial personality, personality or character disorders were included in the first round of article selection. Seventy-five articles were found through conventional database and library searches.

Each of the 75 articles was reviewed and those studies with only anecdotal or qualitative clinical accounts of treatment effects were excluded. With the remaining studies, the design and implementation of each study were evaluated, based on six criteria of adequacy: (a) diagnostic criteria for psychopathy; (b) diagnostic reliability; (c) adequate description of the treatment programme; (d) appropriateness of treatment evaluation; (e) inclusion of a follow-up period; and (f) the use of a no-treatment or matched control group. Each article was rated as adequate (rated 2), somewhat adequate (rated 1) or not adequate (rated 0) on each of the six criteria, based on a rating scheme (Appendix A) developed by Wong (1998). For the purpose of the review, Cleckley's criteria or the PCL-R (original or revised version) was used as the operational definition of psychopathy.

The six evaluation criteria for the studies were developed to ensure that only well designed and implemented empirical studies were used to assess the "treatability" of psychopaths. Also, criterion (c) was included to ensure that if such a programme was identified, others could replicate it. No systematic attempt was made to solicit unpublished articles. Completed but unpublished studies often contain negative or non-significant results. The review, if anything, will be biased in favour of finding positive treatment effects for psychopaths. The articles were initially rated by a trained research assistant, and were re-rated by the author, who resolved any disagreements. Inter-rater agreement of over 95% was obtained.

Only two studies (using the same sample) were considered adequate on all six criteria; therefore, the criteria for adequacy were relaxed, such that a study would be considered for review if it scored "0" on diagnostic reliability, follow-up period and no-treatment control, and at least "1" on treatment programme and treatment evaluation, and "2" on diagnostic criteria. It was felt that some information could be gained by reviewing the outcome of fairly well-defined and evaluated treatment programmes targeted at subjects who are clearly psychopathic. Even with less stringent criteria, and without addressing the nature and quality of the treatment programmes used, only four of the 74 studies were included in this review. The major reason that so few studies were considered to be adequate is that the descriptions of the subjects were either absent or incomplete. It is often unclear whether the subjects were just ordinary criminals, forensic psychiatric patients or psychopaths. Given that we now have much better means of assessing psychopathy, there is no excuse not to use the appropriate tools in the selection of subjects for future studies.

The subjects in six of the 74 studies were diagnosed with APD (DSM). These studies were not included in the present review because APD diagnosis is much more inclusive compared to diagnosis using the PCL-R or similar criteria. Also, the treatment approaches in these studies were focused almost exclusively on substance abuse and not on general antisocial or criminal behaviour.

The four studies (which included three independent samples) are reviewed in the chronological order in which they were published. The ratings of the four studies are presented in Table 4.3, at the end of Appendix A.

Results

Maddocks (1970) followed 52 untreated psychopaths for five years. On follow-up, 17% had "settled down", 66% had "not settled down", 5% had died and 12% could not be found. A psychopath was considered to have settled down if there was a reduction in "impulsiveness", as evidenced by changing job, accommodation, sexual partners, lying, trouble at school or with the law. The evaluation criteria were vague and subjective, and the study sheds no light on the effectiveness of treatment intervention.

Ogloff, Wong and Greenwood (1990) evaluated the treatment outcomes of psychopaths and non-psychopaths in a therapeutic community treatment programme. The programme was not designed specifically for the treatment of psychopathy; however, about 10–15% of the participants in the programme were psychopaths according to the PCL criteria. The programme provided treatment to Canadian offenders serving sentences of two years or more with a history of violence.

A treatment team of mental health professionals delivered treatment within a therapeutic and supportive environment, which discouraged criminal attitudes, in particular, the "con code". Positive peer group pressure (Vorrath & Brendtro, 1985) from more prosocial offenders (Ross & McKay, 1976), were used as the agents of change. Treatment also consisted of group problem-solving sessions, skills training sessions (stress management, assertiveness training) and individual counselling (see Ogloff, Wong & Greenwood, 1990).

Psychopathy was assessed shortly after admission to the programme, using the PCL (Hare, 1980) with good inter-rater reliability (Pearson's $r = .85$). Those who scored 33 or more and 22 or less were considered to be in the psychopathic and non-psychopathic groups, respectively; everyone else was assigned to the mixed group. Treatment staff were blind to the PCL ratings.

Psychopaths ($n = 21$; $M^1 = 31.29$) remained in treatment for a significantly shorter period of time (103.71 days; $p < .05$) than the mixed ($n = 47$; $M = 22.06$; 207.47 days) or the non-psychopathic groups ($n = 12$; $M = 12.50$; 241.67 days). Discharges from the programme were mainly for disciplinary reasons or lack of motivation. The correlation between PCL scores and the number of days in treatment was $-.29$ ($p < .01$). This result was replicated in a sample of federally incarcerated sexual offenders attending a six-month sex offender treatment programme (Gordon et al., 1992). Significantly more psychopaths (23.8%; $n = 21$) than non-psychopaths (5.9%; $n = 34$; $p < .05$) failed to complete the treatment programme independent of offender type (rapist vs. paedophile).

The subjects in the Ogloff, Wong and Greenwood (1990) study were also rated (4-point scale) on level of motivation and effort, and the extent of clinical improvement at the end of treatment. Subjects in the high PCL group showed significantly less motivation and less improvement than those in the mixed and the low PCL groups. Almost 75% of the sample, mainly those in the mixed and low PCL groups, showed clinical improvement and demonstrated good motivation in the programme.

Psychopaths may show some motivation and request treatment for purely administrative reasons, for example, to impress the parole decision makers. However, once in treatment, participants are required to go through a continuous process of self-examination. Since psychopaths typically do not see problems in themselves, such self-examination may become a meaningless and tedious task which they grow to resent. This may result in their discharge from treatment for lack of motivation or other disciplinary actions (Ogloff, Wong & Greenwood, 1990). More innovative approaches must be devised to engage psychopaths in treatment for longer periods of time in order for treatment designed specifically for them to have a positive impact.

Harris, Rice and Cormier (1991) and Rice, Harris and Cormier (1992) describe an intensive therapeutic community programme for mentally disordered offenders, including psychopaths and some psychotics. Fifty-seven per cent of the subjects had been found not guilty by reason of insanity, some of whom were found insane because of a serious personality disorder (Rice, Harris & Cormier, 1992). Other patients were certified according to civil commitment procedures. Twenty-seven per cent of the subjects met the DSM-III criteria for schizophrenia, based on file information[2]. The programme was peer-operated for the most part, independent of input from professional staff. The objective of the programme was to create an environment in which subjects could develop empathy and responsibility

---

[1] Mean PCL scores for the three groups.
[2] Although over a quarter were schizophrenic, it was decided to include this study in the review because of the extensive follow-up period and the use of an appropriate control group.

for one another. Subjects were encouraged to act as "therapist" and to lead therapy groups, and were largely responsible for the day-to-day management of the programme (Barker & Buck, 1977; Barker & Mason, 1968; Barker & McLaughlin, 1977).

So-called "innovative defence disrupting techniques", for example mood-altering drugs, marathon group therapy and nude encounter groups, were used. Subjects who performed well were promoted to leadership positions. There were no structured programmes specifically aimed at changing criminal attitudes and beliefs, or teaching social and problem-solving skills, programmes that are now considered essential for reducing recidivism (Andrews et al., 1990). Although considered innovative at the time, the programme fell far short of what is now considered to be effective correctional programming.

Psychopathy was assessed using the PCL, based on file review alone (mean score PCL = 19.1; SD = 9.7). Inter-rater reliability was .96. Those who scored 25 or more on the PCL were included in the psychopathy group, which consisted of sub-groups of 52 treated and 29 untreated matched controls. The customary cut-off of 30 was not used, as it would have yielded too few psychopaths. The non-psychopath group consisted of 114 treated and 90 untreated matched controls. The mean follow-up period was 10.5 (SD = 4.94) years. Treatment outcome was assessed by the presence or absence of a violent failure, defined as any new charge (*not conviction*) against persons, or any parole revocation or return to the maximum security institution for violent behaviour (Rice, Harris & Cormier, 1992). This is a very liberal definition of violent recidivism. More treated psychopaths (77%) failed violently, compared to untreated psychopaths (55%). The opposite was true for non-psychopaths; more untreated non-psychopaths (39%) failed compared to treated non-psychopaths (22%). The type of treatment described by Rice, Harris and Cormier (1992) had a negative impact on psychopaths but a positive impact on non-psychopaths. It should be noted that it took 55.4 months (SD = 46.4) on average, a long period of time, for those who failed violently to fail.

Why did treated psychopaths have a higher violent recidivism rate than untreated psychopaths who spent a comparable amount of time in a more negative prison setting? An unstructured and undersupervised treatment programme could become a place where psychopaths could hone their skills for manipulating and conning fellow patients. In the therapeutic community programme, described by Ogloff, Wong and Greenwood (1990), psychopaths were not motivated to change, even with close monitoring, continual confrontation and extensive education by staff. It is unrealistic to expect that psychopaths would make any changes if left to govern themselves. Further, by rewarding psychopaths with positions of leadership and responsibility, the programme might have inadvertently reinforced the conning, manipulative skills of the psychopath, behaviours that were associated with subsequent recidivism. The results of this programme provide a good lesson of what *not* to do in the treatment of institutionalized psychopaths.

Conclusions

The number of studies reviewed (Wong, 1998) was much smaller than in previous reviews because more stringent selection criteria were used and the literature on juvenile offenders was excluded. In all, only four out of 74 studies were deemed adequate, even when the criteria of acceptability were relaxed. The programme in two of the four studies (both studies used the same sample treated in the same programme) was designed specifically for the treatment of psychopathy (Rice, Harris & Cormier, 1992) but, as the authors indicated, the programme was the wrong one for treating serious psychopathic offenders. Based on the results of the review (Wong, 1998), it is concluded that an appropriately designed and implemented treatment programme for the Cleckley-type psychopath has yet to be carried out. Also, since no specially designed treatment programme for the psychopath has been attempted, the clinical lore that psychopaths are "untreatable" or unresponsive to treatment is premature and is not based on empirical evidence.

The literature suggests that putting psychopaths in the off-the-shelf treatment programmes available in most prison institutions will not suffice. There is an urgent need to develop intervention strategies that are appropriate for this group of high-risk, high-need offenders.

Where do we go from here? The review of this literature tells us more about what not to do than what to do in providing treatment for psychopaths. To find out what to do in a psychopathy treatment programme, we have to turn to the literature on the effective treatment of offenders and use this information as a foundation to design a programme for psychopaths that will take into account the psychopath's personality and behavioural characteristics.

OUTLINE OF AN INSTITUTIONAL TREATMENT PROGRAMME FOR VIOLENT PSYCHOPATHS

Due to space limitations, I will outline only briefly a proposed institutional treatment programme for violent psychopaths. A comprehensive programme guideline is in preparation (Wong & Hare, 1999).

The programme is based on the integration of the principles of effective intervention with offenders proposed by Gendreau (1996), the literature on the treatment of psychopathy, and the author's experience in working with psychopaths in the last 15 years. Gendreau's seminal work in delineating the principles of effective correctional treatment were derived from results of meta-analyses of the correctional treatment literature, from narrative reviews, communication with colleagues who had run successful programmes, and his own personal experiences.

Programme objectives

The primary objective of a treatment programme for violent psychopaths should be the reduction of the frequency and severity of violent behaviour, rather than the modification of psychopathic personality characteristics. In most cases, psychopaths are not referred for impatient treatment because of their psychopathic personality. Being self-centred, superficial, manipulative, callous and remorseless may be unpleasant for others, but it is not illegal. It is the antisocial and violent behaviours of psychopaths that bring them into contact with the criminal justice or mental health systems. Also, by not trying to change the overall personality structure, the proposed treatment is less threatening to the psychopath with his narcissistic view of himself.

If the goal of treatment is to instill affect (love) and morality (guilt) in the psychopath, the effort will be futile:

> If the therapy goals are to make the psychopath into an upstanding citizen who will care about others, feel what others feel, and feel guilt when he hurts someone (i.e. to increase his superego functioning, to use psychoanalytic terminology), the therapy is doomed to failure. . . . Treatment can alter how psychopaths interact with others, but it cannot teach them to love, to empathize, and to feel guilt when they never have before. Those emotions are minimally felt before treatment, so there is virtually nothing to build on and shape (Doren, 1987, p. 168).

In short, Doren suggests, and I concur, that it is unrealistic to try to change the psychopath's personality structure. Rather, treatment should focus on reducing the risk of violence and destructiveness by modifying the cognitions and behaviours that directly precipitate his violent behaviour.

Can treatment invariably make the psychopath worse? Any treatment programme runs the risk of turning out psychopaths who are more skilled at deceiving and manipulating other individuals than they were before treatment (Harris, Rice & Cormier, 1991). However, the orientation and focus of the proposed programme should minimize the chances of this happening. At worst, the psychopath's repertoire of antisocial behaviour should remain unchanged, no worse than before. However, since others will be watching carefully, there may be a tendency for the psychopath to learn to conceal negative behaviours. The real issue here is that due care and vigilance must be exercised in monitoring and evaluating the programme and its outcomes. Self-reports from psychopaths or changes in psychological test scores cannot be taken as sole measures of treatment outcome (see section on Programme Evaluation).

Theoretical orientation and design

The programme should use a highly structured cognitive-behavioural, relapse prevention approach (Laws, 1990; Marlett & Gordon, 1985; Gendreau, 1996). Positive reinforcement strategies and social learning approaches (e.g. modelling) should be used to strengthen prosocial behaviours and attitudes. It should be prescriptive in nature; that is, it should enable all participants to uncover the idiosyncratic factors that caused them to commit violent acts, and help them to learn specific preventive measures. Traditional "Freudian" psychodynamic and "Rogerian" non-directive or client-centred therapies do not appear to work for offenders or psychopaths (Gendreau, 1996; Lösel, 1998).

- The use of positive reinforcers must predominate over the use of punishment.
- Programmes must be designed by professionals who are trained and experienced in the principles and operation of cognitive-behaviourally based treatment programmes. The designer must also be familiar with the appropriate literature, for example, the risk/need/responsivity principles of correctional assessment and treatment (Andrews, Bonta & Hoge, 1990) and the assessment and treatment of psychopaths.
- Actuarial assessments of risk pre- and post-treatment must be carried out to ensure appropriate evaluation of change in risk level as a result of treatment. Assessment instruments should be able to evaluate both static (historical) and dynamic (changeable) risk factors. Major static risk factors are long criminal history, early onset of criminal behaviours, and unstable and abusive upbringing. Major dynamic risk factors include criminal attitudes, violent life-style, criminal associates, anger and aggressive behaviours. The Level of Service Inventory–Revised (Andrews & Bonta, 1994) for the assessment of recidivism in general and the Violence Risk Scale (Wong & Gordon, 1999) for the assessment of the risk of violence are examples of instruments composed of both static and dynamic risk factors. The Violence Risk Scale can also identify treatment targets and areas of strength of the individual, in addition to measuring changes in risk as a result of treatment.
- Relapse prevention (RP) strategies should be a key part of the programme. Relapse prevention originated in the substance abuse area and

emphasizes the importance of self-monitoring and self-management skills. Elements of the strategy include the following (Gendreau, 1996):

1. Monitoring and anticipating problem situations.
2. Planning and rehearsing alternative prosocial responses to cope with problem situations.
3. Practising new prosocial behaviours in increasingly difficult situations and rewarding improved competencies.
4. Informing significant others, such as family and friends, of problem situations and encouraging them to provide the offender with timely support and reinforcement for prosocial behaviour.
5. Providing maintenance or booster sessions to offenders after they have completed the formal phase of the programme.

Delivery and management

• Programmes should be of a reasonable duration (6–12 months) and should occupy a significant amount of the offender's time (40–60%) to ensure that the intervention impacts on the offender's well-entrenched antisocial behavioural pattern.
• Staff are responsible for the design, maintenance and operation of the programme. However, staff and offenders should function, as much as possible, in a collaborative manner by taking into account input and feedback provided by the offenders. Programme structure and the required programme activities should be implemented in a firm but fair manner.
• Reinforcement contingencies must be under the control of the staff. The "con code" or the criminal subculture often pulls offenders towards actively supporting each other's antisocial behaviours, sometime to the detriment or even exclusion of positive, prosocial contingencies designed by the staff. Some offenders, psychopaths in particular, through intimidation and control of others, may try to exert negative influences over the programme. Staff must maintain control over the programme and the reinforcement contingencies and provide an overall positive prosocial environment for all. It must be clear to everyone that the staff, and not the offenders, are running the programme.
• Clear structure must be provided in the programme to ensure that what is supposed to be delivered in the programme is, in fact, delivered. This is the issue of maintaining programme integrity. Programme structure can be provided by the following approaches:

1. Having available, and following a treatment manual which specifies in sufficient detail the theoretical, operational and evaluation strategies of the programme.

2. Line and functional responsibilities of the staff in the programme are clearly assigned.
3. Staff are trained to a level of competency that will allow them to carry out their assigned duties.
4. Important indicators of a properly functioning programme should be monitored on a continual basis. Indicators, such as the quality and the extent of documentation, the achievement of intermediate treatment targets (e.g. reduction of institutional rule infractions and the reduction of aggressive behaviours), should be monitored.
5. In-service training and regular programme audits and staff performance reviews should be carried out as a matter of course.

Treatment targets

- Treatment must focus on significant targets, which are those that have been shown to be strongly and reliably associated with criminal behaviour. These targets include criminal thinking and attitudes; criminal life-style, friends and associates; substance abuse; anger and aggression. Treatment directed at minor or non-significant targets, for example, self-esteem issues, will not lead to significant change in criminal behaviours. Appropriate treatment targets for the psychopath are the ones that are found to be reliably associated with violence in the offender's criminal or social history. The Violence Risk Scale (Wong & Gordon, 1999) is specifically designed to provide an assessment of such targets.
- The programme must be made comprehensive by addressing a wide range of appropriate treatment targets. For example, an offender with substance abuse problems, criminal attitudes, a violent life-style and criminal friends and associates will benefit more from a programme which targets all these problems than one which addressed only one or another of the problems.

Offender characteristics

- Appropriate candidates for treatment should be selected using a valid and reliable means of assessing psychopathy, for example, the PCL-R.
- Intensive treatment should be delivered to high-risk rather than low-risk offenders. High-risk offenders are those with a high probability of re-offending when released. High risk is generally indicated by the presence of a significant number of static (historical) and dynamic (changeable) risk factors. For inclusion in an intensive programme for violent psychopaths, select psychopaths with violent histories rather than the non-violent

psychopathic con man. The baseline for violence is so low for the latter that a programme for violent psychopaths would be irrelevant to them.

- The programme, including the staff, must be sufficiently flexible to accommodate and respond to the specific and individual needs of the offender: this is the responsivity principle of effective correctional treatment. For example, different learning styles, motivation, cognitive and intellectual strengths and limitations must be taken into account and accommodated by the staff when implementing the programme. The psychopathic personality traits are important responsivity factors. For example, the trait of callousness and shallow emotions would make empathy training very difficult. On the other hand, the tendency of psychopaths to intellectualize interpersonal interactions would suggest strength in their cognitive appraisal abilities.

Staff characteristics

The appropriate staff characteristics are clearly summarized by Gendreau (1996):

- Staff should relate to offenders in interpersonally sensitive and constructive ways, and should be trained and supervised appropriately.
- Staff should be selected on the basis of interpersonal skills associated with effective counselling. These skills include clarity in communication, warmth, humour, openness, the ability to set appropriate behavioural limits, and the ability to see the interconnections between attitudes, affect and behaviour. With these skills, staff can be an effective source of reinforcement and can competently model prosocial skills.
- Staff should have at least an undergraduate degree or equivalent, with training in the theories as well as the prediction and treatment of criminal behaviour, including psychopathy.
- Staff should receive formal instruction and on-the-job or internship training in the general application of cognitive-behavioural interventions, and applications specific to the programme.
- Staff are assessed periodically on the quality of their service delivery.
- Countertransference issues must be openly discussed and resolved with support and understanding from colleagues.

Programme evaluation

- Programme evaluation should be an integral part of the overall programme. Systematic evaluation of the achievement of intermediate targets and the ultimate objectives of treatment, that is, reduction in violent recidivism, should be carried out periodically. The treated group should be compared to an appropriate control group. The methodology of measuring the reduction of violent recidivism (e.g. survival analysis, number of violent convictions/charges pre- and post-treatment) must be clearly specified.

Follow-up services

- Follow-up services should be available to the offender after the end of the formal treatment programme. The follow-up must be accessible, relevant and of sufficient frequency. "Accessible" means that the offender does not have to overcome unreasonable obstacles to access the service, for example travel excessive distances. It must be "relevant" in that the follow-up services should be of similar theoretical and operational orientation as the original programme. It must be of "sufficient frequency" such that the offender can maintain a reasonable level of contact with the service provider.

Overcoming resistance

The psychopath's resistance to treatment and management is almost legendary. However, there will likely be less resistance if the treatment and management efforts capitalize on the psychopath's natural propensities. For example, a reasonable approach would be to make use of the psychopath's egocentric personality by appealing to his incessant need to advance his own interests (Templemann & Wollersheim, 1979). Albert Ellis (1962) has called this approach "socialized hedonism" and has defined it as:

> The philosophy that one should primarily strive for one's own satisfaction while, at the same time, keeping in mind that one will achieve one's own best good, in most instances, by giving up immediate gratification for future gains and by being courteous to and considerate of others so that they will not sabotage one's own ends.

Many of the psychopath's goals, such as having material wealth, power and recognition, are, within limits, socially acceptable. It is what the psychopath does to achieve these goals that causes him to come into conflict with the law. The psychopath's antisocial behaviours are not always in his own best interest—at least in the long run—and often are actually self-defeating (e.g. many incarcerations). It is therefore advantageous for him to explore prosocial ways to achieve his goals. This approach is therapeutically advantageous for three reasons. First, the realization that he has been "shooting himself in the foot" may encourage him to make changes. Second, it prevents power struggles in which the therapist wastes much energy defending moral and social principles. Third, it places the psychopath in a powerful "Catch 22": he cannot reject the therapist's suggestions without rejecting his own best interests (Templemann & Wollersheim, 1979).

Managing attrition

The drop-out rate in programmes for psychopaths has been high (Ogloff, Wong & Greenwood, 1990). The psychopath may decide that treatment is too boring, intrusive, threatening or demanding for him to devote any effort to it. When the "game" is no longer fun or challenging, it is time to switch to something else. Alternatively, psychopaths are often excluded from the programme by staff, either for being unmotivated and disinterested in treatment, or for unacceptable behaviours, usually being too aggressive or manipulative. They cannot benefit from treatment once they are discharged. Those who drop out of treatment are likely those who need it the most. A key part to treating psychopaths, therefore, is to find ways to keep them engaged in treatment and to minimize drop-out.

Drop-out can be minimized by finding innovative and prosocial ways of engaging and challenging the psychopath to stay in treatment. At the same time, staff need to recognize that aggression, manipulation and other kinds of unacceptable behaviours are the reasons why the psychopath is in treatment, and should not be the reasons for discharging them.

The Transtheoretical Model (TM) of change (Prochaska & DiClemente, 1986; Prochaska, DeClemente & Norcross, 1992) provides a useful heuristic towards a better understanding of how we could provide offenders with the appropriate treatment at the appropriate time as they progress through the change process. I will use this model to conceptualize the change process in psychopaths in order to match interventions to their stages of change. Within the framework of the TM, treatment staff could also develop a better understanding and a more realistic expectation of what the psychopath is willing to do or capable of doing at different stages of change, and thus decrease the attrition rate.

The TM has been validated in studies of treatment-facilitated or client-mediated (self-help) modification of addictive and other problem behaviours, including alcohol abuse, cigarette smoking and obesity. The TM postulates that individuals who modify their problem behaviours move through a series of stages: the pre-contemplation, contemplation, preparation, action and maintenance stages. Each stage is characterized by specific client behaviours. Treatment interventions that are effective for one stage may be ineffective or even damaging when applied to clients at other stages. Before being successfully treated, the person may cycle through most or all of the stages a number of times. Relapse or cycling through the stages is considered to be a rule rather than an exception (Prochaska, DiClemente & Norcross, 1992).

In the pre-contemplation stage, the offender has no intention to change the behaviour in the foreseeable future. Many individuals in this stage are unaware or in complete denial of their problems. They deny or attribute the problem to external causes ("If only I had a better lawyer"; "the system is rotten to the core, so no wonder I never get a fair shake"). One tends to find many psychopaths in this stage when they enter treatment. The literature suggests that since the client lacks insight and any commitment to treatment, action-orientated interventions, such as skills-building activities (anger and emotional management, social skills training) will be met with minimal compliance and may even engender resentment or, worse, sabotage. Therapeutic alliances and helping relationships will be difficult to build or maintain. Treatment staff that prescribe action-orientated interventions to offenders will likely be exasperated, see the client as resistant, non-compliant and unmotivated, and they may engage in a power struggle with the offender or revert to heavy-handed enforcement of programme rules in order to break down resistance. Most participants (likely including many psychopaths) probably drop out of programmes at this stage of treatment.

In contrast, activities leading to examination of the negative impact of one's criminal behaviours on oneself and on others (the former would apply more to psychopaths) could be useful. Feedback, together with sensible advice from offenders who have made positive and sustained changes, could also be very valuable. Observation of how others participate in treatment activities may allow the observer to learn vicariously the positive aspects of treatment. Prematurely plunging psychopaths who are in the pre-contemplation stage into active treatment is not advisable. In short, if you want them to drink and they flatly refuse, leading them to the water is probably the best you can do. Forcing them to drink is counterproductive.

Those in the contemplation stage are aware that a problem exists and are seriously thinking about overcoming it but have not yet made a commitment to take action. Many psychopaths at this stage are also found in treatment programmes and they may continue at this stage for a long time. Often, their convincing verbal façade could be mistaken for a demonstration of sincerity and commitment toward treatment, particularly in an outpatient setting, when it is often difficult to verify whether they are, in fact, doing what they are expected to do. Again, action-orientated intervention is likely to be counterproductive. However, realistic, objective and careful re-evaluation of the costs and benefits of continuing a criminal career, the balance between short-term gain and long-term pain, or, alternatively, realistically looking at the price one has to pay for another lengthy period of incarceration, could be beneficial.

The next stage is the preparation stage. In this stage, clients combine serious intention with some treatment-orientated behaviour. They may have tried and failed, or have made some small positive behaviour changes together with a commitment to do something towards reducing problem behaviours. Psychopaths may cycle through the preparation and the contemplation stage many times without progressing further. At this stage, it is important to divide the goal-directed behaviours into manageable chunks, reward small successes, learn to deal with failures, and use commitment-enhancing techniques. Motivational interviewing techniques (Miller & Rollnick, 1991) used by a skilful and empathic therapist could increase the motivation for change and enhance the therapeutic alliance with the client. Motivational interview techniques could also be effective to those at the pre-contemplation and contemplation stages.

During the action stage, individuals actively modify their cognitions, feelings and behaviour or their environment in order to overcome their problems. The most overt behavioural changes will be observed during this stage, wherein the client will expend much time, energy and commitment to effect these changes. Skills-orientated interventions are appropriate and necessary at this stage to assist psychopaths to learn the skills in order to put into action the necessary behavioural changes. Professionals often equate the action stage with change itself, without realizing that it is built on the foundation of the previous three stages and that it has to be followed by the maintenance stage if the changes are to be maintained in the long term. Psychopaths can exert short-term dazzling changes to impress or to achieve immediate objectives, for example, to make a good impression for an upcoming parole hearing. However, for changes to be durable, the new behaviour must be applied and generalized to many different situations and maintained for an extended period of time. The treatment providers should be highly vigilant in monitoring changes and relapses; the word of the psychopath cannot be taken as the sole measure of change.

The last stage is the maintenance stage, in which relapse prevention techniques are used to prevent relapse and to consolidate and strengthen the gains made in the action stage. Again, for the psychopath, behavioural and corroborated evidence indicating that the relapse prevention strategies are being implemented is required. As indicated, staff can use the Transtheoretical Model of change as a conceptual framework to assess the various steps that the offender has taken in his change process. Effective intervention strategies then can be matched with the offenders' ongoing needs.

CONCLUSION

Mental health professionals are faced with a significant challenge to provide effective intervention for institutionalized psychopathic clients with a history of violence. Despite much research and study of this group of highly recalcitrant individuals, there are few signposts to guide us in terms of effective treatment and management. I hope the ideas provided in this chapter represent a small step in the right direction; no doubt, we have a long way to go.

ACKNOWLEDGEMENTS

The author wishes to thank Chantal Di Placido for assembling the literature and Treena Witte for assistance in the preparation of the manuscript.

REFERENCES

American Psychiatric Association (1994).   *Diagnostic and Statistical Manual of Mental Disorders*, 4th edn. Washington, DC: American Psychiatric Association.

American Psychiatric Association (1987).   *Diagnostic and Statistical Manual of Mental Disorders*, 3rd edn (revised). Washington, DC: American Psychiatric Association.

American Psychiatric Association (1980).   *Diagnostic and Statistical Manual of Mental Disorders*, 3rd edn. Washington, DC: American Psychiatric Association.

American Psychiatric Association (1968).   *Diagnostic and Statistical Manual of Mental Disorders*, 2nd edn. Washington, DC: American Psychiatric Association.

Andrews, D. A. & Bonta, J. (1994).   *The Psychology of Criminal Conduct*. Cincinnati, OH: Anderson.

Andrews, D. A., Bonta, J. & Hoge, R. D. (1990).   Classification for effective rehabilitation: rediscovering psychology. *Criminal Justice and Behaviour*, **17**, 19–52.

Andrews, D. A., Zinger, I., Hoge, R. D., Bonta, J., Gendreau, P. & Cullen, F. (1990).   Does correctional treatment work? A clinically relevant and psychologically informed meta-analysis. *Criminology*, **28**(3), 369–404.

Babiak, P. (1995).   When psychopaths go to work. *International Journal of Applied Psychology*, **44**, 171–188.

Barker, E. T. & Buck, M. F. (1977).   LSD in a coercive milieu therapy programme. *Canadian Psychiatric Association Journal*, **22**(6), 311–314.

Barker, E. T. & Mason, M. H. (1968).   The insane criminal as therapist. *Canadian Journal of Corrections*, **10**, 553–561.

Barker, E. T. & McLaughlin, A. J. (1977).   The total encounter capsule. *Canadian Psychiatric Association Journal*, **22**, 355–360.

Blackburn, R. (1993).   Treatment of the psychopathic offender. In C. R. Collins and K. Howells (Eds), *Clinical Approaches to Working with Mentally Disordered Offenders*. Leicester: British Psychological Society.

Cleckley, H. (1976).   *The Mask of Sanity*, 5th edn. St. Louis, MO: Mosby.

Cleckley, H. (1982).   *The Mask of Sanity*. Scarborough, Ontario: Plume.

Dahlstrom, W. M. & Welsh, G. S. (1960).   *An MMPI Handbook: A Guide to use in Clinical Practice and Research*. Minniapolis, MN: University of Minnesota Press.

Doren, D. M. (1987).   *Understanding and Treating the Psychopath*. Toronto: Wiley.

Ellis, A. (1962).   *Reason and Emotion in Psychotherapy*. Secaucus, NJ: Lyle Stewart.

Forth, A. E., Hart, S. D. & Hare, R. D. (1990).   Assessment of psychopathy in male young offenders. *Psychological Assessment: A Journal of Consulting and Clinical Psychology*, **2**, 342–344.

Gendreau, P. (1996).   The principles of effective intervention with offenders. In A. Harland (Ed.), *Choosing Correctional Options that Work.* Thousand Oaks, CA: Sage.

Gordon, A., Templeman, R., Christopher, M. & Hawke, W. (1992).   Psychopathy in sexual offenders. Paper presented at the Annual Meeting of the Association for the Treatment of Sexual Abusers, Portland, OR.

Gough, H. (1969).   *Manual for the California Psychological Inventory.* Palo Alto, CA: Consulting Psychologists Press.

Gray, K. G. & Hutchison, H. C. (1964).   The psychopathic personality: a survey of Canadian psychiatrists' opinions. *Canadian Psychiatric Association Journal*, **9**, 452–461.

Hare, R. D. (1980).   A research scale for the assessment of psychopathy in criminal populations. *Personality and Individual Differences*, **1**, 111–119.

Hare, R. D. (1985).   A comparison of procedures for the assessment of psychopathy. *Journal of Consulting and Clinical Psychology*, **53**, 7–16.

Hare, R. D. (1991).   *The Hare Psychopathy Checklist–Revised.* Toronto: Multi-Health Systems.

Hare, R. D. (1996).   Psychopathy: a clinical construct whose time has come. *Criminal Justice and Behaviour*, **23**, 25–54.

Hare, R. D. & Cox, D. N. (1978).   Clinical and empirical conceptions of psychopathy, and the selection of subjects for research. In R. D. Hare & D. Schalling (Eds), *Psychopathic Behaviour: Approaches to Research* (pp. 107–144). Chichester: Wiley.

Harpur, T. J., Hakistian, R. & Hare, R. D. (1988).   Factor structure of the Psychopathy Checklist. *Journal of Consulting and Clinical Psychology*, **56**, 741–747.

Harpur, T. J., Hare, R. & Hakistian, R. (1989).   A two-factor conceptualization of psychopathy: construct validity and implications for assessment. *Psychological Assessment: A Journal of Consulting and Clinical Psychology*, **1**, 6–17.

Harris, G. T., Rice, M. E. & Cormier, C. A. (1991).   Psychopathy and violent recidivism. *Law and Human Behaviour*, **15**, 625–637.

Hart, S. D., Cox, D. N. & Hare, R. D. (1995).   *Manual for the Hare Psychopathy Checklist—Revised: Screening Version (PCL:SV).* Toronto: Multi-Health Systems.

Hart, S. D. & Hare, R. D. (1997).   Psychopathy: assessment and association with criminal conduct. In D. M. Stoff, J. Breiling & J. D. Maser (Eds), *Handbook of Antisocial Behaviour.* Toronto: Wiley.

Laws, D. R. (Ed.) (1990).   *Relapse Prevention with Sex Offenders.* New York: Guilford.

Lilienfeld, S. O. (1994).   Conceptual problems in the assessment of psychopathy. *Clinical Psychology Reviews*, **14**, 17–38.

Lösel, F. (1998).   Treatment and management of psychopaths. In D. J. Cooke, A. E. Forth & R. D. Hare (Eds), *Psychopathy: Theory, Research and Implications for Society* (pp. 303–354). Dordrecht: Kluwer Academic.

Maddocks, P. D. (1970).   A five year follow-up of untreated psychopaths. *British Journal of Psychiatry*, **116**, 511–515.

Marlett, G. A. & Gordon, J. R. (Eds) (1985).   *Relapse Prevention: Maintenance Strategies in the Treatment of Addictive Behaviours.* New York: Guilford.

McCord, W. & McCord, J. (1956).   *Psychopathy and Delinquency.* New York: Grune & Stratton.

McCord, W. & McCord, J. (1964).   *The Psychopath: An Essay on the Criminal Mind.* Princeton, NJ: Van Nostrand.

Miller, W. R. & Rollnick, S. (Eds) (1991).   *Motivational Interviewing: Preparing People for Change.* New York: Guilford.

Ogloff, J. R. P., Wong, S. & Greenwood, A. (1990).   Treating criminal psychopaths in a therapeutic community programme. *Behavioural Sciences and the Law*, **8**, 181–190.

Prochaska, J. & DiClemente, C. (1986).   Toward a comprehensive model of change. In W. R. Millen & N. Heather (Eds), *Treating Addictive Behaviours: Processes of Change* (pp. 3–27). New York: Plenum.

Prochaska, J., DiClemente, C. & Norcross, J. (1992).   In search of how people change: applications to addictive behaviours. *American Psychologist*, **47**, 1102–1114.

Rice, M. E., Harris, G. T. & Cormier, C. (1992).   An evaluation of a maximum security therapeutic community for psychopaths and other mentally disordered offenders. *Law and Human Behaviour*, **16**(4), 399–412.

Ross, B. & McKay, H. B. (1976).   Adolescent therapists. *Canada's Mental Health*, **24**(2), 15–17.

Suedfeld, P. & Landon, P. B. (1978).   Approaches to treatment. In R. D. Hare & D. Schalling (Eds), *Psychopathic Behaviour: Approaches to Research*. New York: Wiley.

Templeman, T. L. & Wollersheim, J. P. (1979).   A cognitive-behavioural approach to the treatment of psychopathy. *Psychotherapy: Theory, Research, and Practice*, **16**(2), 132–139.

Tennent, G., Tennent, D., Prins, H. & Bedford, A. (1993).   Is psychopathic disorder a treatable condition? *Medicine, Science and the Law*, **33**, 63–66.

Vorrath, M. & Brentro, L. K. (1985).   *Positive Peer Culture*. New York: Aldine.

Wong, S. (1998).   Treatment outcome of psychopaths: a review of the literature (in preparation).

Wong, S. & Gordon, A. (1999).   *Violence Risk Scale* (unpublished manuscript).

Wong, S. & Hare, R. D. (1998).   *Program Guidelines for the Treatment of Institutionalized Violent Psychopathic Offenders* (in preparation).

World Health Organization (1975).   *International Classification of Diseases: Manual of the International Statistical Classification of Diseases, Injuries and Causes of Death*. Geneva: World Health Organization.

World Health Organization (1992).   *The ICD-10 Classification Manual of Mental and Behavioural Disorders: Clinical Descriptions and Diagnostic Guidelines*. Geneva: World Health Organization.

APPENDIX A

Criteria used to determine the adequacy of studies.

1. Diagnostic criteria

Definition of psychopathy/sociopathy/antisocial personality:

0—*Not adequate.* The study gave no description of the subjects or simply labelled the subjects as psychopath, etc., without giving any more descriptions.

1—*Somewhat adequate.* A brief description of the characteristics of psychopathy was given, including a few characteristics according to Cleckley's (1976) criteria or the PCL-R. All DSM-III and DSM-III-R diagnoses of antisocial personality disorder are rated as 1.

2—*Adequate.* Diagnostic criteria of psychopathy were very similar to those given by Cleckley (1976) or the PCL-R.

2. Diagnostic reliability

Measuring the reliability in the assessment of psychopathy:

0—*Not adequate.* The study made no mention of diagnostic reliability.
1—*Somewhat adequate.* Good or acceptable diagnostic reliability was mentioned but no objective measure of inter-rater reliability was given.
2—*Adequate.* Good inter-rater reliability was obtained based on an objective measure of reliability.

3. Treatment programme

Description of the treatment programme:

0—*Not adequate.* The study did not describe the treatment programme or just named a treatment programme but gave no description of it.
1—*Somewhat adequate.* The treatment programme was described but there was insufficient detail to determine clearly the objective, content and process of the programme.
2—*Adequate.* The programme was described in sufficient detail to enable the reader to determine clearly the objective, content and process of the programme.

4. Treatment evaluation

Evaluation of the outcomes of the treatment programme:

0—*Not adequate.* No treatment outcome evaluation measure was used.
1—*Somewhat adequate.* Treatment outcome measure(s) was (were) vague or subjective.
2—*Adequate.* A reliable and objective treatment outcome measure(s) was (were) provided.

5. Follow-up

A follow-up period of at least one year including at least 50% of the cases:

0—*Not adequate.* No follow-up period was provided.

1—*Somewhat adequate.* A follow-up period was provided; however, it did not comply with the one year, 50% stipulation.

2—*Adequate.* A follow-up period of at least one year and included no less than 50% of the cases.

6. Control group

The use of an appropriate control/comparison group:

0—*Not adequate.* No control/comparison group was used.

1—*Somewhat adequate.* The appropriateness of the control/comparison group(s) was (were) questionable.

2—*Adequate.* Appropriate control/comparison group(s) was (were) used.

Table 4.3   Rating of the four studies in Wong (1998)

Study	Diagnostic criteria	Diagnostic reliability	Treatment programme	Treatment evaluation	Follow-up	Control group
Harris et al. (1991)	2	2	2	2	2	2
Maddocks (1970)	2	0	1	1	2	0
Ogloff et al. (1990)	2	2	2	2	0	0
Rice et al. (1992)	2	2	2	2	2	2

Chapter 5

OFFENDERS WITH SCHIZOPHRENIA

Joseph D. Bloom and William H. Wilson

School of Medicine, Oregon Health Sciences University, Portland, Oregon, USA

INTRODUCTION

Schizophrenia is a common, severe, debilitating mental illness. Once thought to be due to psychological factors, schizophrenia is now recognized to be a disorder of brain structure and function (Carpenter & Buchanan, 1994; Pinals & Breier, 1997) caused by a combination of incompletely characterized genetic and environmental factors (Tamminga, 1997). The great majority of individuals with schizophrenia do not pose a risk of violence. However, a minority commit violent (Lindqvist & Allebeck, 1990b; Eronen, Hakola & Tiihonen, 1996; Eronen, Tiihonen & Hakola, 1996) and other types of illegal acts and become involved in the criminal justice system (Hodgins, 1992, 1993; Hodgins et al., 1996).

Treatment of schizophrenia consists of antipsychotic medication in conjunction with comprehensive psychosocial support. Recent development of a new generation of more effective medications has increased the effectiveness of treatment of schizophrenia. Co-morbid conditions such as substance abuse complicate treatment and contribute to violence (Cuffel et al., 1994).

Violence, Crime and Mentally Disordered Offenders. Edited by S. Hodgins and R. Müller-Isberner.
© 2000 John Wiley & Sons, Ltd.

HISTORY OF THE DISORDER

Classification of mental illness in Western medicine dates back to the Ancient Greeks. However, the current concept of schizophrenia has evolved over the past 100 years (Pinals & Brier, 1997). Early in this century, the German psychiatrist Emil Kraepelin characterized a syndrome of severe chronic psychosis which he termed "dementia praecox", and which he differentiated from manic depressive illness. Eugen Bleuler, a Swiss psychiatrist, elaborating on the concept of dementia praecox, named the illness "schizophrenia" to emphasize the fragmentation of various mental functions in the disorder. The current notion of schizophrenia is a refinement of these ideas.

DIAGNOSIS

While schizophrenia is considered to be due to dysfunction of the central nervous system, there are not as yet biologically based diagnostic criteria. Rather, diagnosis is based on symptoms and natural history. Officially recognized diagnostic criteria are those of the World Health Organization's International Statistical Classification of Diseases and Related Health Problems, 10th edn (ICD-10; World Health Organization, 1992) and the similar criteria of the American Psychiatric Association's Diagnostic and Statistical Manual, 4th edn (DSM-IV; American Psychiatric Association, 1994).

In order to make a diagnosis, characteristic symptoms of schizophrenia must have been present for at least one month. These symptoms include hallucinations, delusions, disorganized speech or disorganized behavior and/or symptoms such as social withdrawal, emotional indifference and decreased speech. In addition, there must be evidence of significant social dysfunction and a continuous disturbance of functioning for at least six months. Schizophrenia is not diagnosed if the symptoms are better accounted for by a major mood disorder, a general medical disorder (such as a brain tumor) or substance abuse. The disorder is categorized into subtypes (paranoid, disorganized, catatonic, undifferentiated, residual) based on the predominant symptoms expressed in a particular case.

EPIDEMIOLOGY AND NATURAL HISTORY

Schizophrenia occurs with a similar prevalence throughout the world, afflicting approximately 1% of the population (Pinals & Brier, 1997). Thus, of the 250 million people in the USA, 2.5 million are or will be afflicted with the disorder. The economic impact of schizophrenia in the USA has been estimated at $40–60 billion annually. Characteristic symptoms of the illness usually have their onset in late adolescence or early adulthood. The appearance of frank psychotic symptoms is frequently preceded by a pro-dromal period of decreasing social functioning, which may be a few months in duration. Retrospectively, individuals with schizophrenia have often seemed odd or awkward in comparison to their siblings, long before the onset of frank psychosis. The antecedents of frank schizophrenia is a fruitful area of inquiry (Cannon, Mednick & Parnas, 1990), which may lead to a better understanding of those who develop schizophrenia and ultimately become involved in the criminal justice system.

Symptoms of schizophrenia wax and wain over the years. For individuals whose illness meets DSM-IV criteria for schizophrenia, the illness is almost always life-long. Treatment with medication allows long periods of relative freedom from major symptoms, but these recur periodically. Such "re-lapses" are apt to occur at times of increased social stress or because of medication treatment non-compliance.

ETIOLOGY

The cause or causes of schizophrenia are poorly understood, but genetic factors play an important role (Tamminga, 1997). Transmission of the illness doe not follow simple Mendelian genetics. Rather, transmission is complex and is assumed to be polygenic. Genetics confer a vulnerability to the illness, but some additional environmental event may be required for actual expres-sion of the illness. Individuals with one first-degree relative with schizo-phrenia have a 10-fold greater risk of developing schizophrenia than does the general population. In fraternal twins with one affected member, the risk to the other twin is 10%, the same as with any other first-degree relative. Mono-zygotic twins have identical genetic material, and have a concordance rate of 50–60%. Infants adopted away at birth have rates of schizophrenia in line with their biological relatives, not with their adoptive families. Numerous environ-mental factors have been proposed as triggers for the expression of schizo-phrenia in genetically susceptible individuals. These include viruses, intrauterine insults and toxins, but none has yet been identified. Sporadic cases of schizophrenia without family history also occur.

A number of structural and functional brain abnormalities are associated with schizophrenia, although none is so robust and unique that it could serve as a diagnostic tool. The ratio of the fluid-filled spaces within the brain (ventricles) to brain tissue is termed the ventricular brain ratio (VBR). On average, the VBR of individuals with schizophrenia is higher than the VBR of normal controls, although there is considerable overlap among the groups. Twin studies have provided further evidence that increased VBR is a feature of schizophrenia. Among monozygotic twins who are discordant for schizophrenia, the schizophrenic twin almost always has larger ventricles than his/her non-schizophrenic twin. Increased ventricular size indicates a relative lack of brain tissue. Such a lack of tissue could be due to maldevelopment of the brain *in utero* or to destruction of tissue later in life. It seems likely that the former accounts for the increase VBR in schizophrenia. Autopsy studies tend to confirm the hypothesis that brain development *in utero* is abnormal. Nerve cells in the medial temporal lobe tend to be decreased in number and are abnormally orientated. These findings are consistent with improper development before the fifth month of gestation and would be unlikely to be caused by later injury to the brain.

High technology brain imaging techniques, such as xenon regional cerebral blood flow (Xe rCBF), positron emission tomography (PET), single photon emission computed tomography (SPECT) and functional magnetic resonance imaging (fMRI), now allow study of the functioning of human brains. These techniques consistently demonstrate abnormalities in brain function in schizophrenia. The most robust of these findings is "hypofrontality".

The frontal lobes of the brain are involved in judgment and problem solving. The Wisconsin Card Sort is an experimental task which targets these frontal lobe functions. Individuals with schizophrenia and normal control subjects show similar levels of frontal lobe activity at rest. When normal subjects are then asked to perform the Wisconsin Card Sort, there is a marked increase in metabolic activity in the frontal lobes. When schizophrenic subjects attempt the same task, there is no increase in frontal lobe activity, and subjects do very poorly in solving the problems presented by the task. This lack of frontal lobe activity helps to explain why individuals with schizophrenia show bewilderment with judgment and problem solving in everyday situations.

CLINICAL FEATURES

Symptoms of schizophrenia are classified in four domains: positive symptoms, negative symptoms, cognitive symptoms and affective symptoms. These domains are relatively independent of each other. Symptoms within each domain respond differentially to certain medications, and are thought to be the result of different neurological abnormalities. The terms "positive" and "negative" were assigned to the major symptoms of schizophrenia due to neurological theories which are no longer current. The terminology is now arbitrary, but the distinction remains useful.

Positive symptoms are hallucinations, delusions and thought disorder. Hallucinations are sensory experiences which occur in the absence of external stimuli. Hallucinations may occur in any sensory modality, but auditory hallucinations are the most common. Often, these are in the form of voices commenting on a person's behaviour, or giving commands. Delusions are irrational ideas which are held with deep conviction despite rational evidence to the contrary. These ideas may be quite bizarre. For example, a patient treated by one of the authors (WHW) believed that government agents had implanted an electronic device in her jaw which transmitted her thoughts to the police. She came to an emergency room demanding surgical excision of the device. When the doctors showed her X-rays of her jaw, which were normal, she concluded that the doctors were conspiring with the government to deceive her.

Negative symptoms include social withdrawal, lack of motivation, spare speech and emotional indifference. These negative symptoms are often quite debilitating and impede rehabilitation, even when positive symptoms are in remission. Cognitive symptoms include poor attention and decreased short-term memory. Long-term memory is not impaired. These cognitive difficulties clearly impede progress in rehabilitation, vocational advancement and educational achievement. Affective disturbances are primarily related to discouragement and demoralization.

VIOLENCE AS A SYMPTOM

The majority of individuals with schizophrenia do not pose a risk of violence (Swanson et al., 1990). The popular misconception to the contrary adds to the burden of social stigma which individuals with schizophrenia must shoulder on a daily basis (Fink & Tasman, 1992). However, there is a well-documented increased incidence of violence and arrest among some individuals with schizophrenia (Tardiff, 1989; Torrey, 1994, 1995). This was demonstrated in the numerous studies that reviewed arrest data of individuals with severe mental disorders (for review, see Link & Stueve, 1994) and in the more recent epidemiological studies in Europe (Lindqvist and Allebeck, 1990b; Hodgins, 1992; Hodgins et al., 1996) and in the USA (Swanson et al., 1990). Link, Andrews and Cullen (1992) sampled rates of violence among current and former patients and a community sample and found increased rates of violence largely related to an association of violence with psychotic symptomatology.

Recent studies have attempted to investigate the relationship to violence of severe mental illness in general and of schizophrenia in particular. Taylor (1993) summarized findings from a study of violent and non-violent prisoners, including some with schizophrenia. She found that the majority of violent schizophrenic men became aggressive at some time after the onset of their illnesses, and that there was a relationship between the criminal activity and psychotic symptomatology (Taylor, 1985). Hodgins (1993) reports data from Sweden that suggests that the onset of criminal activity in individuals with major mental disorders falls into two groups, those that begin a career of offending prior to the onset of psychiatric symptoms and those whose symptomatology precedes criminal justice involvement. Such findings have important implications for criminal justice and for forensic mental health systems.

A different line of investigation looks at the dimension of major mental illness and violence as it relates to hospital admission and discharge. Studies have found a relationship between severe psychopathology and violence occurring just before or early into hospital admission (McNeil, Binder & Greenfield, 1988; Beck, White & Gage, 1991). This was confirmed by Tardiff et al. (1997). Violence occurring immediately after discharge was associated with personality disorder rather than lingering effects of the major mental disorder.

Further investigations have begun to look for links between violence and specific symptoms of schizophrenia. These include the presence or absence of delusions (Tardiff, 1989; Taylor et al., 1994) and hallucinations (McNeil, 1994) or to particular variables related to aspects of acute psychosis. These investigations are particularly important because of the often discussed clinical association between violence and command hallucinations. McNeil (1994) reported that while some individuals appear to commit violent acts in response to command hallucinations, most do not respond to such commands.

Link and Stueve (1994) moved beyond the question of the presence or absence of a particular psychotic feature by postulating a relationship between violence and certain psychotic symptoms, based on what they termed the "principle of rationality-within-irrationality". They operationalized this principle using three of 13 items on a psychotic symptomatology scale (Dohrenwend et al., 1980) and found a strong association between these scale items and the violent behaviours of their study sample. This is a promising line of research which places violence and schizophrenia in a matrix of symptoms and settings (McNeil, 1994). This type of approach formed the basis of one of the areas of investigation in the recently completed McArthur Foundation study of risk (Monahan & Steadman, 1994).

A very important area in relation to schizophrenia and violence has been the question of the co-morbid conditions, such as alcoholism and/or substance abuse (Lindqvist & Allebeck, 1990a; Abram & Teplin, 1991; Cuffel et al., 1994; Drake et al., 1993). Borum et al. (1997) investigated the relationship between medication compliance and arrest in a sample of severely ill individuals, of whom 70% suffered from schizophrenia. In one of the models tested, the authors found that neither substance abuse alone nor medication non-compliance alone was significant in predicting violent behaviour, but occurrence of the two together was highly significant for violent behaviour.

In other tested models, substance abuse alone was significantly related to police encounters and violent behaviour. The authors suggest that medication non-compliance together with substance abuse form an important substrate that leads to heightened chance of police encounter and/or violent behaviour. This study confirmed views of family members' reporting of situations that led their severely ill relatives into problems with the criminal justice system (McFarland et al., 1989). Although not specifically focused on schizophrenia, Steadman et al. (1998) confirm an association between mental illness, violence and substance abuse.

TREATMENT

To the extent that a significant degree of criminality and violence associated with schizophrenia is related to its symptomatology, then the treatment of the illness will have a salutary effect on such negative consequences. As yet there is no cure for schizophrenia and no treatment which completely eliminates symptoms. The current approach to treatment combines pharmacological, psychological and social interventions, and results in a marked amelioration of symptoms and improvement in social functioning.

Medications

Although medications alone are rarely sufficient to treat schizophrenia, antipsychotic medication is the cornerstone of the treatment and is a prerequisite for the success of psychological and social treatment (Buckley & Meltzer, 1995). The newer or "atypical" antipsychotic medications introduced within the last few years are more effective and have far fewer side effects than the older antipsychotic medications (Marder, Wirshing & Ames, 1997). Treatment with antipsychotic medication results in a marked decrease in symptoms over a time period of about six weeks. Continued maintenance treatment is effective in forestalling and moderating subsequent relapses.

The original antipsychotic medications were developed in the 1950s and 1960s. The prototypic drugs in this class are chlorpromazine and haloperidol. These medications provide effective relief from positive symptoms for about two-thirds of the population with schizophrenia. They are substantially less effective for the other symptom domains. The therapeutic efficacy of these agents is thought to be due to their ability to block the action of the neurotransmitter dopamine at D2 dopamine receptors in the limbic areas of the brain.

These agents also block dopamine transmission within the basal ganglia, giving rise to motor system side effects which mimic the symptoms of

Parkinson's disease. Signs of drug-induced Parkinsonism include slow speech, decreased behaviour, muscle stiffness, tremor and a wide-based gait. Drug-induced Parkinsonism is lessened by concurrent use of anti-cholinergic medications, such as benztropine (Cogentin) and remits if the antipsychotic medication is withdrawn.

Treatment with these antipsychotic medications over the course of weeks to months may lead to a syndrome of choreoathetoid movements and non-rhythmic motor tics, known as tardive dyskinesia. Tardive dyskinesia is usually mild, but may be severely disfiguring and disabling. Frequently it does not remit, even when the medication is withdrawn. The incidence of tardive dyskinesia is approximately 5% of treated patients per year for young, otherwise healthy, patients, and upward of 50% per year in the elderly.

Since 1990, several "atypical" antipsychotic medications have become available for routine use worldwide. Clozapine was introduced for clinical use in the USA in 1990, although it had been in use in some European countries since the mid-1970s. Clozapine is demonstrably more effective as an antipsychotic than are the typical agents. It is highly effective in treating positive symptoms, and also has beneficial effects on negative, cognitive and affective symptoms. Clozapine has specific therapeutic effects on aggression, and hence decreases violence (Anonymous, 1996; Buckley et al., 1995; Ratey et al., 1993; Wilson & Claussen, 1995). Clozapine's neurochemical mechanism of action is not completely characterized. It is neurochemically distinct from the original antipsychotic agents, having a rather lower affinity for dopamine receptors and a distinctly higher affinity for certain serotonin receptors. Therapeutic effects are thought to be due to dopamine blockade within the limbic system and dopamine system activation within the cerebral cortex. Clozapine does not inhibit dopamine activity within the basal ganglia, and thus it does not cause either drug-induced Parkinsonism or tardive dyskinesia.

Clozapine does have some problematic side effects, the most serious of which is a reduction in white blood cell production by the bone marrow (agranulocytosis). This side effect occurs in just under 1% of treated patients. If unrecognized, agranulocytosis would leave the body defenseless against life-threatening bacterial infections. Frequent monitoring of the white blood cell count allows for early recognition of agranulocytosis. If clozapine is discontinued at the first indication of agranulocytosis, individuals typically recover without infection. However, they may not take clozapine in the future, due to a high rate of recurrence of agranulocytosis. In the USA, governmental regulations require blood count monitoring for the duration of treatment with the drug. The required monitoring is weekly for the first six months of use and then every other week for the duration of treatment.

Clozapine treatment is complicated by a number of less serious but uncomfortable side effects. Epileptic seizures occur in approximately 5% of patients treated with clozapine, usually when doses have been raised too quickly. Anticholinergic side effects (dry mouth, blurry vision, constipation, urinary retention) are common, as are orthostatic hypotension (dizziness on standing) and sedation. Increased salivary volume may be annoying. Not infrequently these side-effects, combined with the required blood tests, lead patients to refuse treatment with clozapine or to have poor adherence to the prescribed dosage schedule.

The therapeutic effectiveness of clozapine has led to the development of other antipsychotic medications which have fewer side effects. As of this writing, risperidone, olanzapine and quetiapine have been released for clinical use, and others are in the late stages of development. These are effective anti-psychotic medications with beneficial effects on all four symptom domains. These agents have little to no effect on the motor system, and do not cause agranulocytosis. Neurochemically, they differ somewhat from each other and from clozapine, with the result that a particular individual may derive more benefit from one than from another of these medicines. Because they ameliorate rather than eliminate symptoms, the treatment of schizophrenia remains partial. Nonetheless, the atypical antipsychotic medications represent a quantum advance.

Psychosocial support

Psychosocial support remains an essential element of treatment, even when patients are receiving optimal medication management. Despite the advances in antipsychotic medication, most individuals with schizophrenia continue to have difficulty with social adjustment. Substantial advances in effective psychosocial care for schizophrenia have been made in the past decade (Mueser, Drake & Bond, 1997). Characteristics of successful programs include location within patients' own communities; direct behavioral interventions focused on specific desired behaviors rather than generalized improvement; and a combination of skills training and environmental support. Attention to psychological and social factors allows individuals with schizophrenia to make the best adjustment possible, despite disability. Efforts to "cure" schizophrenia through psychotherapy, which were common in the mid-century, have been replaced by proven methods of providing support and rehabilitation (Solomon & Meyerson, 1997). Current psychosocial methods focus on helping individuals to access support for concrete needs (e.g. housing, food, money, medical care, socialization) and on developing social competence through specifically designed psychiatric rehabilitation programmes (Stein & Test, 1980). Individual supportive psychotherapy, focused on problems of adjustment, has been shown to have a positive effect on broad components of social adjustment (Hogarty et al., 1997).

Assertive community treatment programs (ACT) and intensive case management (ICM) are psychosocial rehabilitation programs designed to focus on more severely mentally ill individuals with more pronounced deficits, who, for various reasons, such as lack of insight or motivation, need extra effort to keep them involved in treatment (Scott & Dixon, 1995, Herincks et al., 1997). The long-standing Program for Assertive Community Treatment (PACT) in Madison, Wisconsin, was designed to provide services in the community which replicate the services traditionally provided in long-term hospitals (Stein & Test, 1980). Staff are available to patients on a 24-hour basis and function much as an interdisciplinary team on an inpatient service.

Programs derived from this model often do not have the intensity of the PACT program, but nonetheless provide an alternative to institutionalization for all but the most severely symptomatic patients. A recent meta-analysis of outcome studies of ACT and ICM programs (Mueser et al., 1998) noted that the programs clearly reduce time spent in hospitals, improve housing stability, reduce symptoms and increase quality of life. This analysis found that the programs were less successful in improving vocational functioning and in reducing arrests and time spent in jail. However, the authors noted that specialized versions of these programs may have a positive effect on substance abuse and social functioning. This appears to be the case, as demonstrated by outcome studies of ICM programs in Vancouver, BC, Canada, and New York (Dvoskin & Steadman, 1994). After 18 months, subjects in the Canadian program had spent an average of 80 days in prison, while a comparison group had averaged 214 days. Similar results were reported for the 5121 subjects in the New York study. These programs are well suited for the treatment component of outpatient civil commitment and the conditional release of insanity acquitees described below.

As mentioned, substance abuse commonly complicates the treatment of schizophrenia. Studies have found that the percentage of individuals with schizophrenia who abuse drugs or alcohol varies from 10% to 70%, depending upon the population and the particular diagnostic criteria (Mueser et al., 1990). The Epidemiologic Catchment Area Study of community and institutionalized patients in the USA found that 47% of all individuals with a lifetime diagnosis of schizophrenia meet criteria for some form of substance abuse or dependence (Regier et al., 1990). Substance abuse increases the risk of violent behaviour among individuals with schizophrenia (Steadman et al., 1998). Thus, treatment of substance abuse is an important component of reducing violence in individuals with schizophrenia. The current emphasis is on combined or dual-diagnosis treatment. Treatment programs which integrate substance abuse treatment and schizophrenia treatment foster remission or recovery from substance abuse at more rapid rates than would otherwise be expected (Drake et al., 1996).

Other co-morbidities may affect the rate of violence among individuals with schizophrenia. For example, co-morbid antisocial personality disorder, or childhood conduct disorder, leads to higher rates of substance abuse, aggression and legal problems (Mueser et al., 1997). As with treatment of any mental disorder, co-morbid disorders need to be considered and treatment individualized to address the totality of the person's problems.

Legal-interventions facilitating treatment

In the USA and in most countries, both the civil and criminal law make special provisions for severely mentally ill individuals. These special provisions exist within the law for multiple purposes (Appelbaum, 1994). For example, competency to stand trial or the insanity defense exist within the criminal justice system to facilitate the trial process, to provide fairness to the accused who must face the power of the state, and to uphold the dignity of the legal process (Morris, 1982; Bloom & Rogers, 1987). In these situations treatment of mental illness is important, but as a secondary consideration.

Other legal provisions are more directly related to the treatment of the mentally ill (Slobogin, 1994). Two areas, civil commitment and the management and treatment of insanity acquittees, are extremely important because of the large number of schizophrenic individuals who are involved in these legal processes (Williams & Bloom, 1989). Each will be discussed briefly.

Civil commitment

Civil commitment is the most important legal procedure because on a daily basis it influences the lives of an extremely large number of individuals suffering from schizophrenia and other mental illnesses. Civil commitment generally allows for the involuntary hospitalization of mentally ill persons for both evaluation and treatment, based on criteria of dangerousness to self or others or on grave disability and being in need of care and custody. Over the last 30 years in the USA and many other Western industrialized countries, civil commitment statutes have been a battleground fought over by various groups who have advocated one side or the other of the various themes related to more treatment vs. more liberty and less coercion (Miller, 1987; Issac & Armat, 1990; LaFond & Durham, 1992). These battles continue to the present time and are currently focused on an extended debate over outpatient civil commitment (see below).

Regardless of the extent of the debate, civil commitment remains an important reality in the lives of many schizophrenic individuals in most

Western industrialized countries, and will remain so into the foreseeable future. Involuntary treatment will continue to be an important component of the treatment system for schizophrenic persons as long as there are no definitive cures for the illness, and as long as lack of insight into illness remains as a feature of some individuals suffering from the illness (McEvoy et al., 1989; Ness and Ende, 1994; Neumann et al., 1996; Dickerson et al., 1997).

Recently, outpatient civil commitment has received a great deal of attention in the American psychiatric and legal literature (Appelbaum, 1986; Hiday & Scheid-Cook, 1987; Miller, 1992). However, from a recent survey of US jurisdictions (Torrey & Kaplan, 1995), this form of commitment is underutilized and presents several problems which are difficult to overcome. These include questions of whether the criteria for commitment should be the same as, or different from, criteria governing inpatient commitment. This is particularly important when the question of non-compliance with a treatment plan becomes an issue. There is also a significant question regarding treatment (medication) refusal and whether the same rules that govern competency and treatment refusal on an inpatient basis should apply in the outpatient setting (Appelbaum, 1988, 1994).

Because the rules governing release from civil commitment are not nearly as stringent as those that generally apply to insanity acquitees (see below), there are many more theoretical and practical obstacles impeding the implementation of strong programs in outpatient civil commitment. Nonetheless, this mechanism is potentially very useful (Swanson et al., 1997), especially if combined with assertive case management and an adequate mechanism for medication monitoring.

The treatment of insanity acquittees

Insanity acquittees are individuals who have raised an insanity defense in a court and who have been found not guilty (of crimes) by reason of insanity (NGRI). There is a long tortured history of the insanity defense in the USA and an acrimonious debate about its moral underpinnings (Bonnie, 1983) and its functional necessity (Keilitz & Fulton, 1984). Again, regardless of the intensity of the debate, the insanity defense continues in some way as a part of the criminal law and the majority of those found NGRI suffer from schizophrenia (Bloom, Williams & Bigelow, 1992; Bloom & Williams, 1994).

Subsequent to an insanity verdict, most insanity acquittees are involuntarily committed for care and treatment until such time as they are no longer mentally ill and/or no longer dangerous. Commitment status provides an opportunity for treatment, usually in highly restrictive hospital-based treatment programs, but in some jurisdictions treatment might also allow conditional release in community settings.

The last two decades have seen the growth of these conditional release programs for insanity acquittees (Bloom, Williams, & Bigelow, 1991; McGreevy et al., 1991; Griffin, Steadman & Heilbrun, 1991; Tellefsen et al., 1992; Lamb, Weinberger & Gross, 1988; Wiederanders, 1992; Bluglass, 1993; Bloom & Williams, 1994; Wiederanders, Bromley & Choate, 1997). Such programs have proved to be effective in the reduction of dangerous behaviours and arrests of insanity acquittees.

The essential features of these programs involve monitored care in the community, where the ideal treatment program is designed along the lines of the assertive case management programs described above, with clear guidelines for medication monitoring and psychosocial rehabilitation and including selected prohibitions, such as the use of alcohol and drugs. An important feature of conditional release programs, which exist to a greater or lesser degree depending on the jurisdiction, include a mechanism for prompt revocation of the conditional release with return of the insanity acquittee to the forensic hospital, should problematic behaviors develop in the community.

Based on these models and on the empirical data cited above, we believe that these programs are greatly effective for persons suffering from schizophrenia and have great potential applicability for the involuntary civil population. However, the difference between a civil and criminal court confinement makes these programs more problematic for civil populations where adequate programming has been generally frustrated by the acrimonious debates surrounding treatment and liberty interests.

CONCLUSION

Schizophrenia is a severe debilitating mental illness that affects about 1% of the population worldwide. Unfortunately, during initial symptoms or relapse individuals may demonstrate highly impaired reality testing and may exhibit bizarre behaviour. Individuals may resist help from family, community members, health care professionals and law enforcement officials. Purposeless, disorganized agitation and violence, such as physical altercations, are common and may result in arrest. Prompt and effective treatment of the illness is the answer, most often in a short-term hospital or community crisis service. This approach usually alleviates the agitation and aggression in a matter of hours to days.

In the middle of the century, most people with schizophrenia lived their lives in large, poorly financed, understaffed public mental hospitals. The conditions in these hospitals led, in the USA and elsewhere, to an era of rapid deinstitutionalization, fueled by changes in commitment law and the introduction of antipsychotic medication. Now the great majority live in various circumstances in community settings. Many are significantly disabled and social and medical resources are sorely lacking for the long-term mentally ill. In the USA we view the police and criminal justice system as the court of last resort. They are often called on to help with problems which would be better addressed by low-cost housing, disability income and comprehensive community mental health services. We believe that much of the criminalization of the mentally ill in general, and of persons suffering from schizophrenia in particular, results from this process, from inadequate mental hospitals to inadequate community resources to the criminal justice system.

This is extremely unfortunate. We live in an era where treatment of schizophrenia has never been better, where medications and conceptual models of psychosocial interventions have dramatically improved. We believe that adequate treatment of acute and chronic schizophrenia would again lead to finding that schizophrenic individuals are no more dangerous than the general population.

REFERENCES

Abram, K. M. & Teplin, L. A. (1991). Co-occurring disorders among mentally ill jail detainees: implications for public policy. *American Psychologist*, **46**, 1036–1045.

American Psychiatric Association (1994). *Diagnostic and Statistical Manual of Mental Disorder, 4th edn (DSM-IV)*. Washington DC: American Psychiatric Press.

Anonymous (1996). Schizophrenia, violence, clozapine and risperidone: a review. *British Journal of Psychiatry*, **169** (31), 21–30.

Appelbaum, P. S. (1986). Outpatient commitment: the problems and the promise. *American Journal of Psychiatry*, **143**, 1270–1272.

Appelbaum, P. S. (1988). The right to refuse treatment with antipsychotic medications: retrospect and prospect. *American Journal of Psychiatry*, **145**, 413–419.

Appelbaum, P. S. (1994). Almost a Revolution—Mental Health Law and the Limits of Change. New York, Oxford University Press.

Beck, J. C., White, K. A. & Gage, B. (1991). Emergency psychiatric assessment of violence. *American Journal of Psychiatry*, **148**, 1562–1565.

Bloom, J. D. & Rogers, J. L. (1987). The legal basis of forensic psychiatry: statutorily mandated psychiatric diagnosis. *American Journal of Psychiatry*, **144**, 847–853.

Bloom, J. D., Williams, M. H. & Bigelow, D. A. (1991). Monitored conditional release of persons found Not Guilty by Reason of Insanity. *American Journal of Psychiatry*, **148**, 444–449.

Bloom, J. D., Williams, M. H. & Bigelow, D. A. (1992). The involvement of schizophrenic insanity acquittees in the mental health and criminal justice systems. *Psychiatric Clinics of North America*, **15**, 591–604.

Bloom, J. D. & Williams, M. H. (1994). *Management and Treatment of Insanity Acquittees: A Model for the 1990s*. Washington, DC: American Psychiatric Press.

Bluglass, R. (1993). Maintaining the treatment of mentally ill people in the community. *British Medical Journal*, **306**, 159–160.

Bonnie, R. J. (1983). The moral basis of the insanity defense. *American Bar Association Journal*, **69**, 194–197.

Borum, R., Swanson, J., Swartz, M. & Hiday, V. (1997). Substance abuse, violent behavior, and police encounters among persons with severe mental disorder. *Journal of Contemporary Criminal Justice*, **13**, 236–249.

Buckley, P., Bartrell, J., Donenwirth, K. & Lee, S. (1995). Violence and schizophrenia: clozapine as a specific antiaggressive agent. *Bulletin of the American Academy of Psychiatry and the Law*, **23**(4), 607–611.

Buckley, P. F. & Meltzer, H. Y. (1995). Treatment of schizophrenia: In Schatzberg, A. F. & Nemeroff, C. B. (Eds), *The American Psychiatric Press Textbook of Psychopharmacology* (pp. 615–640). Washington, DC: American Psychiatric Press.

Carpenter, W. T. & Buchanan, R. W. (1994). Medical progress: schizophrenia. *New England Journal of Medicine*, **330**(10), 681–690.

Cannon, T. D., Mednick, S. A., Parnas, J. (1990). Antecedents of predominantly negative- and predominantly positive-symptom schizophrenia in a high-risk population. *Archives of General Psychiatry*, **47**, 622–632.

Cuffel, B. J., Shumway, M., Chouljian, T. L. & MacDonald, T. (1994). A longitudinal study of substance use and community violence in schizophrenia. *Journal of Nervous and Mental Disease*, **182**(12), 704–708.

Dickerson, F. B., Boronow, J. J., Ringel, N. & Parente, F. (1997). Lack of insight among outpatients with schizophrenia. *Psychiatric Services*, **48**, 195–199.

Dohrenwend, B. P., Shrout, P., Egri, G. & Mendelsohn, F. (1980). Measures of nonspecific psychological distress and other dimensions of psychopathology in the general population. *Archives of General Psychiatry*, **37**, 1229–1236.

Drake, R., Bartels, S., Teague, G., Noordsy, D. & Clark, R. (1993). Treatment of substance abuse in severely mentally ill patients. *Journal of Nervous and Mental Disorders*, **181**, 606–611.

Drake, R. E., Mueser, K. T., Clark, R. E. & Wallach, M. E. (1996). The course, treatment, and outcome of substance disorder in persons with severe mental illness. *American Journal of Orthopsychiatry*, **66**, 42–51.

Dvoskin, J. A. & Steadman, H. J. (1994). Using intensive case management to reduce violence by mentally ill persons in the community. *Hospital & Community Psychiatry*, **45**, 679–684.

Eronen, M., Hakola, P. & Tiihonen, J. (1996). Mental disorders and homicidal behavior in Finland. *Archives of General Psychiatry*, **53**, 497–501.

Eronen, M., Tiihonen, J. & Hakola, P. (1996). Schizophrenia and homicidal behavior. *Schizophrenia Bulletin*, **22**, 83–89.

Fink, P. J. & Tasman, A. (Eds) (1992). *Stigma in Mental Illness*. Washington, DC: American Psychiatric Press.

Griffin, P. A., Steadman, H. J., Heilbrun, K. (1991). Designing conditional release systems for insanity acquittees. *Journal of Mental Health Administration*, **18**, 231–241.

Herinckx, H. A., Kinney, R. F., Clarke, G. N. & Paulson, R. I. (1997). Assertive community treatment versus usual care in engaging and retaining clients with severe mental illness. *Psychiatric Services*, **48**, 1297–1306.

Hiday, V. A. & Scheid-Cook, T. L. (1987). The North Carolina experience with outpatient commitment: a critical appraisal. *International Journal of Law and Psychiatry*, **10**, 215–232.

Hodgins, S. (1992). Mental disorder, intellectual deficiency and crime: evidence from a birth cohort. *Archives of General Psychiatry*, **49**, 476–483.

Hodgins, S. (1993). The criminality of mentally disordered persons. In Hodgins, S. (Ed.), *Mental Disorder and Crime* (pp. 3–21). Newbury Park, CA: Sage.

Hodgins, S., Mednick, S. A., Brennan, P. A., Schulsinger, F. & Engberg, M. (1996). Mental disorder and crime. *Archives of General Psychiatry*, **53**, 489–496.

Hogarty, G. E., Greenwald, D., Ulrich, R. R., Kornblith, S. J., DiBarry, A. L., Dooley, S., Carter, M. & Flesher, S. (1997). Three-year trials of personal therapy among schizophrenic patients living with or independent of family. II. Effect of adjustment of patients. *American Journal of Psychiatry*, **154**, 1514–1524.

Issac, R. J. & Armat, V. C. (1990). *Madness in the Streets—How Psychiatry and the Law Abandoned the Mentally Ill.* New York: Free Press.

Keiltiz, I. & Fulton, J. P. (1984). *The Insanity Defense and its Alternatives*, R-085. Washington, DC. National Center for State Courts.

LaFond, J. Q. & Durham, M. L. (1992). *Back to Asylum: The Future of Mental Health Law and Policy in the United States.* New York: Oxford University Press.

Lamb, H. R., Weinberger, L. E. & Gross, B. H. (1988). Court-mandated community outpatient treatment for persons found Not Guilty by Reason of Insanity: a five-year follow-up. *American Journal of Psychiatry*, **145**, 450–456.

Lindqvist, P. & Allebeck, P. (1990a). Schizophrenia and assaultive behavior: the role of alcohol and drug abuse. *Acta Psychiatrica Scandinavia*, **82**, 191–195.

Lindqvist, P. & Allebeck, P. (1990b). Schizophrenia and crime: a longitudinal follow-up of 644 schizophrenics in Stockholm. *British Journal of Psychiatry*, **157**, 345–350.

Link, B. G., Andrews, H. A., Cullen, F. T. (1992). The violent and illegal behavior of mental patients reconsidered. *American Sociological Review*, **57**, 275–292.

Link, B. G. & Stueve, A. (1994). Psychotic symptoms and the violent/illegal behavior of mental patients compared to community controls. In Monahan, J. and Steadman, H. J. (Eds), *Violence and Mental Disorder*, (pp. 137–159). Chicago, IL: University of Chicago Press.

Marder, S. R., Wirshing, W. C. & Ames, D. (1997). New antipsychotics. *Psychiatric Clinics of North America: Annals of Drug Therapy*, **4**, 195–207.

McGreevy, M. A., Steadman, H. J., Dvoskin, J. A. et al. (1991). New York State's system of managing insanity acquittees in the community. *Hospital and Community Psychiatry*, **42**, 512–517.

McEvoy, J. P., Appelbaum, P. S., Apperson, L. J., Geller, J. L. & Freter, S. (1989). Why must some schizophrenic patients be involuntarily committed? The role of insight. *Comprehensive Psychiatry*, **30**, 13–17.

McFarland, B. H., Faulkner, L. R., Bloom, J. D., Hallaux, R. & Bray, J. D. (1989). Chronic mental illness and the criminal justice system. *Hospital and Community Psychiatry*, **40**, 718–723.

McNeil, D. E., Binder, R. L. & Greenfield, T. K. (1988). Predictors of violence in civilly committed acute psychiatric patients. *American Journal of Psychiatry*, **145**, 965–970.

McNiel, D. E. (1994). Hallucinations and violence. In Monahan, J. and Steadman, H. J. (Eds), *Violence and Mental Disorder* (pp. 183–202). Chicago, IL: University of Chicago Press.

Miller, R. D. (1987). *Involuntary Civil Commitment of the Mentally Ill in the Post-Reform Era.* Springfield, IL: Charles C. Thomas.

Miller, R. D. (1992). An update on involuntary civil commitment to outpatient treatment. *Hospital and Community Psychiatry*, **43**, 79–82.

Monahan, J. & Steadman, H. J. (1994). Toward a rejuvenation of risk assessment research. In Monahan, J. & Steadman, H. J. (Eds), *Violence and Mental Disorder.* Chicago, IL: University of Chicago Press.

Morris, N. (1982).   *Madness and the Criminal Law.* Chicago, IL: University of Chicago Press.

Mueser, K. T., Yarnold, P. R., Levinson, D. R. et al. (1990).   Prevalence of substance abuse in schizophrenia: demographic and clinical correlates. *Schizophrenia Bulletin*, **16**, 31–56.

Mueser, K. T., Drake, R. E. & Bond, G. R. (1997).   Recent advances in psychiatric rehabilitation of patients with severe mental illness. *Harvard Review of Psychiatry*, **5**, 123–137.

Mueser, K. R., Drake, R. E., Ackerson, T. H., Alterman, A. I. et al. (1997).   Antisocial personality disorder, conduct disorder, and substance abuse in schizophrenia. *Journal of Abnormal Psychology*, **106**, 473–477.

Mueser, K. T., Bond, G. R., Drake, R. E. & Resnick, S. D. (1998).   Models of community care for severe mental illness: a review of research on case management. *Schizophrenia Bulletin*, **24**, 37–74.

Ness, D. E. & Ende, J. (1994).   Denial in the medical interview: recognition and management. *JAMA*, **272**, 1777–1781.

Neumann, C. S., Walker, E. F., Weinstein, J. & Cutshaw, M. A. (1996).   Psychotic patients' awareness of mental illness: implications for legal defense proceedings. *Journal of Psychiatry & Law*, **Fall**, 421–442.

Pinals, D. A. & Breier, A. (1997).   Schizophrenia. In Tasman, A., Kay, J. & Lieberman, J. A. (Eds), (pp. 927–965). Philadelphia, PA: Saunders.

Ratey, J. J., Leveroni, C., Kilmer, D., Gutheit, C. et al. (1993).   The effects of clozapine on severely aggressive psychiatric inpatients in a state hospital. *Journal of Clinical Psychiatry*, **54**(6), 219–223.

Regier, D. A., Farmer, M. E., Rae, D. S. et al. (1990).   Comorbidity of mental disorders with alcohol and other drug abuse: results from the Epidemiologic Catchment Area Study. *JAMA*, **264**: 2511–2518.

Scott, J. E. & Dixon, L. B. (1995).   Assertive community treatment and case management for schizophrenia. *Schizophrenia Bulletin*, **21**, 657–668.

Slobogin, C. (1994).   Involuntary community treatment of people who are violent and mentally ill: a legal analysis. *Hospital and Community Psychiatry*, **45**, 685–689.

Solomon, P. & Meyerson, A. T. (1997).   Social stabilization: achieving satisfactory community adaptation for the disabled mentally ill. Tasman, A., Kay, J. & Lieberman, J. A. (Eds), *Psychiatry* (pp. 1727–1750). Philadelphia, PA: Saunders.

Steadman, H. J., Mulvey, E. P., Monahan, J., Robbins, P. C., Appelbaum, P. S., Grisso, T., Roth, L. H. & Silver, E. (1998).   Violence by people discharged from acute psychiatric inpatient facilities and by others in the same neighborhoods. *Archives of General Psychiatry*, **55**, 393–401.

Stein, L. I. & Test, M. A. (1980).   Alternative to mental hospital treatment. I. Conceptual model, treatment program and clinical evaluation. *Archives of General Psychiatry*, **41**, 175–179.

Swanson, J. W., Holzer, C. E., Ganju, V. K. et al. (1990).   Violence and psychiatric disorder in the community: evidence from the epidemiologic catchment area surveys. *Hospital and Community Psychiatry*, **41**, 761–770.

Swanson, J. W., Swartz, M. S., George, L. K., Burns, B. J., Hiday, V. A., Borum, R. & Wagner, H. R. (1997).   Interpreting the effectiveness of involuntary outpatient commitment: a conceptual model. *Journal of American Academy Psychiatry and Law*, **25**, 5–16.

Tamminga, C. A. (1997).   Neuropsychiatric aspects of schizophrenia. In Yudofsky, S. A. & Hales, R. E. (Eds), *The American Psychiatric Press Textbook of Neuropsychiatry*, 3rd edn (pp. 855–882). Washington, DC: American Psychiatric Press.

Tardiff, K. (1989). *Assessment and Management of Violent Patients*. Washington, DC: American Psychiatric Press.

Tardiff, K., Marzuk, P. M., Leon, A. C. & Portera, B. A. (1997).   A prospective study of violence by psychiatric patients after hospital discharge. *Psychiatric Services*, **48**, 678–681.

Taylor, P. J. (1985).   Motives for offending among violent and psychotic men. *British Journal of Psychiatry*, **147**, 491–498.

Taylor, P. J. (1993).   Schizophrenia and crime: distinctive patterns in association. In Hodgins, S. (Ed.), *Mental Disorder and Crime* (pp. 63–85). Newbury Park, CA: Sage.

Taylor, P. J., Garety, P., Buchanan, A., Reed, A., Wessley, S., Ray, K., Dunn, G. & Grubin, D. (1994).   Delusions and violence. In Monahan, J. and Steadman, H. J. (Eds), *Violence and Mental Disorders* (pp. 161–182). Chicago, IL: University of Chicago Press.

Tellefsen, C., Cohen, M. I. & Silver, S. B. (1992).   Predicting success on conditional release for insanity acquittees: regionalized versus non-regionalized hospital patients. *Bulletin of the American Academy of Psychiatry and Law*, **20**, 87–100.

Torrey, E. F. (1994).   Violent behavior by individuals with serious mental illness. *Hospital and Community Psychiatry*, **45**, 653–662.

Torrey, E. F. (1995).   Editorial: Jails and prisons—America's new mental hospital. *American Journal of Public Health*, **85**, 1611–1613.

Torrey, E. F. & Kaplan, R. J. (1995).   A national survey of the use of outpatient commitment. *Psychiatric Services*, **46**, 778–784.

Wiederanders, M. R. (1992).   Recidivism of disordered offenders who were conditionally vs. unconditionally released. *Behavioral Sciences and the Law*, **10**, 141–148.

Wiederanders, M. R., Bromley, D. L. & Choate, P. A. (1997).   Forensic conditional release programs and outcomes in three states. *International Journal of Law and Psychiatry*, **20**, 249–257.

Williams, M. H. & Bloom, J. D. (1989).   Mental health services research with forensic populations. In Bloom, J. D. (Ed.), *State–University Collaboration: The Oregon Experience. New Directions for Mental Health Services*. San Francisco, CA: Jossey-Bass.

Wilson, W. H. & Claussen, A. M. (1995).   Outcome of 18 month of clozapine treatment for 100 state hospital patients. *Psychiatric Services*, **46**, 386–389.

World Health Organization (1992).   *International Statistical Classification of Diseases and Related Health Problems (ICD-10)*. Geneva: World Health Organization.

Chapter 6

OFFENDERS WITH MAJOR AFFECTIVE DISORDERS

Derek Eaves, George Tien and Derek Wilson

Forensic Psychiatric Services Commission, Vancouver, British Columbia, Canada

INTRODUCTION

Affective disorders encompass a wide group of disorders in which alterations of mood, together with motor disturbances and vegetative states, form the predominant clinical picture. The terms "mood disorder" and "affective disorder" are usually used interchangeably, the former term being used in the current edition of the Diagnostic and Statistical Manual of Mental Disorders (DSM-IV). DSM-IV recognizes 12 different kinds of mood disorder. Although depression is a dominant feature of many forms of mood disorder, it can also be a major symptom of other disorders classified under the DSM-IV (e.g. adjustment disorder). The milder forms of depression—dysthymia, cyclothymia—will not be considered in this chapter. Emphasis will be placed on the more serious forms of affective disorders (major depression, bipolar disorder).

CHARACTERISTICS

The core features of major or unipolar depression include a pervasive low mood, loss of interest and enjoyment (anhedonia) and reduced energy or

Violence, Crime and Mentally Disordered Offenders. Edited by S. Hodgins and R. Müller-Isberner.
© 2000 John Wiley & Sons, Ltd.

diminished activity. Other features common to depression include poor concentration and attention, poor self-esteem and self-confidence, ideas of guilt and unworthiness, bleak and pessimistic views of the future, ideas or acts of self-harm or suicide, disturbed sleep and diminished appetite. Many patients present initially with physical symptoms. Indeed, the presence of a somatic syndrome may be inferred if patients suffer from four or more of the following physical symptoms: anhedonia, loss of reactivity, early waking (two hours or more), psychomotor retardation or agitation, marked loss of appetite, weight loss or loss of libido.

Mania is defined as a distinct period during which there is an abnormally and persistently elevated, expansive or irritable mood. Symptoms include grandiosity, insomnia, pressure of speech, disinhibition and increased motor activity. Persons with such symptoms may take inordinate risks and can find themselves in conflict with other persons or, indeed, in conflict with the law.

Other forms of mood disorders include bipolar disorders, sometimes referred to as manic depression in North America. This usage of the term "manic depression" differs from the continental European usage, where the term refers to both bipolar disorder and recurrent major depression. By definition, a patient with bipolar disorder is one who displays mania, with or without a period of depression. Most patients, however, have both manic and depressive episodes in various sequences and frequencies. Patients in the manic phase of bipolar disorders are hyperactive, easily distracted and grandiose. They may exhibit flight of ideas, pressured speech, tangentiality and have a diminished need for sleep. Bipolar disorders tend to be more severe than major depression. Compared to patients who suffer from a major depression, depressed patients with bipolar disorders stay depressed longer, relapse more often, display more depressive and more severe symptoms. Such patients also tend to have more delusions and hallucinations, are more likely to commit suicide, require more hospitalizations and experience more incapacitation (Coryell et al., 1985). As their mental organization worsens, patients with bipolar disorders may develop persecutory and grandiose ideas of reference leading, in some cases, to delusions. It is interesting to note that persecutory ideas among schizophrenics are frequently not aimed at anyone specific. However, manics often believe that specific individuals or organizations are the source of impending harm (Maxmen & Ward, 1995).

ONSET AND EPIDEMIOLOGY

In unipolar depression, onset can occur as early as childhood. However, approximately 50% of all cases have an onset between the ages of 20 and 50, with the mean age of onset being approximately 40. Bipolar disorders begin somewhat earlier. The mean age of onset is approximately 30 years, with a range from childhood to 50 years. The peak age of onset of first symptoms is said to be between the ages of 15 and 19. Estimates of the prevalence of Bipolar I disorders range between 0.4% and 1.6%, and bipolar II disorders are said to affect approximately 0.5% of the population over the lifetime. Bipolar I and bipolar II disorders are distinguished in the following way: bipolar I disorders involve one or more manic episodes, often with one or more depressive spells, whereas bipolar II disorders involve recurrent major depression and hypomanic spells, but with frank mania or mixed episodes. Current evidence suggests that bipolar disorders often go undetected, untreated or under-treated, and there is often a 3–10 year lag between time of onset and first treatment or hospitalization. In bipolar disorders, the initial episode tends to be depression in females and mania in males, although early onset bipolar disorder is more commonly associated with depression as the first mood disorder episode. In general, patients suffering from bipolar disorders may experience several episodes of depression before the onset of an actual manic episode (Akiskal, 1995; Strober et al., 1993). Mood disorders are among the most common mental disorders of adults. In general, mood disorders strike twice as many females as males, although this ratio varies depending on the type of mood disorder. For example, approximately 90% of "atypical depression" occurs in women. Major depression affects about two to three times more women than men, while bipolar disorders afflict as many men as women. Estimates of prevalence rates vary. Maxmen and Ward (1995) indicated that during a lifetime, approximately 20% of women and 10% of men will suffer a major depressive episode, and about one-third of these individuals may be hospitalized. Kaplan and Sadock (1991), on the other hand, reported the lifetime prevalence rate for unipolar depression to be approximately 6%.

CRIMINALITY AND AFFECTIVE DISORDER

Mood disorders can be precipitated by organic states and can often be the result of substance abuse (e.g. cocaine consumption can cause a manic-like syndrome). Substance abuse is not usually the sole cause of a major affective disorder, but it and other co-morbid conditions often complicate the clinical picture, making it difficult to establish clearly a direct link between affective disorders and other behavioural characteristics, such as criminal or violent behaviour. For example, heavy alcohol consumption may be associated with depression and mania, as well as aggressive or violent behaviour. Moreover, it is important to recognize that persons with mood disorders may well have other underlying problems, such as personality disorders (antisocial or borderline types), which can also be associated with aggressive or criminal behaviour. Therefore, the relationship between affective disorders and violent or aggressive behaviour may be extremely complex, and other factors play an important part in this interplay. However, there is no doubt that mood disorders can be implicated in many criminal acts of violence. In fact, most mental health practitioners who work with forensic cases can cite numerous examples based on their own experience. Kaplan and Sadock (1991), for example, reported that 75% of manic patients are assaultive or threatening, and Benezech (1991) presented a review of the relationship between depression and homicide, and murder and suicide. The latter author also presented an in-depth discussion of two cases of familial murders committed during a state of depression. He concluded that depression as a factor in homicidal acts has been underestimated and made a case for the inclusion of depression and suicidal tendencies as indicators of dangerousness, and also argued that these factors should be included in forensic psychiatric assessments. Malmquist (1995) wrote an extensive discussion paper on the relationship between depression and homicidal violence, and he also indicated that the presence of delusions and hallucinations should be seen as significant. The term "psychotic depression" is frequently used to describe depressed patients who suffer from delusions and hallucinations. Delusions, along with hallucinations are, in fact, considered to be central features of psychotic depression. A variety of symptoms in psychotic depression are said to bear on homicidal behaviour. For example, some delusions in depressed individuals with a psychosis have a paranoid quality, with ideas of reference, suspiciousness and persecutory themes. In others, delusions may have a guilt-ridden quality derived from a sense of sinfulness, or have a nihilistic component. Such patients may hear voices suggesting or commanding them to commit violent acts. Persons with frank mania may have grandiose delusions, and if challenged can become irritable, angry, or overtly aggressive. These symptoms, combined with a tendency for failure to respond to treatment, increase the likelihood for unpredictable outcomes.

The presumed relationship between affective disorders and criminality is also suggested by a variety of research. For example, Petrich (1976), Piotrowski, Losacco and Guze (1976), Lamb and Grant (1982), Glaser (1985), Roesch (1995) and Ogloff (1996) have reported prevalence rates for mood disorders that range from about 3% to 25% among jail populations. Similarly, studies on those found not guilty by reason of insanity indicate that the prevalence rates for mood disorders ranged from 7% to 10% (Bogenberger et al., 1987; Hodgins, 1983; Lamb, Weinberger & Gross, 1988; McGreevy et al., 1991; Nicholson, Norwood & Enyart, 1991; Pasewark, Pantle & Steadman, 1982; Rodenhauser & Khamis, 1988; Russo, 1994).

Krakowski, Volavka and Brizer (1986) reviewed the literature regarding psychopathology and violence. In particular, the authors reviewed 13 studies involving individuals who were committed to a hospital or a forensic psychiatric centre by court order. Of those individuals, a small but significant proportion (1.8–12.9%) were diagnosed as manic depressives. Similarly, in other studies of the prevalence of affective disorders in male criminal populations, the rates ranged from 1–7% (Schuckit, Herman & Schuckit, 1977; Taylor & Gunn, 1984; Abrams & Teplin, 1991) to over 20% (Bland et al., 1990; Côté & Hodgins, 1990). In inmates referred for psychiatric assessment or pretrial psychiatric hospitalizations, the percentage of affective disorders ranged from 2% to 10% (Pfeiffer, Eisenstein & Dabbs, 1967; Guze, 1976; Good, 1978; Seltzer & Langford, 1984). In individuals charged with or convicted of murder, the proportion of those who suffer from affective disorders tends to be somewhat higher and figures of 3–37% have been reported (Dell & Smith, 1983; Taylor, 1986). Modestin, Hug and Ammann (1997) compared a group of individuals who suffered from affective disorders with a group of matched comparison subjects. Of the 261 patients, 82 suffered from bipolar disorder, 112 from unipolar major depression and 67 from unipolar minor depression. The authors reported that the probability of criminal involvement for the affective disorders group was 1.65 times higher than the comparison group. Moreover, the affective disorders group were more likely to be sentenced to prison (30% vs. 15%) and were more likely to recidivate (6.2 sentences vs. 3.9).

Not all researchers believe that affective disorders contribute in a significant manner to violent offending (Taylor, 1986). But Modestin, Hug and Ammann (1997) believe that there is an increased risk associated with affective disorders. On the whole, given the positive results generated by a significant body of research, it is reasonable to suggest that there does appear to be a reliable, although modest, relationship between affective disorders and criminality. However, the number of such patients involved in violent crimes is, undoubtedly, relatively small within the overall violent crime context. Indeed, Monahan (1981) observed that, as a group, mentally disordered persons were responsible only for a small fraction of the crimes in society. This is certainly the case in many North American cities where the overall violent crime rate is high.

TREATMENT ALTERNATIVES

For the most part, contemporary treatments and the conceptual models for mood disorders tend to be biochemical in nature. Akiskal and Mckinney (1975), for example, have described the major contemporary models of depression, and although there have been more recent significant advances in the understanding of the aetiology of affective disorders, their basic classification remains intact. Of the 10 conceptual models of depression they describe, the most significant with regard to major depression is the biogenic amine hypothesis, first advanced by Schildkraut (1965). Numerous studies have compared the frequency of affective disorders between monozygotic and dizygotic twins. These studies have confirmed that there is a strong genetic predisposition to affective disorders, and that genetic factors contribute to the underlying biochemical disturbances in depression and mania. Others have also suggested that biochemical changes underlie mood disorders, and that chemical substances such as catecholamines (especially dopamine) and the indoleamines (serotonin) have been implicated.

Electroconvulsive therapy

Earlier in the century, electroconvulsive therapy (ECT) was the only effective treatment for affective disorders. Murkherjee, Sackheim and Schnurr (1994) found that 80% of acute mania cases showed significant clinical improvement, and Small et al. (1988) found that in a controlled study, ECT was as effective as the use of lithium. ECT has also been used effectively and safely in the treatment of depression with psychotic symptoms. Moreover, double-blind studies have shown ECT to be more effective in treating unipolar and bipolar depression, in comparison to anaesthesia alone (Sackheim, 1989). The historical background of ECT and its utility in preventing relapse when used as maintenance therapy was reviewed by Rabheru and Persad (1998). Although the use of ECT as a therapeutic modality has gradually declined, it may still have a significant role in the treatment of refractory disorders, and in the reduction of relapse and re-hospitalization.

Pharmacotherapy

Antidepressants

The discovery of the mood elevation properties of the monoamine oxidase inhibitors (MAOIs) led to the search for more chemical treatments for depression. Yatham and colleagues (1997) reported that the use of imipramine, a tricyclic antidepressant, resulted in an average positive response rate of 55% in bipolar depression. Tricyclic antidepressants unfortunately have a high incidence of side effects, including weight gain, dry mouth, constipation, difficulties in urination and blurred vision, hence their use has diminished. Since the introduction of a new generation of drugs such as fluoxetine (and subsequently other selective serotonin reuptake inhibitors—SSRIs) their use have become widespread. A review by Lader (1988) indicated that fluoxetine was as effective as tricyclic agents but with fewer side effects.

In a more recent review of emerging trends in the treatment of depression, Nemerhoff (1994) noted that antidepressant medications can now achieve a

65–75% positive response within six to eight weeks in patients suffering from major depression. He concluded that SSRIs are now the treatment agents of choice. This view was supported by Richelson (1994), who also pointed out that these drugs have other advantages, including fewer side effects and drug interactions, as well as lower toxicity associated with overdose. Moreover, these drugs have a broader spectrum of efficacy compared with older antidepressants. However, with respect to bipolar illnesses, Zarate and colleagues (1995) suggested that the same conclusion cannot be drawn as too few studies have been undertaken. Antidepressants should be used with caution in treating affective disorders associated with criminal or aggressive behaviour. Tricyclic antidepressants have been shown to trigger mania and may have a deleterious effect on rapid cycling states. These effects can actually contribute to disordered behaviour. SSRIs have in fact been implicated in increasing suicidal risk in depressed patients, and in triggering violent acts. However, evidence for this is not conclusive. A more general view, also yet to be confirmed, is that SSRIs have a positive effect on controlling the impulsivity and aggressive proneness of depressed patients.

Mood stabilizers

For many years, lithium was the treatment of choice for mania, and is practically the standard drug for the treatment of bipolar illness. The use of lithium and its impact on the course of manic illnesses was first described by Schou, Neilson & Stromgren (1954), and Schou (1997) has reviewed its utility in the treatment of both unipolar and bipolar affective disorders. Schou (1997) concluded that despite the availability of other therapies, lithium remains the treatment of choice for the prophylaxis of recurrent manic depressive illnesses. Soares and Gershon (1998), following a review of all controlled trials of the use of lithium for the treatment of mania, bipolar disorders, unipolar depression, schizophrenia and schizo-affective disorders since 1966, concluded that lithium's efficacy is restricted entirely to bipolar disorders. Lithium had little or no impact on other neuropsychiatric disorders. Bowden (1998) confirmed the effectiveness of lithium in alleviating mania, and further suggested that there is ample support for the efficacy of lithium when used for maintenance. However, with respect to the rapid cycling forms of the disorder, or when substance abuse is also involved, lithium appears to be less effective (Calabrese et al., 1996). Calabrese and Woyshville (1995) reported failure rates as high as 80% for lithium when it was used to treat the rapid cycling variant of the affective disorders. Calabrese suggested instead valproic acid and carbamazepine as alternatives.

Once commenced, lithium should normally be continued over a lengthy period and a decision to discontinue should be carefully considered, since rapid discontinuance is known to be associated with higher relapse rates (Baldessarini et al., 1996). Interruption of long-term treatment carries an extraordinary high risk of recurrence within several months, even after several years of stability. In view of the association between affective disorders and violence, this is a crucial issue. Gradual discontinuance is recommended, although this is not always feasible; for example, if there is evidence of renal toxicity, a significant and not uncommon complication of long-term lithium treatment.

Despite the effectiveness of lithium in the treatment of mood disorders, its use has decreased in recent years because of serious side effects (e.g. damage to the kidneys and thyroid gland), especially since affective alternatives are now available. With respect to the treatment of bipolar illnesses, two other agents are emerging as effective alternatives to lithium, although more controlled studies need to be conducted. Divalproex sodium has been shown to be as effective as lithium in bipolar disorder (Bowden et al., 1994), and is useful not only in acute mania but also when rapid cycling is involved. Additionally, risperidone has been proved effective in cases where personality disorder and substance abuse are also involved. With respect to criminal recidivism, divalproex may be especially appropriate, since this drug appears to be an effective agent in the management of aggression (Wilcox, 1994). A second agent, carbamazepine, has also been used in acute mania and as a prophylactic agent. It is not as effective in rapid cycling states, and may not be as effective as lithium for maintenance. Both divalproex sodium and carbamezapine are far less toxic than lithium, although the former has been associated with bleeding disorders and white cell suppression. Emilien and colleagues (1995) contrasted the utility of lithium in the treatment and maintenance of bipolar disorder with two anticonvulsants, carbamazepine and valproic acid. Their review suggested that carbamazepine is similar in its relative specificity in treating mania, often acts faster, and has fewer side effects, so that it is a satisfactory alternative for patients not responding to or intolerant of lithium, and especially where renal problems contraindicate the use of lithium. They suggested that both carbamazepine and valproic acid might be the best agents to use in rapid cycling cases. Post and colleagues (1996) identified 19 double-blind studies suggesting that carbamazepine is effective in acute mania, six controlled studies reporting the efficacy of valproate in the treatment of mania too, and 14 controlled or partly-controlled studies of prophylaxis, suggesting that carbamazepine is effective in preventing both manic and depressive episodes. Valproate has not been studied as rigorously, but uncontrolled studies suggested it might be as effective as carbamazepine. They also described the possible utility of clonazepam as an adjunct to lithium or anticonvulsant therapy or as an alternative to neuroleptics in mania, and that calcium channel blockers may have mood-stabilizing qualities. Solomon and colleagues (1996) pointed out that, whereas it is known that monotherapy with lithium, valproate or carbamazepine can be effective, not all patients respond, and to improve outcome, polypharmacy is commonly used, indeed to the extent of being the rule rather than the exception in routine clinical care. They indicated that the literature on polypharmacy consists mostly of case reports and chart reviews. The only controlled studies they could identify indicated that: (a) lithium plus imipramine is no better than lithium alone; (b) lithium plus flupenthixol is no better than lithium alone; and (c) lithium plus carbamazepine might be as effective as lithium plus haloperidol for acute and continuation treatment. However, there was some evidence in favor of combinations such as lithium plus valproate, lithium plus carbamazepine, and valproate plus carbamazepine being effective. Treatment of co-morbid conditions and substance abuse improves response (Sachs, 1996). Risperidone has been proved effective in cases where personality disorder and substance abuse are involved, and divalproex may be especially appropriate with respect to criminal recidivism, since it can be an effective agent in the management of aggression (Wilcox, 1994).

Psychotherapy

Miklowitz (1996) has reviewed the movement toward delivering psychotherapy in combination with pharmacological maintenance in the treatment of bipolar disorder, and in particular he described family educational approaches as well as individual treatment. While psychotherapy may have a valuable adjunctive effect, it has not been shown to be an effective treatment alone, and its impact on modifying risk factors for violence is unknown. He does suggest that psychotherapy might promote adherence to drug regimens. Medication compliance is an important issue, given the fact that non-compliance often leads to relapse. Smith (1989), for example, noted that 60% of those who were readmitted to a forensic facility in New York relapsed because they refused to continue their medication. Our own experience indicates that assertive case management promotes medication compliance.

Most studies indicate that a combination of psychotherapy and pharmacotherapy is the most effective approach to treating mood disorders (Kaplan & Sadock, 1991). Moreover, recent studies seem to indicate that for milder depressive illnesses, psychotherapy may be virtually as effective as pharmacotherapy. The more common psychotherapies used to treat mood disorders include interpersonal psychotherapy, behavior therapy, cognitive therapy and marital/family therapy. While the different psychotherapies described below may not have a significant impact on major mental illnesses by themselves, they may be useful under specific circumstances.

Interpersonal psychotherapy

Interpersonal psychotherapy is based on the premise that almost all individuals who suffer from depression have a major interpersonal problem, such as conflict with a spouse or a boss. Interpersonal psychotherapy is a short-term psychotherapy, lasting 12–16 sessions. It was developed specifically to treat unipolar and non-psychotic depression, as well as ambulatory depressed patients. Interpersonal psychotherapy focuses on current interpersonal matters and social functioning. Intrapsychic phenomena, such as defence mechanisms and internal conflicts, are not addressed (Kaplan & Sadock, 1991; Maxmen & Ward, 1995). Some studies have shown that a combination of interpersonal psychotherapy and tricyclic antidepressants yields superior results. Additionally, by teaching patients coping skills, interpersonal psychotherapy may reduce the rate of later relapse (Frank, Kupfer & Perel, 1989).

Behavioural therapy

The reinforcement principle is thought to be a key element in the treatment of depression. Although behavioural therapy approaches vary in terms of specific techniques and foci, they share common assumptions and strategies.

Lewinsohn et al. (1984) developed a framework for the treatment of depression with the use of behavioural therapy. Generally, behavioural therapy approaches assume that depressed patients lack positive reinforcement. Therefore, patients are first taught to recognize relationships between events and feelings. They are taught to focus on opportunities that maximize praise from self and from others, and to avoid situations or events that may lead to self-punishment. Patients are also taught to set goals that are more realistic. The overall effect that can be achieved by changing and redirecting the patients' behaviour towards positive goals that are attainable is considered to be an effective way to alleviate depression. As part of behavioural therapy, some patients are also given social skills training so as to increase the opportunity for positive reinforcement and reduce the likelihood for negative encounters.

Cognitive therapy

Cognitive therapy usually lasts 10–25 sessions and is generally used to treat patients with mild to moderately severe depression (Beck et al., 1979). The cognitive theory of depression assumes that the signs and symptoms of depressions are a result of cognitive dysfunction. That is, cognitive theory assumes that patients' faulty perceptions and attitudes about the world and about themselves precede and produce the pathological mood. The goal of cognitive therapy is, therefore, to assist patients to identify and recognize these negative cognitions, to help them devise more rational and healthy ways to view themselves and the world, and to encourage them to rehearse new cognitive and behavioural responses. It has been reported that cognitive therapy is frequently effective when combined with behavioural therapy (Maxmen & Ward, 1995).

Marital/family therapy

Marital discord or separation often precedes depression, persists after the depressive episode, and often precedes relapses. In fact, in more than half of the couples who are in the process of divorce or who are contemplating divorce, one spouse may show signs of clinical depression (Maxmen & Ward, 1995). Marital therapy may, therefore, be used to treat the depression, as well as address the precipitating condition, the marital discord (Jacobson, Holtzworth-Munroe & Schaling, 1989). While marital/family therapy is not, generally, viewed as a primary therapy for the treatment of depression, it may be indicated in cases where marital discord or family interactions are identified as significant factors in the genesis and the maintenance of the depression. It may also be indicated in cases where the depression is seriously jeopardizing a patient's marital and family functioning. Marital or family therapy focuses on the role of the depressed patient in the overall psychological well-being of the marriage or of the family. It also focuses on the role of the spouse or that of the entire family in the maintenance of the depression.

Other forms of psychotherapy

Other forms of psychotherapy that have been used to treat mood disorders and deserve some mention include psychoanalytically-orientated therapy, brief psychodynamic psychotherapy, and group therapy. Psychoanalytically orientated therapy attempts to change the personality or character structure of the patient, and not simply to relieve the symptoms of depression. The goal of brief psychodynamic psychotherapy is to resolve the core conflicts based on personality and situational variables (Maxmen & Ward, 1995). Group psychodynamic, behavioural and cognitive therapy are also used to treat mood disorders, although they tend to be slightly less effective than their individual versions.

A COMMUNITY MANAGEMENT APPROACH

Not all individuals who suffer from a particular mental disorder commit acts of criminal violence. This suggests that there are factors other than those that are directly related to the mental disorder which are of at least equal importance in the genesis of criminal recidivism, that is, criminal recidivism, in all probability, has multiple causes. Simply treating the affective disorder, or any mental disorder for that matter, will hardly guarantee that the individual will no longer act in a manner that might lead to criminal recidivism. It is more than likely that in such situations, factors exist that must also be addressed if treatment is to be successful. Within this context, it seems reasonable to suggest that, to be effective, treatment should focus on the target disorder, as well as the other factors and conditions that lead to criminal recidivism. The remaining sections of this chapter present a treatment and community management approach designed to prevent or retard recidivism. This approach is based on research in a number of different areas, including criminal recidivism and assertive case management. It is based on observation of techniques that are known to be effective in some of the most difficult populations in the criminal justice system and the mentally disordered offender populations.

The prevention of criminal recidivism

Criminal recidivism has been the subject of intensive research and model building in recent years. Much of this work has been undertaken in the correctional setting and therefore most efforts have focused on correctional protocols related to the supervision of offenders on conditional release. Nevertheless, these efforts have resulted in new insights regarding the process of recidivism that may have significance in the broader context of treatment directed towards the reduction of violent criminal recidivism and the reduction of criminal recidivism in general. Many researchers now agree that, under given circumstances, recidivism can be successfully predicted. Indeed, certain factors such as age at first offence, gender, criminal history, early childhood factors, alcohol and drug abuse and criminal associates, for example, are relatively good predictors of recidivism (Gendreau, Little & Goggin, 1996). Composite measures made up of a variety of predictors appear to provide even better reliability as well as better predictive accuracy (Zamble & Quinsey, 1997).

Framework for treatment and community management

Until recently, researchers focused almost exclusively on predictors that were of the static or "tombstone" variety (Gendreau, Little & Goggin, 1996; Zamble & Quinsey, 1997). Static variables include factors such as age, gender or history of substance abuse, which are defined by past events and either do not change or change slowly and incrementally. Prediction based on the use of static variables is essentially actuarial in nature, rather than being based on some theoretical framework or on an understanding of the nature and the process of recidivism. Work undertaken by Andrews and his colleagues (Andrews & Bonta, 1994; Andrews, Bonta & Hoge, 1990), as well as others such as Gendreau (1996) and Zamble and Quinsey (1997) have shed new light on the issue of the prediction of recidivism. Their prediction scheme is based on the premise that, in addition to personal characteristics, psychological processes play an important role in the determination of behaviour. In the case of the offender, such factors as emotional state, stress, coping skills and the interplay between environmental conditions and the psychological processes to a large extent determine the choice of behaviours. These events are said to be dynamic, transitory and may change over time, depending on the local circumstances. Such dynamic factors can be related to criminal behaviour. By their definition, dynamic risk factors or needs that are related to recidivism are termed "criminogenic needs". Criminogenic needs act as links to recidivism. Therefore, such needs can be used as predictors of recidivism. While the value of static predictors of recidivism is still recognized, the move towards the use of dynamic risk factors has fundamentally altered the thinking behind the prediction of recidivism. Clearly, with respect to recidivism, the role of historical events has been deemphasized, and the role of current events and psychological state in the causation of new offences or the process of recidivism is now a principal focus. In this regard, the more recent literature seems to indicate that a focus on criminogenic needs is fundamental to the success of correctional treatment and rehabilitation programmes. Some of these factors have been empirically identified, and since they are dynamic and can be modified, criminogenic needs can serve as targets for correctional intervention (Bonta, 1996) and in general can serve as targets for treatment and intervention. Therefore, once an offender has been assessed, the criminogenic needs can form the basis of treatment goals for offenders. The effectiveness of this approach has already been illustrated by meta-analyses of the rehabilitation literature (Andrews & Bonta, 1994; Andrews et al., 1990; Gendreau, 1996).

It was suggested earlier that the actuarial method of predicting recidivism is not theory-driven. Theories are important because they structure thinking, guide further theorizing and create insight concerning the processes in question. This newer strategy for predicting recidivism based on the use of dynamic criminogenic needs, on the other hand, is theory-driven. Indeed, Zamble and Quinsey suggested that the process of recidivism can be adequately explained by a theoretical framework called the coping–criminality hypothesis, and cited studies that appear to support this framework (Louks & Zamble, 1994; Hughes & Zamble, 1993). The coping–criminality hypothesis links recidivism to inadequate coping responses. It is hypothesized that offenders are often unable to recognize and resolve their problems and, as a result, a considerable amount of stress is generated. Such offenders are likely to lash out or react in maladaptive, often criminal ways. Thus, poor coping skills eventually lead to behaviours that lead in turn to re-offending. While the coping–criminality hypothesis explains the process of recidivism in terms of the origins of a breakdown into renewed criminal behaviour, it does not address the recidivism process after coping responses fail. To account for the latter part of the recidivism process, Zamble and Quinsey (1997) called on the relapse prevention model developed by Marlatt and George (1984). Relapse prevention was originally developed for treatment programmes involving alcohol and drug addiction, and in this regard "relapse" was defined as a failure to maintain behaviour change. Relapse essentially begins with a failure to cope. Relapse theory is useful in this instance because it focuses on factors responsible for the maintenance of behavioural change. Of concern to relapse theory is the sequence of behaviours and events that form critical junctures on the path back to a former non-adaptive mode of behaviours. Understanding these events leads to the possibility of better control. From this perspective, recidivism can be viewed as a relapse process whereby the offender falls back on old habitual behaviour patterns, and therefore relapse prevention theory can be used to guide the search for critical junctures in the recidivism process.

Relapse theory is said to complement the coping–criminality theory. The coping–criminality hypothesis links inadequate coping with criminal relapse, while relapse theory suggests that situations that lead to relapse are produced by inappropriate or inadequate coping behaviours. However, each emphasizes a different stage of the recidivism process. The coping–criminality hypothesis addresses the recidivism process up to the point of failure. In this respect the coping–criminality hypothesis is incomplete. It offers no direction for remedial treatment or intervention. Fortunately, relapse theory takes over at the point where the coping–criminality hypothesis loses its definition. It is principally concerned with the sequence of behaviours and events that lead to a former non-adaptive mode of behaviours, and therefore provides an explicit focus for remedial treatment or intervention.

A combination of the coping–criminality hypothesis and the relapse prevention approach can serve as the basis of a treatment model that explicitly targets criminal recidivism. This approach can be referred to as the Coping/ Relapse Prevention Treatment Model. The Coping/Relapse Prevention Treatment Model provides a broader framework for treatment and directs attention to the fact that criminal recidivism is not the result of some singular factor. In this regard, simply by treating the affective disorder, or any psychiatric disorder for that matter, will hardly guarantee that the individual will no longer act in a manner that might lead to criminal recidivism. It is more than likely that in such situations, other criminogenic needs exist and must also be addressed if treatment is to be successful. Experienced clinicians, no doubt, know this intuitively. This model, however, makes this explicit and provides a framework for assessment, and directs treatment efforts to target the constellation of criminogenic needs that may be at the basis of future criminal recidivism.

Intensive case management

From a practical perspective, the concept of intensive or assertive case management ought to serve as an excellent vehicle for implementing the Coping/Relapse Prevention Treatment Model for the prevention of criminal recidivism. Intensive case management or assertive case management differs from traditional case management in many important aspects. Marshall and Lockwood (1998), and Marshall et al. (1998), following an extensive review, concluded that there was little evidence to suggest that traditional case management can result in clinically significant improvements in mental state, social functioning, or quality of life. In contrast, assertive case management was found to be an effective way of caring for severely mentally ill people in the community. The assertive case management approach was said to dramatically reduce the use of inpatient care, as well as improve some aspects of outcome.

The conceptual framework for intensive case management was originally developed by Stein and Test (1980). Enhancements to the original concepts were later undertaken by Witheridge and Dincin (1985), as well as many others. Intensive case management was developed as an alternative to traditional "office-based" treatment services that were often inadequate for meeting the needs of chronic mentally ill individuals (Stein & Test, 1980; Witheridge & Dincin, 1985). It was developed to provide support where and when it is needed, and to enable chronically mentally ill individuals to extend the length of their community tenure and improve their quality of life. Over the years, assertive case management has been adapted to serve patients with numerous types of mental illnesses. However, most have retained the essential features of the original assertive case management project. These include close contacts with clients, intensive support, a long-term commitment to patients, and doing whatever is necessary to maintain the patient in the community setting.

During the past decade, many studies of assertive case management have been undertaken. While it is true that not all researchers have found this model to be effective (Inciardi, Martin & Scarpitti, 1994; Ford et al., 1997), many have found that assertive case management is effective with diverse patient groups. For example, Toro et al. (1997) reported that subjects improved in terms of their experience with homelessness as well as their physical health and stressful life events. In a review of the research on intensive case management, Mueser et al. (1998) reported that controlled intensive case management studies have yielded positive results. Intensive case management is effective in reducing time spent in hospital and in improving housing stability. Intensive case management also was moderately successful in symptomatology and quality of life. Similarly, Holloway and Carson (1998) reported positive results. In this case, both quality of life and satisfaction with care were significantly improved. In another study, Quinlivan and colleagues (1995) reported that clients who received intensive case management had fewer inpatient days, as well as reduced overall cost for mental health services. Patients in intensive case management groups were also found to require significantly fewer emergency visits, and their relatives reported a significantly reduced burden of care associated with caring for the patient (Aberg-Wistedt et al., 1995).

Our own research (Wilson, Tien & Eaves, 1995) suggests that assertive case management applied to mentally disordered offenders (14% were diagnosed with an affective disorder) can delay recidivism, increase community tenure and decrease time spent in prison. In this study, in the group that received assertive case management, the mean number of days spent in the criminal justice system was lower. More specifically, the average number of jail days (remand days and days served) of the assertive case management group at six months following release was 8.2 days as opposed to 50.6 days for the comparison group ($t(46) = -2.70$, $p = 0.1$). At 12 months after their release from prison, assertive case management clients had spent an average of 40.4 days in jail and the comparison cases had spent 136.8 days ($t(34) = -2.32$, $p = 0.3$). Finally, the assertive case management group spent 80.4 days and the comparison group 213.6 days in correctional facilities during the 18 months following initial release into the community ($t(29) = -2.01$, $p = 0.05$). Not only did the assertive case management group spend fewer days in correctional institutions compared to the comparison group, they also spent a greater number of days in the community following release before coming into conflict with the criminal justice system. The comparison group were in the community an average of 119.6 days before being re-convicted, whereas the assertive management group were in the community an average of 270.9 days ($t(27) = 3.21$, $p = 0.003$) prior to re-conviction.

In a recent but as yet unpublished study, involving mentally ill persons who are frequent hospital users, preliminary data gathered at the end of the first year of assertive case management indicates that significant results can be achieved in terms of a reduction in emergency room visits, hospital admissions and hospital days. The reduction of hospital admissions is a primary goal of this latter study. Thus far, data from two time periods (pre-intake period—12 months prior to admission to the assertive case management project; and post-intake period—12 months during participation in the assertive case management project) have been analysed. These include hospital utilization data for 14 clients who have participated in the assertive case management project for at least 12 months. Assertive case management clients averaged 7.5 visits to the emergency room at a local hospital during the 12 months prior to their admission to the assertive case management project. Once in the programme, this figure dropped to an average of 2.4 visits ($t = 2.35$, $p = 0.04$). This represents a 68% decrease in emergency room visits. In terms of the total number of emergency room visits, assertive case management clients visited the emergency room 142 times during the pre-intake period but only 32 times during their involvement with the assertive case management project. In the year prior to project participation, only one (7%) of the clients had no admissions to a psychiatric unit. However, during the first year of project participation, seven (50%) of the clients had no psychiatric inpatient admissions. With respect to bed-days, the mean number of psychiatric unit bed-days utilized by clients receiving assertive case management during the pre-intake period was 46.2, compared to 20 during the post-intake period. This represents a 57% decrease in inpatient bed utilization.

Many of the characteristics of assertive case management are ideally suited to the Coping/Relapse Prevention Model. Although it has not been viewed in this fashion, the assertive case management process is one that focuses on risk indicators, and corrective actions are undertaken when warranted. In this sense, assertive case management is a good structure in which to implement the Coping/Relapse Prevention Model. That is, close and intensive contacts will be necessary to monitor the status of criminogenic risk factors, so that those situations that can lead to recidivism can be addressed. Moreover, the assertive case management approach can easily accommodate the traditional treatment modalities to address the patient's mental illness. In this regard, assertive case management can be adapted to focus on all relevant factors, including symptoms of mental disorders. It is our personal experience that this is an important aspect of the care and management of patients with major affective disorders. Depressed patients are often unmotivated, and when left to their own devices may refrain from attending appointments and may take medication irregularly or not at all. Both these events are risk factors that need to be closely monitored. In an assertive case management programme, case workers visit daily, if necessary, to encourage patients to keep appointments, take their medication, join social support groups, and attend to all aspects of their personal and mental health needs. Manic patients whose symptoms have been controlled may actually miss the experience of being "high" and therefore stop their medication regimen, making the risk of relapse and the risk of aggressive, irresponsible or criminal behaviour more likely. Again, case workers provide support and encouragement and reinforce the need to maintain stability. They can be effective in directing patients away from high-risk behaviours that might lead to criminal recidivism, such as alcohol or substance use or consorting with known criminals. Case workers are in a unique position to monitor such risk factors, and take expeditious action when necessary.

CONCLUDING REMARKS

Although there is a vast literature on the treatment of affective disorders using a wide range of modalities and approaches such as cognitive-behavioural, psychoanalytic and interpersonal, as well as the drug approaches described earlier, little of it has been directed towards the associated aggression or criminality. In this chapter, we are suggesting that the criminal justice literature and the literature on case management strategies may offer useful insights regarding the treatment of affective disorders as it relates to the process of criminal recidivism and violence. The aetiology of criminality and violence is complex, and treatment regimens must address all the factors involved in a systematic way. It is not sufficient merely to treat the underlying mental disorder. Traditional and effective strategies, particularly medication regimens, need to be supplemented by interventions focusing on criminogenic needs. We would suggest that the Coping/ Relapse Prevention Model borrowed from the criminal justice area, together with the assertive case management approach, should provide an appropriate basis for intervention.

ACKNOWLEDGEMENTS

We would like to thank Patricia Fortin and Debbie Monkman of Riverview Hospital and Heidi Dysarsz of the Forensic Psychiatric Institute for their invaluable assistance in gathering the numerous articles that were reviewed in the preparation of this manuscript.

REFERENCES

Aberg-Wistedt, A., Cressell, T., Lidberg, Y., Liljenberg, B. & Osby, U. (1995). Two-year outcome of team-based intensive case management for patients with schizophrenia. *Psychiatric Services*, **46**(12), 1263–1266.

Abrams, K. M. & Teplin, L. (1991). Co-occurring disorders among mentally ill jail detainees. *American Psychologist*, **46**, 1036–1045.

Akiskal, H. S. (1995). Developmental pathways to bipolarity: are juvenile-onset depressions pre-bipolar? *Journal of the American Academy of Child and Adolescent Psychiatry*, **34**, 754–763.

Akiskal, H. & Mckinney, W. (1975).   Overview of recent research in depression: integration of 10 conceptual models into a comprehensive clinical frame. *Archives of General Psychiatry*, **32**, 285–305.

Andrews, D. A. & Bonta, J. (1994).   The Psychology of Criminal Conduct. Cincinnati, OH: Anderson.

Andrews, D. A., Bonta, J. & Hoge, R. D. (1990).   Classification for effective rehabilitation: rediscovering psychology. *Criminal Justice and Behaviour*, **17**(1), 19–52.

Andrews, D. A. et al. (1990).   Does correctional treatment work? A psychologically informed meta-analysis. *Criminology*, **28**, 369–404.

Baldessarini, R. J., Faedda, G. L., Floris, G. & Rudas, N. (1996).   Effects of the rate of discontinuing lithium maintenance treatment in bipolar disorders. *Journal of Clinical Psychiatry*, **57**, 441–448.

Beck, A. T., Rush, A. J., Shaw, B. F. & Emery, G. (1979).   *Cognitive Therapy of Depression: a Treatment Manual*. New York: Guilford.

Benezech, M. (1991).   Depression et crime. Revue de la litterature et observations originales. *Annales Medico-Psychologiques*, **149**(2), 150–165.

Bland, R. C., Newman, S. C., Dyck, R. J. & Om, H. (1990).   Prevalence of psychiatric disorders and suicide attempts in a prison population. *Canadian Journal of Psychiatry*, **35**, 407–413.

Bogenberger, R. P., Pasewark, R. A., Gudeman, H. & Beiber, S. L. (1987).   Follow-up of insanity acquitees in Hawaii. *International Journal of Law and Psychiatry*, **10**, 283–295.

Bonta, J. (1996).   Risk–needs assessment and treatment. In A.T. Harland (Ed.), *Choosing Correctional Options that Work: Defining the Demand and Evaluating the Supply* (pp. 18–32). Thousand Oaks, CA: Sage.

Bowden, C. L. (1998).   Key treatment studies in manic-depressive illness: efficacy and side effects. *Journal of Clinical Psychiatry*, **59**, 13–19.

Bowden, C. L., Brugger, A. M., Swann, A. C. & Calabrese, J. R. (1994).   Efficacy of divalproex vs. lithium and placebo in the treatment of mania. *Journal of American Medical Association*, **271**(12), 918–924.

Calabrese, J. R., Fatemi, S. H., Kujawa, M. & Woyshville, M. J. (1996).   Predictors of response to mood stabilizers. *Journal of Clinical Psychopharmacology*, **16**(2), 24–30.

Calabrese, J. R. & Woyshville, M. J. (1995).   A medication algorithm for treatment of bipolar rapid cycling. *Journal of Clinical Psychiatry*, **56**, 11–18.

Côté, G. & Hodgins, S. (1990).   Co-occurring mental disorders among criminal offenders. *Bulletin of the American Academy of Psychiatry and Law*, **18**, 271–281.

Coryell, W., Endicott, J., Keller, M. & Andreasen, N. C. (1985).   Phenomenology and family history in DSM-III psychotic depression. *Journal of Affective Disorder*, **9**(1), 13–18.

Dell, S. & Smith, A. (1983).   Changes in the sentencing of diminished responsibility homicides. *British Journal of Psychiatry*, **142**, 20–34.

Emilien, G., Maloteux, J. M., Seghers, A. & Charles, G. (1995).   Lithium therapy in the treatment of manic-depressive illness: present status and future perspectives—a critical review. *Archives Internationales de Pharmacodynamie et de Therapie*, **330**(3), 251–278.

Ford, R., Ryan, P., Beadsmoore, A., Craig, T. & Muijen, M. (1997).   Intensive case management for people with serious mental illness—Site 2: clinical and social outcome. *Journal of Mental Health*, **6**(2): 181–190.

Frank, E., Kupfer, D. J. & Perel, J. M. (1989).   Early recurrence in unipolar depression. *Archives of General Psychiatry*, **46**, 397–400.

Gendreau, P. (1996).   Offender rehabilitation: what we know and what needs to be done. *Criminal Justice & Behaviour*, **23**, 144–161.

Gendreau, P., Little, T. & Goggin, C. (1996).   A meta-analysis of adult offender recidivism: what works. *Criminology*, **34**, 575–607.

Glaser, D. (1985).   Who gets probation and parole—case study versus actuarial decision making. *Crime and Delinquency*, **31**, 367–378.

Good, M. I. (1978).   Primary affective disorder, aggression, and criminality: a review and clinical study. *Archives of General Psychiatry*, **35**, 954–960.

Guze, S. B. (1976).   *Criminality and Psychiatric Disorders*. New York: Oxford University Press.

Hodgins, S. (1983). A follow-up study of persons found incompetent to stand trial and/or not guilty by reason of insanity in Quebec. *International Journal of Law and Psychiatry*, **6**, 399–411.

Holloway, F. & Carson, J. (1998).   Intensive case management for the severely mentally ill: controlled trial. *British Journal of Psychiatry*, **172**, 19–22.

Hughes, G. & Zamble, E. (1993).   A profile of Canadian correctional workers: how they experience and respond to job stress. *International Journal of Offender Therapy and Comparative Criminology*, **37**, 99–113.

Inciardi, J. A., Martin, S. S. & Scarpitti, F. R. (1994).   Appropriateness of assertive case management for drug-involved prison releasees. *Journal of Case Management.* **3**(4), 145–149.

Jacobson, N. S., Holtzworth-Munroe, A. & Schaling, K. B. (1989).   Marital therapy and spouse involvement in the treatment of depression, agoraphobia, and alcoholism. *Journal of Consulting and Clinical Psychology*, **57**(1), 5–10.

Kaplan, H. I. & Sadock, B. J. (1991).   *Synopsis of Psychiatry*. Baltimore, MD: Williams & Wilkins.

Krakowski, M., Volavka, J. & Brizer, D. (1986).   Psychopathology and violence: a review of literature. *Comprehensive Psychiatry*, **27**(2), 131–148.

Lader, M. (1988).   Fluoxetine efficacy comparative drugs: an overview. *British Journal of Psychiatry*, **153**, 51–58.

Lamb, H. & Grant, R. (1982).   The mentally ill in an urban county jail. *Archives of General Psychiatry*, **39**, 17–22.

Lamb, H. R., Weinberger, L. E. & Gross, B. H. (1988).   Court-mandated community outpatient treatment for persons found Not Guilty by Reason of Insanity: a five-year follow-up. *American Journal of Psychiatry*, **145**(4), 450–456.

Lewinsohn, P. M., Antonuccio, D. A., Steinmetz, J. & Teri, L. (1984).   *The Coping with Depression Course: A Psychoeducational Intervention for Unipolar Depression*. Eugene, OR: Castalia.

Louks, A. & Zamble, E. (1994).   Some comparison of male and female serious offenders. *Forum on Correctional Research*, **6**, 22–25.

Malmquist, C. P. (1995).   Depression and homicidal violence. *International Journal of Law and Psychiatry*, **18**(2), 145–162.

Marlatt, G. A. & George, W. H. (1984).   Relapse prevention: introduction and overview of the model. *British Journal of Addiction*, **79**(3), 261–273.

Marshall, M., Gray, A., Lockwood, A. & Green, R. (1998).   Case management for people with severe mental disorders. *The Cochrane Library*, **3**. Oxford: Update Software.

Marshall, M. & Lockwood, A. (1998).   Assertive community treatment for people with severe mental disorders. *The Cochrane Library*, **3**. Oxford: Update Software.

Maxmen, J. S. & Ward, N. G. (1995).   *Essential Psychopathology and Its Treatment*. New York: W.W. Norton.

McGreevy, M. A., Steadman, H. J., Dvoskin, J. A. & Dollard, N. (1991).   New York State's system of managing insanity acquittees in the community. *Hospital and Community Psychiatry*, **42**(5), 512–517.

Miklowitz, D. J. (1996).   Psychotherapy in combination with drug treatment for bipolar disorder. *Journal of Clinical Psychopharmacology*, **16**(2), 56–66.

Modestin, J., Hug, A. & Ammann, R. (1997).   Criminal behavior in males with affective disorders. *Journal of Affective Disorders*, **42**, 29–38.
Monahan, J. (1981). *Predicting Violent Behavior: An Assessment of Clinical Techniques.* Beverly Hills, CA: Sage.
Mueser, K. T., Bond, G. R., Drake, R. E. & Resnick, S. G. (1998).   Models of community care for severe mental illness: a review of research on case management. *Schizophrenia Bulletin*, **24**(1), 37–74.
Mukherjee, S., Sackheim, H. A. & Schnurr, D. B. (1994).   Electroconvulsive therapy of acute mania episodes: a review. *American Journal of Psychiatry*, **151**, 169–176.
Nemeroff, C. B. (1994). Evolutionary trends in the pharmacotherapeutic management of depression. *Journal of Clinical Psychiatry*, **55**(12), 3–15.
Nicholson, R. A., Norwood, S. & Enyart, C. (1991).   Characteristics and outcomes of insanity acquitees in Oklahoma. *Behavioral Sciences and the Law*, **9**, 487–500.
Ogloff, J. R. P. (1996).   *The Surrey Pretrial Mental Health Program: Community Component Evaluation.* Vancouver: British Columbia Forensic Psychiatric Services Commission.
Pasework, R. A., Pantle, M. L. & Steadman, H. J. (1982).   Detention and rearrest rates of persons found not guilty by reason of insanity and convicted felons. *American Journal of Psychiatry*, **139**(7), 892–897.
Petrich, J. (1976). Psychiatric treatment in jail: an experiment in healthcare delivery. *American Journal of Psychiatry*, **133**, 1439–1440.
Pfeiffer, E., Eisenstein, R. B. & Dabbs, E. G. (1967).   Mental competency evaluation for federal courts: methods and results. *Journal of Nervous and Mental Disorders*, **144**, 320–328.
Piotrowski, K. W., Losacco, D. & Guze, S. B. (1976).   Psychiatric disorders and crime: a study of pretrial psychiatric examinations. *Diseases of the Nervous System*, **37**(5), 3009–3011.
Post, R. M., Ketter, T. A., Denicoff, K., Pazzaglia, P. J., Leverich, G. S., Marangell, L. B., Callahan, A. M., George, M. S. & Frye, M. A. (1996).   The place of anticonvulsant therapy in bipolar illnesses. *Psychopharmacology*, **128**, 115–129.
Quinlivan, R., Hough, R., Crowell, A., Beach, C., Hofstetter, R. & Kenworthy, K. (1995).   Service untilization and costs of care for severely mentally ill clients in an intensive case management program. *Psychiatric Services*, **46**, 365–371.
Rabheru, K. & Persad, K. (1998).   A review of continuation and maintenance electroconvulsive therapy. *Canadian Journal of Psychiatry*, **43**, 305–306.
Richelson, E. (1994).   Pharmacology of antidepressants—characteristics of the ideal drug. *Mayo Clinic Proceedings*, **69**, 1069–1081.
Rodenhauser, P. & Khamis, H. J. (1988).   Predictors of improvement in maximum security forensic hospital patients. *Behavioral Sciences and the Law*, **6**(4): 531–542.
Roesch, R. (1995).   Mental health interventions in pretrial jails. In G. Davies, S. Lloyd-Bostock, M. McMurran & C. Wilson (Eds), *Psychology, Law, and Criminal Justice: International Developments in Research and Practice.* (pp. 520–531). Berlin: Walter De Gruyter.
Russo, G. (1994).   Follow-up of 91 mentally ill criminals discharged from the maximum security hospital in Barcelona P.G. *International Journal of Law and Psychiatry*, **71**, 279–301.
Sachs, G. S. (1996).   Treatment-resistant bipolar depression. *Psychiatric Clinics of North America*, **19**, 215–236.
Sackheim, H. A. (1989).   The efficacy of electroconvulsive therapy in the treatment of major depressive disorder. In S. Fisher, R. P. Greenberg & N. J. Hillsdale (Eds), *The Limits of Biological Treatments for Psychological Distress* (pp. 275–307). Hillsdale, NJ: Erlbaum.
Schildkraut, J. J. (1965).   The catecholamine hypothesis of affective disorders: a review of supporting evidence. *American Journal of Psychiatry*, **122**, 509–522.

Schou, M. (1997).   Forty years of lithium treatment. *Archives of General Psychiatry*, **54**, 9–13.

Schou, M., Neilson, N. & Stromgren, E. (1954).   The treatment of manic psychoses by the administration of lithium salts. *Journal of Neurology, Neurosurgery and Psychiatry*, **17**, 250–260.

Schuckit, M. A., Herman, G. & Schuckit, J. J. (1977).   The importance of psychiatric illness in newly arrested prisoners. *Journal of Nervous and Mental Disorders*, **165**, 118–125.

Seltzer, A. & Langford, A. (1984).   Forensic psychiatric assessments in the Northwest Territories. *Canadian Journal of Psychiatry*, **29**, 665–668.

Small, J. G., Klopper, M. H., Kellams, J. J., Miller, M. J., Milstein, V., Sharpley, P. H. & Small, I. F. (1988).   Electroconvulsive treatment compared with lithium in the management of manic states. *Archives of General Psychiatry*, **45**, 727–732.

Smith, L. D. (1989).   Medication refusal and the rehospitalized mentally ill inmate. *Hospital and Community Psychiatry*, **40**, 491–496.

Soares, J. C. & Gershon, S. (1998).   The lithium ion: a foundation for neuropsychopharmacological specificity. *Neuropsychopharmacology*, **19**, 167–182.

Solomon, D. A., Keitner, G. I., Ryan, C. E. & Miller, I. W. (1996).   Polypharmacy in bipolar I disorder. *Psychopharmacology Bulletin*, **32**, 579–587.

Stein, L. I. & Test, M. A. (1980).   Alternative to mental hospital treatment. *Archives of General Psychiatry*, **37**, 392–397.

Strober, M., Lampert, C., Schmidt, S. & Morrell, W. (1993).   The course of major depressive disorder in adolescents: recovery and risk of manic switching in followup of psychotic and non-psychotic subtypes. *Journal of the American Academy of Child and Adolescent Psychiatry*, **32**, 34–42.

Taylor, P. J. (1986).   Psychiatric disorder in London's life-sentenced offenders. *British Journal of Criminology*, **26**, 63–78.

Taylor, P. J. & Gunn, J. (1984).   Violence and psychosis: risk of violence among psychotic men. British Medical Journal, **288**, 1945–1949.

Toro, P. A., Passero Rabideau, J. M., Bellavia, C. W., Daeschler, C. V., Wall, D. D. & Smith, S. J. (1997).   Evaluating an intervention for homeless persons: result of a field experiment. *Journal of Consulting and Clinical Psychology*, **65**(3), 476–484.

Wilcox, J. (1994).   Divalproex sodium in the treatment of aggressive behaviour. *Annals of Clinical Psychiatry*, **6**, 17–20.

Wilson, D. A., Tien, G. & Eaves, D. (1995).   Increasing the community tenure of mentally disordered offenders: an assertive case management program. *International Journal of Law and Psychiatry*, **18**(1), 61–69.

Witheridge, T. F. & Dincin, J. (1985).   The Bridge: an assertive outreach program in an urban setting. In L. I. Stein & M. A. Test (Eds), *The Training in Community Living Model: A Decade of Experience* (pp. 65–76). New Directions for Mental Health Services, No. 26. San Francisco, CH: Jossey-Bass.

Yatham, L. N., Kusumaker, V., Parikh, S., Haslam, D. R. S., Matte, R., Sharma, V. & Kennedy, S. (1997).   Bipolar depression: treatment options. *Canadian Journal of Psychiatry*, **42**, 97–91.

Zamble, E. & Quinsey, V. L. (1997).   *The Criminal Recidivism Process*. Cambridge: Cambridge University Press.

Zarate, C. A., Token, M., Baraibar, G. & Kando, J. C. (1995).   Prescribing trends of antidepressants in bipolar depression. *Journal of Clinical Psychiatry*, **56**, 260–264.

Chapter 7

PHARMACOLOGICAL TREATMENTS FOR PSYCHOTIC OFFENDERS

Leslie Citrome and Jan Volavka

Nathan S Kline Institute for Psychiatric Research, Orangeburg, New York, USA

INTRODUCTION

Persons with Psychotic disorders can be violent due to a multiplicity of factors. Clinical treatment of the violent patient with a diagnosis of a psychotic disorder begins by examining the possible reasons for the violent behaviour. Although the disease process itself may produce hallucinations and delusions that can drive violent behaviour, these patients may also suffer from a co-morbid substance use disorder and/or a co-morbid personality disorder that may be the principal causative factor for the patient's violent behaviour. Thus, acute intoxication or withdrawal may be the presenting clinical problem. Antisocial personality traits may be the most important factor in some instances of patient violence where goal-directed

Portions of this article draw on Dr Volavka's book, *Neurobiology of Violence* (New York: American Psychiatric Press, 1995): on Citrome, L. and Volavka, J. Psychopharmacology of violence. Part I: Assessment and acute treatment (*Psychiatric Annals*, **27**(10). 691–695, 1997; and Citrome L. and Volavka J., Psychopharmacology of violence. Part II: Beyond the acute episode (*Psychiatric Annals*, **27**(10), 696–703, 1997).

behaviour, such as extortion of money, sex or cigarettes, are evident. Neuropsychiatric deficits may facilitate the discharge of aggressive impulses. Where the patient is residing may also influence behaviour—a structured psychiatric intensive care unit might inhibit aggressive behaviour, while a chaotic living situation may encourage it.

Violent or threatening behaviour is a frequent reason for the admission to a psychiatric inpatient facility, and that behaviour may continue after the admission. The distinction between transient and recidivistic assaultiveness is important; a small group of repeatedly violent patients may cause the majority of violent incidents.

Treatment beyond acute sedation needs to address the underlying cause of the violent behaviour. Thus, a person who is violent as the result of command auditory hallucinations ought to be treated with an antipsychotic. For a person with co-morbid antisocial personality disorder and schizophrenia, control of psychotic symptoms with an antipsychotic may not be adequate to prevent violent behaviour.

The efficacy of psychotropic medication in controlling violent behaviour is difficult to measure. The literature is replete with uncontrolled case reports advocating the use of one agent or another. Few controlled double-blind studies exist. Overall, the information available on the efficacy of pharmacological treatments in preventing violence among persons with psychotic disorders is limited. Caution must be exercised before extrapolating from the results of studies on aggressivity in patients with other diagnoses, such as mental retardation, dementia or post-traumatic stress disorder. These results may not be generalizable to patients with schizophrenia or other psychotic disorders.

PATIENT ASSESSMENT AND DIFFERENTIAL DIAGNOSIS

A singular acute episode of violent behaviour needs to be differentiated from a chronic pattern of aggressive behaviour. Historical information about past behaviour is obtained from the patient, family, other providers and, where available, criminal justice services arrest records.

Repetitive episodes of violent behaviour in patients already receiving treatment in a structured environment, such as a secure unit in a hospital, may be related to neuropsychological deficits. Impairments in measures of stereognosis and visual–spatial functioning may be seen in formal neuropsychological testing (Krakowski et al., 1989a, 1989b).

Newly admitted patients may exhibit transient violence in response to their new environment. For example, crowding on the ward may encourage violence (Palmistierna, Huitfeldt & Wistedt, 1991).

Differentiating the persistently violent from the transiently violent may have therapeutic implications. It appears that the transiently violent are more responsive to typical neuroleptic medication and have less neurological impairment than the persistently violent patient (Volavka & Krakowski, 1989).

Patients with schizophrenia living in the community may decompensate and present with aggressive and violent behaviour. Overt or covert non-compliance with treatment may be a factor. Failure to respond to the prescribed medication may also be possible: as many as 30% of patients with schizophrenia fail to respond, or respond only partially. The clinical picture accompanying the violent behaviour in these instances would be an exacerbation of psychotic symptoms.

Violent acts by psychotic patients may also be attributable to co-morbidity with substance abuse (Lindqvist & Allebeck, 1990; Swanson, 1994). Co-occurrence of substance abuse with medication non-compliance is strongly related to violent behaviour among the severely mentally ill (Swartz et al., 1998). Substance abuse increases the probability of violent behaviour substantially more than schizophrenia alone (Swanson, 1994). Schizophrenia and substance use disorders co-occur more frequently than expected by chance. Data from a USA-based epidemiological study (which may not generalize to other countries) indicate that 47% of all individuals with a lifetime diagnosis of schizophrenia have also met criteria for substance abuse or dependence (Regier et al., 1990). Schizophrenia was found to elevate very significantly the risks for alcohol dependence as well as for drug dependence. Conversely, substance use disorders elevated the risk for schizophrenia. The importance of these findings is underscored by the reported increase of the prevalence estimates of co-morbid substance abuse with schizophrenia over several decades (Cuffel, 1992). The risk of violence is particularly elevated for schizophrenic or schizoaffective patients having a pattern of polysubstance abuse (Cuffel et al., 1994). Alcohol, cocaine, phencyclidine or amphetamine intoxication may present with aggressive behaviour (Smith & Hucker, 1994). A recent report from Finland revealed that although the risk of committing a homicide was about 10 times greater for schizophrenic patients than for the general population, the risk increased to greater than 17 times for male patients with schizophrenia and co-existing alcoholism, and more than 80 times for female patients with schizophrenia and co-existing alcoholism (Eronen, Tiihonen & Hakola, 1996). In hospitals and prisons, access to drugs and alcohol, although difficult, is not impossible and may be a factor in violence in those settings. Intoxication with caffeine, water, antihistamines, deodorants and other aerosols has also been described in institutional settings (Koczapski et al., 1990).

Antisocial personality traits or disorders may co-exist with schizophrenia or other psychotic disorders. There are strong cross-sectional associations between schizophrenia and antisocial personality disorder, as evidenced by the Epidemiologic Catchment Area Study data showing, in males diagnosed with antisocial personality disorder, that schizophrenia occurs at a rate seven times higher (and in females, 12 times higher) than the expected rate (Robins, Tipp & Przybeck, 1991). This finding is consistent with the observation of frequent conduct problems in the pre-morbid history of schizophrenic patients (Robins, 1966). Engagement in illegal activities, rule-breaking, lying and a lack of remorse are only a few of the criteria in the diagnosis of Antisocial Personality Disorder in DSM-IV (American Psychiatric Association, 1994). These characteristics may be found in both inpatient and outpatient populations. Thus, examining the context of the aggressive incident is important. A pattern of intimidation of others for material gain may be seen. For example, there may be fighting over money, cigarettes or access to sexual partners. Care-givers may be at risk when trying to set limits. Misdiagnosis of schizophrenia as antisocial personality disorder can occur, possibly missing an opportunity for treatment (Travin & Protter, 1982). Chronically psychotic patients can also make sociopathic adaptations to the environments imposed on them as a result of their illnesses, and this can distort the clinical picture, an example being the individual whose psychotic symptoms diminish when his welfare check is due to arrive (Geller, 1980).

Superimposed metabolic disturbances, brain tumours, or brain injury may lead to violent behaviour in patients with a history of docility. Ongoing attention to somatic complaints and abnormalities found on routine physical examination and laboratory screening may provide diagnostic clues for the diagnosis responsible for the abnormal behaviour.

Superimposed epilepsy does not appear to be a primary causative factor in violent behaviour. Interictal violence is associated more with psychopathology and mental retardation than with an abnormal electroencephalogram (Mendez, Doss & Taylor, 1993).

Bipolar disorder with psychotic features needs to be distinguished from schizophrenia; this distinction has important consequences for treatment planning and prognosis (Pope & Lipinski, 1978). Clinically, the irritable manic patient has posed a serious risk to the evaluating emergency room psychiatrist, especially if the patient does not agree with a recommendation for hospital admission. Mania has been associated with violent behaviour in a study of 40 male psychiatric inpatients (Yesavage, 1983). In a comparison of 20 inpatients with mania and 856 with other diagnoses, agitation (but not assaultiveness) was seen more frequently in the manic group (Craig, 1982).

Major depression with psychotic features is another entity that can be associated with violent behaviour. The association between homicide and depression has also been reported (Husain, Anasseril & Harris, 1983; Rosenbaum & Bennett, 1986; Bourget & Bradford, 1990). Co-morbidity with alcohol/substance abuse and/or personality disorders appears to be a prominent feature in these cases.

MANAGEMENT OF ACUTE AGGRESSION

Practical clinical information and advice on the management of agitated patients can be found in a number of reviews (Tupin, 1983; Lehmann et al., 1983; Citrome & Green, 1990; Gertz, 1980; Eichelman & Hartwig, 1995; Thackrey, 1987; Tardiff, 1992). Physical restraints and seclusion remain an important option in assuring the safety of both the patient and those around him/her (Fisher, 1994). A comprehensive biopsychosocial approach, involving the multidisciplinary team, is key in optimally managing crisis situations.

There is no specific drug treatment for violent behaviour; however, non-specific sedation is often used in the management of an acutely agitated patient. The selection of the sedating agent is made using the best available information about the patient and the specific pharmacological activities of the potential drug. Availability of an intramuscular preparation is factored into the decision-making process when a fast onset of action is required and/or when the patient is actively resisting oral or sublingual administration. Rate of onset of action is sometimes difficult to interpret—a patient may calm down readily after an oral dose, knowing that action has been taken and help is being provided.

The choice of sedating agent generally falls between either a benzodiazepine or an antipsychotic. Other agents commonly used include chloral hydrate, diphenhydramine, hydroxyzine and sodium amytal. Lorazepam, a benzodiazepine, is commonly used when treating an acute episode of agitation (Salzman, 1988). Its main advantage lies in the relative lack of untoward side effects when compared with the acute use of an antipsychotic, such as acute dystonic reactions and the lowering of the seizure threshold. The latter makes antipsychotics particularly unsuitable for agitation secondary to withdrawal from alcohol. In these instances an antipsychotic can precipitate a seizure, while a benzodiazepine would have a protective effect regarding seizure activity and also sedate the patient. A comparison between a single dose of haloperidol (10 mg) with a single dose of lorazepam (2 mg) in violent psychiatric patients led to a conclusion that lorazepam was at least as effective as haloperidol in controlling violent behaviour (Bick & Hannah, 1986). Of all the benzodiazepines available, lorazepam is the only one reliably absorbed when administered intramuscularly (Greenblatt et al., 1979; Greenblatt et al., 1982). Its half-life is relatively short (10–20 hours) and its route of elimination produces no active metabolites. Typical doses are 0.5–2.0 mg every 1–6 hours and this may be given orally, sublingually, intramuscularly or intravenously. Older patients and those who are medically compromised may require one-quarter to one-half the regular adult dose. Particular care is required when prescribing a benzodiazepine to a patient with respiratory difficulties, as respiratory depression can result. A deleterious interaction of benzodiazepines with clozapine has been reported, with this combination implicated in producing respiratory depression (Friedman et al., 1991; Klimke & Klieser, 1994) and marked sedation, excessive sialorrhea and ataxia (Cobb, Anderson & Seidel, 1991). Other practitioners have used this combination of clozapine and lorazepam with some success, but caution is still warranted (Kanofsky & Lindenmayer, 1993). There have been reports of a paradoxical reaction to benzodiazepines, as evidenced by an increase in hostility on the part of the patient receiving one or several doses of the agent in question (Bond & Lader, 1979). This appears to be relatively uncommon (Dietch & Jennings, 1988), and even more unlikely to occur when given within the context of single or limited doses in a crisis situation (Volavka, 1995). In current clinical practice, chronic administration of benzodiazepines is discouraged because of a diminution of clinical effect with time due to the ease with which physiological tolerance develops and the difficulties involved in titrating a patient off the drug because of this iatrogenic dependence. However, benzodiazepines remain an indispensable tool for the short-term quick reduction of severe motor agitation.

Antipsychotics have traditionally been used as sedating agents, even though their main indication is for the treatment of psychotic symptoms. The use of antipsychotics as sedatives is complicated by their wide array of potential side effects, which may accompany the desired sedative effect. Haloperidol, a butyrophenone, has been commonly used for agitation in emergency department settings for a wide variety of patients (Clinton et al., 1987). It is available as an intramuscular medication and causes less hypotension, fewer anticholinergic side effects, and less of a decrease in the seizure threshold compared with low-potency neuroleptics (e.g. chlorpromazine).

Neuroleptics may have a longer-lasting effect on the reduction of agitation by treating the underlying psychosis. Akathisia may limit this benefit. Akathisia is the unpleasant sensation of inner restlessness, often leading the patient to move his/her legs and arms, squirm in his/her seat, and pace about. Akathisia increases irritability and has been reported to be associated with violence in several cases (Kechich, 1978; Siris, 1985). Akathisia may have been the mediating variable associated with violence and high-dose haloperidol treatment in patients with chronic schizophrenia (Herrera et al., 1988). Moreover, over 30% of patients with schizophrenia are treatment-resistant to typical antipsychotics. For them, there are no (or limited) benefits in the use of these agents beyond the acute sedative effect.

Antipsychotics have been used with success as sedating agents in patients with mania (Chou, 1991), the elderly (at low doses) (Yudofsky, Silver & Hales, 1990; De Cuyper, Van Praag & Verstraeten, 1985), in patients who develop violent, aggressive behaviour after a severe closed head injury (Rao, Jellinek & Woolston, 1985) and in mental retardation. For the latter their effectiveness is questionable. Small studies of various neuroleptics reported some success (Hacke, 1980; De Cuyper et al., 1985; Zapletalek, Hametova & Rydlova, 1989) but a large, placebo-controlled study has demonstrated a significant worsening of aggressiveness with thioridazine at a dose of 200 mg/day (Elie et al., 1980). Although common, the administration of neuroleptics to control behaviour of non-psychotic, mentally retarded individuals may be neither effective nor safe (Aman, 1989) and the practice remains controversial (Rasmussen, 1989; Beermann & Thelander, 1989).

A pre-anaesthetic agent, droperidol, may be effective for the acute sedation of an agitated patient. It is a neuroleptic in the butyrophenone class. There is some experience of using this agent in the emergency room setting (Thomas, Schwartz & Petrilli, 1992). However, there is a case report of coma following intravenous droperidol given to a patient with post-electroconvulsive therapy delirium (Koo & Chien, 1986). Adequate medical back-up and the availability of intubation and oxygen is urged (Schatzberg & Cole, 1991). Thus, droperidol should not be used in psychiatric hospitals where such back-up is not immediately available.

PHARMACOLOGICAL MANAGEMENT OF CHRONIC VIOLENT BEHAVIOUR

Treatment directed at the longer-term management of violent behaviour is dependent on the underlying diagnosis. When the primary psychiatric problem is treated effectively, the associated aggressive behaviour is reduced. For example, the utilization of a mood stabilizer, such as lithium, valproate or carbamazepine, would be the first choice for a patient diagnosed with bipolar disorder. Likewise, a neuroleptic would be the first choice of agent for a patient with schizophrenia. Unfortunately, treatment with the recommended agent is no guarantee of success—as many as one-third of all patients with schizophrenia are treatment-resistant to typical antipsychotic medication. In these instances, new and novel psychotherapeutic approaches are necessary to effectuate control of aggressive behaviour. Theoretical rationales for treatment strategies have included the serotonin hypothesis. The atypical antipsychotics (such as clozapine, risperidone, olanzapine and quetiapine), β-adrenergic blockers, mood stabilizers (lithium, carbamazepine and valproic acid), antidepressants and buspirone have been used in patients with psychosis in order to prevent violence.

The serotonin neurotransmitter system emerges as a common theme amongst many putative anti-aggressive agents. The modulation of aggressive behaviour involves the serotonergic system in many species and a disturbance of this system has been implicated in impulsive violence in humans. The impulsive aggressivity may be directed towards self or against others (Apter et al., 1990; Roy & Linnoila, 1988). Disturbance of the serotonergic system in humans has been inferred from low levels of cerebrospinal fluid (CSF) 5-hydroxyindoleacetic acid (5-HIAA) (Linnoila et al., 1983; Virkkunen & Linnoila, 1990; Virkkunen et al., 1989, 1995), or from a blunted response to neuroendocrine challenges (Coccaro et al., 1989). The majority of this work was not done with psychotic patients, but rather with patients with personality disorders and substance use disorders. Nonetheless, if we generalize these findings to all patients with impulsive, violent behaviour, the serotonin system provides a theoretical rationale for the observation that atypical antipsychotics are helpful in decreasing hostility and aggressivity among psychotic patients. Medications that affect the serotonin neurotransmitter system, and that may reduce aggressive behaviour in psychotic patients, include antipsychotics, such as clozapine and risperidone, and antidepressants, such as fluoxetine and citalopram. These and other medications are described in more detail below.

Antipsychotics: the atypicals

In the past, clinicians had to choose between high potency antipsychotics, such as haloperidol, with the attendant risk of extrapyramidal side effects, and low-potency drugs such as thioridazine, with the risk of excessive sedation, hypotension and anticholinergic side effects. Several new antipsychotics have recently become available, including clozapine, risperidone, olanzapine and quetiapine. These new antipsychotic medications are often referred to as *"atypical antipsychotics"*. "Atypical" refers to their differences from the typical antipsychotics (such as haloperidol and chlorpromazine) and generally implies few or no extrapyramidal side effects, efficacy in reducing the negative symptoms of schizophrenia (blunted affect, emotional and social withdrawal, lack of motivation), efficacy in treatment-refractory schizophrenia, and a lower risk of the development of tardive dyskinesia (a usually irreversible disorder characterized by disabling or disfiguring abnormal movements). Note that not all currently available and forthcoming "new" antipsychotics meet all of these criteria. Atypical antipsychotics, as compared to traditional (typical) antipsychotic medication, generally have a different affinity profile for the various neurotransmitter receptors in the brain; they usually have an increased affinity for the serotonergic system and a reduced affinity for the dopamine D2 receptor, compared with typical agents. This is consistent with the clinical observation of fewer or absent extrapyramidal side effects. Thus, the availability of these new treatment options offers many advantages, despite their cost (Citrome, 1997). Information on the effectiveness of clozapine, risperidone and quetiapine in the control of aggressivity is available and will be described below.

Clozapine

The atypical antipsychotic clozapine has been the gold standard for the effective treatment of patients refractory to typical neuroleptics, and may also have specific anti-aggressive effects. It is the oldest of the available atypical antipsychotics. Because of the risk of agranulocytosis, there is a mandatory monitoring programme in the USA requiring clozapine recipients to undergo a weekly white blood cell count. This has limited its use to patients refractory to, or intolerant of, typical antipsychotics. The state hospital has become an important resource in the evaluation of the effectiveness of clozapine because, as the state hospital population shrinks, the patients that remain tend to be treatment-resistant. Often, the major obstacle preventing discharge to the community is aggressive and violent behaviour. Thus, most of the studies reported below have taken place in the state hospital setting.

A USA retrospective record review of 100 state hospital patients, all diagnosed with a chronic psychotic disorder, found that the number of violent episodes decreased in the 18 month period after they began clozapine treatment, as measured by the number of reported incidents involving self-harm or aggression against others (Wilson & Claussen, 1995). Similar results were found in another retrospective record review of five patients with chronic schizophrenia housed on a specialized unit for the severely aggressive (Ratey et al., 1993).

An open retrospective review of Brief Psychiatric Rating Scale (BPRS) ratings among 223 patients with schizophrenia, spanning 21 state hospitals in New York State, found a selective effect of clozapine on hostility (Volavka et al., 1993). A review of restraint and seclusion data for 139 patients, diagnosed with either schizophrenia or schizoaffective disorder, revealed a reduction in the use of these restrictive measures in the 12 weeks after the start of clozapine treatment (Chiles, Davidson & McBride, 1994). This reduction in the utilization of restraints and seclusion was also observed among 107 "chronic" patients in state hospitals in Missouri after they began receiving clozapine (Mallya, Roos & Roebuck-Colgan, 1992). Buckley et al. (1995), in their report of 11 patients with schizophrenia treated with clozapine, suggested that because the magnitude of the reduction in aggression (again measured by the utilization of restraints and seclusion) was greater than the modest improvement noted in the BPRS scores, clozapine had a selective anti-aggressive effect.

Forensic patients were the subjects in another retrospective record review where the security level of 25 patients with either schizophrenia or schizoaffective disorder was evaluated before and after the start of clozapine therapy (Maier, 1992); marked improvement and movement to a less secure unit was noted in over half the subjects. Another retrospective review of records in 27 forensic patients diagnosed with schizophrenia or schizoaffective disorder found a decrease in BPRS scores, an increased likelihood of achieving higher levels of patient privileges, and a reduction in the utilization of restraints and seclusion in the six months following the start of treatment with clozapine (Ebrahim et al., 1994).

Although no controlled studies of the anti-aggressive effects of clozapine are yet available, the preponderance of evidence does not indicate that this drug reduces aggressive behaviour in schizophrenia and schizoaffective disorder. These effects cannot be fully explained by sedation or by general antipsychotic effects.

Risperidone

Studies are currently under way comparing risperidone with clozapine under double-blind conditions. Until these results are known, clinicians must rely on the information available so far, mainly uncontrolled open (that is, not double-blind) studies and case reports. Clinical experience so far points to the supremacy of clozapine for treatment-refractory schizophrenia. There is some evidence, however, that risperidone may also have specific anti-aggressive properties, but the magnitude of this effect compared with that for clozapine is not yet known. This selective effect of risperidone on hostility was demonstrated by utilizing the data gathered as part of a large multicenter pharmaceutical company-sponsored phase III clinical trial (Czobor, Volavka & Meibach, 1995). The study design was a double-blind, placebo-controlled, parallel group, nine-week clinical trial of risperidone vs. haloperidol (Marder & Meibach, 1994). Hostility was measured by the Positive and Negative Syndrome Scale. One hundred and thirty-nine patients had a baseline hostility score of at least "mild", and all had a diagnosis of schizophrenia. Risperidone was found to have a greater selective effect on hostility than haloperidol. This effect was not evident in a retrospective case-control study of 27 patients with schizophrenia or schizoaffective disorder (Buckley et al., 1997). In these patients a similar response between risperidone and typical antipsychotics was found, as measured by the utilization of restraints and seclusion.

Quetiapine

Quetiapine may also preferentially reduce hostility and aggression in acute schizophrenia. Utilizing the data gathered on 351 patients in a six-week placebo-controlled, double-blind, randomized, efficacy and safety phase III clinical trial, quetiapine was compared with haloperidol in measures of aggression and hostility assessed by the BPRS (Cantillon & Goldstein, 1998). Quetiapine and haloperidol were both superior to placebo in reducing positive symptoms, but only quetiapine was superior to placebo in the measures of aggression and hostility.

β-Adrenergic blockers: propanolol, nadolol, metoprolol and pindolol

Although β-blockers (e.g. propranolol) have been extensively studied as an anti-aggressive agent in brain-injured patients (Yudofsky, Williams & Gorman, 1981; Yudofsky et al., 1984), their use in schizophrenia have not been as well examined (Volavka, 1988; 1995).

Propanolol has been used as an adjunctive treatment for schizophrenia and a reduction in symptoms, including aggression, was found (Sheppard, 1979). At one institution, a retrospective chart review of all patients diagnosed with schizophrenia and receiving β-blockers (nadolol or propranolol) for the treatment of chronic aggressivity revealed a 70% decrease in actual assaults for four of the seven patients (Sorgi, Ratey & Polakoff, 1986). Forty-one patients, 29 of whom were schizophrenic, participated in a double-blind placebo-controlled study of adjunctive nadolol (40–120 mg/day) and a decline in the frequency of aggression was found when compared with controls (Ratey et al., 1992). This supported an earlier report of a double-blind, placebo-controlled study of adjunctive nadolol (80–120 mg/day) in 30 violent inpatients, of whom 23 were schizophrenic, where a trend was found demonstrating lower hostility for the active treatment group (Alpert et al., 1990). In the latter study, the authors noted a decrease in extrapyramidal symptoms, leading to the conclusion that anti-aggression and anti-akathisia effects were associated, consistent with the idea that akathisia can be a cause of violent behaviour. However, in the investigators' final report of 34 acutely aggressive male schizophrenic patients (Allan et al., 1996), this association was not maintained. Nadolol did appear to induce a more rapid decrease of overall psychiatric symptoms independent of any effect on extrapyramidal side effects.

Titration of propranolol to an effective dose may require some time because the build-up must be gradual in order to avoid hypotension. The current literature suggests that the onset of the anti-aggressive effects can be seen four to eight weeks after the effective dose is reached (Yudofsky, Silver & Hales, 1990). It is unclear what dose is most effective. Doses above 600 mg/day are used only exceptionally. The dose–response relationship has not been systematically studied.

As noted, the main practical problem with the administration of propranolol for aggression is the high frequency of cardiovascular side effects (reduction of pulse rate and blood pressure). In addition, propranolol has a relatively short half-life requiring multiple dosing during the course of the day (this property being moot since the availability of a long-acting preparation, Inderal LA). This has led to the examination of the utility of other β-blockers, such as pindolol, which has a partial agonist effect (intrinsic sympathomimetic activity) in addition to its non-selective β-adrenergic blocking activity. This accounts for a reduction of cardiovascular side effects of pindolol in normotensive population, making it a safer and more attractive compound for psychiatric indications than propranolol. Other β-blockers besides propranolol that have been investigated for the treatment of aggressivity include metoprolol and nadolol. Unfortunately, except for the latter, these other agents have not been systematically evaluated in psychotic patients.

Mood stabilizers: lithium, carbamazepine and valproic acid

Mood stabilizers such as lithium, valproic acid and carbamazepine are used as the primary medication treatment for bipolar disorder and as adjuncts to neuroleptic treatment for patients with schizophrenia. Although they are not prototypical anti-aggressive drugs, they are commonly used for this purpose in clinical practice. At one 500 bed state hospital (Citrome, 1995; Citrome, unpublished data) 25% of all patients in 1993 were receiving lithium, carbamazepine or valproate. Approximately 15% of the patients diagnosed with schizophrenia received at least one of these agents (usually carbamazepine), and 86% of the time the indication was poor impulse control or assaultive/aggressive behaviour. The measure of effectiveness in reducing aggressivity was hampered by the reliance on data contained in the medical record, but the overall impression was that there was a tangible clinical benefit. Mood stabilizers continue to be extensively prescribed in patients with schizophrenia. In 1996, among the 5973 patients with schizophrenia hospitalized within the New York State psychiatric hospital system, 38.5% received at least one type of mood stabilizer, with 28.3% receiving valproate, 11.6% lithium and 5.4% carbamazepine (Citrome, 1998).

Lithium

Lithium is a first-line agent for the treatment of bipolar disorder (manic-depressive illness). Aggressivity is common during manic episodes (Yesavage, 1983). Consequently, the reduction of aggressivity is an important goal of lithium treatment in manic patients. In contrast to bipolar disorder, the effectiveness of lithium therapy in schizophrenia is not established. Methodological problems, such as small sample size and lack of strict diagnostic criteria, plague older studies demonstrating benefit (Atre-Vaidya & Taylor, 1989). Active affective symptoms, previous affective episodes and a family history of affective disorder may predict a favourable response to lithium (Atre-Vaidya & Taylor, 1989), but also provides clues that the diagnosis may be something other than schizophrenia (Citrome, 1989). A double-blind placebo-controlled, parallel design clinical trial, involving 21 seriously ill state hospital patients with schizophrenia, who had not responded to prior trials of typical neuroleptics, demonstrated no advantage of lithium (levels around 1.0 mEq/l) combined with haloperidol over haloperidol alone (Wilson, 1993). These patients did not have a concurrent affective disorder. When lithium was added to neuroleptics for the treatment of resistant schizophrenic patients classified as "dangerous, violent or criminal" in a single-blind randomized design, no benefits were seen after four weeks of adjunctive lithium (Collins, Larkin & Shubsachs, 1991). Another group described a case series where lithium was useful as a single agent in ameliorating psychosis in three patients with chronic schizophrenia, who suffered from intractable akathisia with accompanying agitation, restlessness and irritability when on standard neuroleptics (Shalev, Hermesh & Munitz, 1987). These three patients were considered treatment-refractory to antipsychotics, were free of affective symptoms and no major affective disorders in their families were known, thus making this group somewhat comparable to the patients described above (Wilson, 1993). For some schizophrenic patients, the impact of lithium on core psychotic symptoms (hallucinations, delusions, formal thought disorder) may be evident after the first seven days (Zemlan et al., 1984). Both schizoaffective disorder and patients with schizophrenia were included in this open study. Lithium responders comprised 26 of the 61 subjects, but it is not clear which of the responders were diagnosed as having schizoaffective disorder. There is a report of two cases of patients with chronic paranoid schizophrenia with aggressive or disorderly behaviours who have responded to the addition of lithium to their neuroleptic treatment, then deteriorated after the lithium was discontinued but subsequently improved when it was reinstituted (Prakash, 1985). In conclusion, the literature on the use of lithium in patients with schizophrenia is mixed.

Carbamazepine

The effectiveness of carbamazepine in managing violent behaviour has been investigated, but has involved relatively few subjects (Volavka, 1995). In a Finnish forensic hospital, eight women diagnosed with schizophrenia (some with abnormalities in their electroencephalograms (EEGs) and exhibiting violent behaviour (two had committed murder before admission; the others had committed serious assaults) were given carbamazepine in addition to their regular neuroleptic medication (Hakola & Laulumaa, 1982). With carbamazepine, the violent behaviour was almost completely eliminated, and in four patients the symptoms of schizophrenia also decreased. Three of the patients were discharged, two went to an open ward, and one returned to an "ordinary mental hospital". On two chronic psychiatric hospital wards, a retrospective look at violent patients, most diagnosed with schizophrenia, with and without abnormalities on the EEG, revealed significant reductions in aggressivity with carbamazepine, regardless of EEG status (Luchins, 1984). The number of subjects was again small, with seven subjects in one study and 19 in the other. A four-week double-blind trial of adjunctive carbamazepine vs. placebo with standard neuroleptic treatment was done on 162 patients across several facilities (Okuma et al., 1989). All subjects had a diagnosis of either schizophrenic or schizoaffective disorder, and all showed excited states or aggressive/violent behaviour that responded unsatisfactorily to neuroleptic treatment. No statistically significant difference was found in response among the patients receiving either adjunctive carbamazepine or placebo, but a trend towards moderate improvement with carbamazepine was noted ($p < 0.10$). Adjunctive carbamazepine in non-epileptic chronic inpatients with EEG temporal lobe abnormalities was the focus of a 15-week double-blind randomized within-patient cross-over study involving 13 patients (Neppe, 1983, 1988). Only nine of the subjects had schizophrenia, of whom seven completed the study. Overt aggression was rated as twice as severe and one and a half times as common on placebo compared with carbamazepine. Response was not correlated with EEG deterioration or improvement.

It is difficult to make firm conclusions regarding the effectiveness of carbamazepine in controlling violent behaviour in patients with a psychotic disorder. Most of the published studies of carbamazepine and aggressivity have not used a double-blind design and are uncontrolled for the placebo effect. Plasma levels of concomitant neuroleptics are not measured, leaving open the possibility for undetected pharmacokinetic interactions. Despite these limitations, carbamazepine does appear to be a useful adjunct to neuroleptic therapy (Simhandl & Meszaros, 1992) and may lower aggression in a broad spectrum of disorders (Young & Hillbrand, 1994). Like lithium, it may be worth a brief trial, but again, chronic administration of carbamazepine may needlessly expose the patient to side effects if no therapeutic advantage is offered. Moreover, given carbamazepine's property of inducing its own metabolism (and that of other psychotropics, including haloperidol and clozapine), dosing issues may complicate treatment planning.

Valproate

Valproate's two formulations, valproic acid and divalproex sodium, have become commonly used in bipolar disorder, schizoaffective disorder, schizophrenia and other disorders (Citrome, 1998). Support for its use as an effective agent in the management of the manic phase of bipolar disorder is compelling, and in 1995 led the USA Food and Drug Administration to formally approve divalproex sodium for this indication. In contrast to the literature on the use of valproate in the treatment of bipolar and schizo-affective disorder, very little is available on its use in schizophrenia (McElroy et al., 1989). Clinical lore suggests that valproate can be used to manage aggressivity, and this has been described in several case reports. Four cases of treatment-resistant schizophrenia were given valproate in addition to their neuroleptic medication, resulting in a reduction of positive symptoms as measured by the BPRS, and a reduction of hostile/disruptive behaviour (Morinigo et al., 1989). Two patients with schizophrenia and one with schizoaffective disorder were given valproic acid in addition to neuroleptics in an effort to control severe neuroleptic-resistant psychotic symptoms, with good results (Wassef et al., 1989). A comparison of valproate and carbamazepine in hospitalized patients (diagnosis not reported) revealed a decrease in the number of hours spent in mechanical restraints for both groups, with valproate being more effective than carbamazepine (Alam et al., 1995). An open design study involving 35 individuals randomly selected from consecutive admissions to a large state hospital found that divalproex sodium reduced agitation in patients with bipolar disorder and in those with borderline personality disorder, as measured by the number of hours spent in seclusion per week (Wilcox, 1994).

The extent of use of valproate cries out for more definitive studies on its effectiveness as an adjunctive agent for the control of agitation in psychotic patients. Double-blind placebo-controlled studies are needed to prove efficacy for this indication. Pending the availability of this information, we have only uncontrolled studies and case reports, and many of them do not include patients with schizophrenia. As with both lithium and car-bamazepine, an empirical trial of valproate may be considered for an individual patient, but chronic use, without demonstrable benefit, only exposes the patient to the possibility of side effects.

Mood stabilizers: summary

Thus, the available evidence indicates that mood stabilizers may reduce aggressive behaviour in patients with a broad spectrum of diagnoses. For patients with bipolar disorder the issue is relatively straightforward, as a mood stabilizer is routinely used for the management of these conditions. Combination therapy with another agent, either another mood stabilizer or another type of psychotropic, may be helpful but exposes the patient to possible toxicity secondary to drug interactions (Freeman & Stoll, 1998). For patients with schizophrenia, the use of a mood stabilizer is more problematic because of the lack of definitive information. The evidence is relatively firm for carbamazepine; it is less conclusive for valproic acid and lithium.

Mechanisms of the specific anti-aggressive action of mood stabilizers are unclear. Since most of the reported trials used mood stabilizers as adjunctive treatment, it is possible that some of the effects depend on pharmaco-dynamic and pharmacokinetic interactions with antipsychotics or other concomitant medications.

Benzodiazepines: clonazepam

In a single case report of a schizophrenic patient with a complex partial seizure disorder, clonazepam was used as an adjunct to haloperidol to con-trol both seizure activity and persistent violent hallucinations (Keats & Mukherjee, 1988). Both phenytoin and carbamazepine had been ineffective. This result is in marked contrast to a double-blind placebo-controlled trial of adjunctive clonazepam in 13 schizophrenic patients receiving neuroleptics (Karson et al., 1982). Nine patients completed the entire protocol. No addi-tional therapeutic benefit was observed and in fact four patients behaved aggressively during the study. Three of these four had not been violent previously. This finding speaks against the chronic use of clonazepam in schizophrenia. Like other benzodiazepines, it can be used as a sedating agent; however, lorazepam is probably more suitable for this use because of its shorter half-life and availability in parenteral form.

Anti-depressants: selective serotonin re-uptake inhibitors (SSRIs)

Major depression, with or without psychotic features, can present with agi-tation. Care must be taken not to miss this diagnosis when evaluating a psychotic patient who is violent. This is because the indicated therapy would be an antidepressant. There have also been observations that some antidepressants may reduce agitated and threatening behaviour in other psychotic disorders. The current interest in certain antidepressants' role in aggression is based on the crucial role of serotonergic regulation of impul-sive aggression against self and others. Now that antidepressants with spe-cific effects on serotonin (5-HT) receptors have become available, a number of reports have emerged.

Fluoxetine

In a retrospective, uncontrolled study, adjunctive fluoxetine was given to five patients with chronic schizophrenia, with a decrease in violent incidents observed for four cases (Goldman & Janecek, 1990). An open study of 85 patients with unipolar depression receiving fluoxetine for eight weeks identified a subgroup of highly irritable and hostile patients (Fava et al., 1993). Anger and hostility was reduced by fluoxetine.

The above findings have been of significant interest because of an early case report of six depressed patients, free of recent serious suicidal ideation, who developed intense and violent suicidal preoccupations after starting fluoxetine treatment (Teicher, Glod & Cole, 1990), leading the authors to recommend that fluoxetine be used with caution. Other psychotropic medications were being used concurrently and there were wide individual differences in fluoxetine drug response. As a consequence to this uncertainty, fluoxetine has been blamed for inducing murder or suicide, and has been used as a legal defence and as a plaintiff's argument in seeking compensatory and punitive damages in a variety of court cases (Burton, 1991; Grinfeld, 1995). In an attempt to put this issue to rest, Lilly Research Laboratories published a meta-analysis of 3992 subjects with several different diagnoses (depression, obesity, bulimia nervosa, obsessive-compulsive disorder, smoking cessation and alcoholism) enrolled in several double-blind placebo-controlled clinical trials of fluoxetine. They demonstrated a four-fold higher likelihood for an aggressive event for patients receiving placebo compared with fluoxetine (Heilgenstein, Beasley & Potvin, 1993). Using pooled data from some of these same trials, fluoxetine was found not to be associated with increased suicidality during pharmacotherapy for depression (Tollefson, 1994).

Citalopram

Citalopram is another selective serotonin re-uptake inhibitor. A 48-week, double-blind, placebo-controlled, cross-over study looking at the anti-aggressive effects of adjunctive citalopram in 15 chronically violent hospitalized schizophrenic patients revealed a decrease in the number of aggressive incidents during active treatment (Vartiainen et al., 1995).

CONCLUSION

Rational pharmacological treatment is dependent on accurate assessment and diagnosis. Treatment of the underlying mental disorder will often lead to a reduction in violent behaviour. Antipsychotics can be used to treat individuals with a variety of diagnoses when the symptomatic control of pyschosis is required, but they will do little else if the underlying problem has its origins in a metabolic disorder, a space-occupying lesion in the brain or an infection. An antipsychotic alone will not stabilize the disturbed mood of a patient with bipolar disorder or major depression. Care must be taken to identify co-morbid substance use disorders and co-morbid antisocial personality disorder, as both increase the risk of violent behaviour.

β-blockers, well studied in the treatment of aggressive behaviour in brain-injured patients, may also be helpful as an adjunctive agent to neuroleptics for aggression and schizophrenia. Mood stabilizers are increasingly utilized as an adjunct to antipsychotic therapy for schizophrenia but they have not been extensively studied under double-blind placebo-controlled conditions.

A significant problem is the number of patients with schizophrenia who do not respond to typical antipsychotic drugs. The atypical antipsychotics may be more effective for this group of patients. In addition, clozapine appears to be more effective than typical neuroleptics in reducing aggressivity in patients with schizophrenia or schizoaffective disorder. Risperidone also appears promising in reducing hostility. Both of these agents appear to have selective anti-aggressive activity in addition to their antipsychotic properties, making them particularly suitable for patients who are both aggressive and have schizophrenia. For this group of patients, clozapine should be considered first, before using adjuvant β-blockers or adjuvant mood stabilizers.

Regardless of the medication strategies used, it is imperative to address co-morbid alcohol and drug use by also offering a full array of treatments that includes education, peer groups (such as Alcoholics Anonymous), and medications such as disulfiram and methadone for selected patients. Compliance or adherence to a treatment regimen may be facilitated by outpatient commitment, a legal framework for supervising patients in the community that is being utilized in some jurisdictions in the USA.

REFERENCES

Alam, M. Y., Klass, D. B., Luchins, D. J., Aleem, Y. & Enich, G. (1995). Effectiveness of divalproex sodium, valproic acid and carbamazepine in aggression (poster). NCDEU 35th Annual Meeting.

Allan, E., Alpert, M., Sison, C., Citrome, L., Laury, G. & Berman, I. (1996). Adjunctive nadolol in the treatment of acutely aggressive schizophrenic patients. *Journal of Clinical Psychiatry*, **57**(10), 455–459.

Alpert, M., Allan, E. R., Citrome, L., Laury, G., Sison, C. & Sudilovsky, A. (1990). A double-blind, placebo-controlled study of adjunctive nadolol in the management of violent psychiatric patients. *Psychopharmacology Bulletin*, **26**(3), 367–371.

Aman, M. G. (1989). Neuroleptics. In American Psychiatric Association (Eds), *Treatment of Psychiatric Disorders. A Task Force Report of the American Psychiatric Association* (pp. 71–77). Washington, DC: American Psychiatric Association.

American Psychiatric Association (1994). *Diagnostic and Statistical Manual of Mental Disorders, 4th edn (DSM-IV)*. Washington, DC: American Psychiatric Association.

Apter, A., Van Praag, H. M., Plutchik, R., Sevy, S., Korn, M. & Brown, S. L. (1990). Interrelationships among anxiety, aggression, impulsivity, and mood: a serotonergically linked cluster? *Psychiatry Research*, **32**, 191–199.

Atre-Vaidya, N. & Taylor, M. A. (1989). Effectiveness of lithium in schiozphrenia: do we really have an answer? *Journal of Clinical Psychiatry*, **50**(5), 170–173.

Beermann, B. & Thelander, S. (1989). The effect of neuroleptics in the mentally retarded is poorly documented [in Swedish]. *Lakartidningen*, **86**, 4320.

Bick, P. A. & Hannah, A. L. (1986). Intramuscular lorazepam to restrain violent patients (letter). *Lancet*, **1**, 206.

Bond, A. & Lader, M. (1979). Benzodiazepines and aggression. In M. Sandler (Ed.), *Psychopharmacology of Aggression* (pp. 173–182). New York: Raven.

Bourget, D. & Bradford, J. M. W. (1990). Homocidal parents. *Canadian Journal of Psychiatry*, **35**(3), 233–238.

Buckley, P., Bartell, J., Donenwirth, K., Lee, S., Torigoe, F. & Schulz, S. C. (1995). Violence and schizophrenia: clozapine as a specific antiaggressive agent. *Bulletin of the American Academy of Psychiatry and the Law*, **23**(4), 607–611.

Buckley, P. F., Ibrahim, Z. Y., Singer, B., Orr, B., Donenwirth, K. & Brar, P. S. (1997). Aggression and schizophrenia: efficacy of risperidone. *Journal of the American Academy of Psychiatry and the Law*, **25**, 173–181.

Burton, T. M. (1991). Medical flap: anti-depression drug of Eli Lilly loses sales after attack by sect. *Wall Street Journal*, Friday, April 19.

Cantillon, M. & Goldstein, J. M. (1998). Quetiapine fumarate reduces aggression and hostility in patients with schizophrenia. American Psychiatric Association 151st Annual Meeting. New Research Poster Session NR444, June 3, Toronto, Canada.

Chiles, J. A., Davidson, P. & McBride, D. (1994). Effects of clozapine on use of seclusion and restraint at a state hospital. *Hospital and Community Psychiatry*, **45**(3), 269–271.

Chou, J. C. (1991). Recent advances in treatment of acute mania. *Journal of Clinical Psychopharmacology*, **11**, 3–21.

Citrome, L. & Green, L. (1990). The dangerous agitated patient: what to do right now. *Postgraduate Medicine 87*(2), 231–236.

Citrome, L. (1989). Differential diagnosis of psychosis. *Postgraduate Medicine*, **85**(4), 273–280.

Citrome, L. (1995). Use of lithium, carbamazepine, and valproic acid in a state-operated psychiatric hospital. *Journal of Pharmacy Technology*, **11**, 55–59.

Citrome, L. (1997). New antipsychotic medications: what advantages do they offer? *Postgraduate Medicine*, **101**(2), 207–214.

Citrome, L. (1998). Valproate: extent of use within the in-patient population of the New York State Office of Mental Health psychiatric hospital system. *Psychiatric Quarterly*, **69**(4), 283–300.

Clinton, J. E., Sterner, S., Stelmachers, Z. & Ruiz, E. (1987). Haloperidol for sedation of disruptive emergency patients. *Annals of Emergency Medicine*, **16**(3), 319–322.

Cobb, C. D., Anderson, C. B. & Seidel, D. R. (1991). Possible interaction between clozapine and lorazepam (letter). *American Journal of Psychiatry*, **148**(11), 1606–1607.

Coccaro, E. F., Siever, L. J., Klar, H. M., Maurer, G., Cochrane, K., Cooper, T. B., Mohs, R. C. & Davis, K. L. (1989). Serotonergic studies in patients with affective and personality disorders. *Archives of General Psychiatry*, **46**, 587–599.

Collins, P. J., Larkin, E. P. & Shubsachs, A. P. W. (1991). Lithium carbonate in chronic schizophrenia—a brief trial of lithium carbonate added to neuroleptics for treatment of resistant schizophrenic patients. *Acta Psychiatrica Scandinavica*, **84**, 150–154.

Craig, T. J. (1982). An epidemiologic study of problems associated with violence among psychiatric inpatients. *American Journal of Psychiatry*, **139**(10), 1262–1266.

Cuffel, B. J., Shumway, M., Chouljian, T. L. & Macdonald, T. (1994). A longitudinal study of substance abuse and community violence in schizophrenia. *Journal of Nervous and Mental Disease*, **182**(12), 704–708.

Cuffel, B. J. (1992). Prevalence estimates of substance abuse in schizophrenia and their correlates. *Journal of Nervous and Mental Disease*, **180**, 589–592.

Czobor, P., Volavka, J. & Meibach, R. C. (1995). Effect of risperidone on hostility in schizophrenia. *Journal of Clinical Psychopharmacology*, **15**, 243–249.

De Cuyper, H., Van Praag, H. M. & Verstraeten, D. (1985). The effect of milenperone on the aggressive behaviour of oligophrenic patients. A double-blind placebo-controlled study. *Neuropsychobiology*, **13**, 101–105.

Dietch, J. T. & Jennings, R. K. (1988). Aggressive dyscontrol in patients treated with benzodiazepines. *Journal of Clinical Psychiatry*, **49**(5), 184–188.

Ebrahim, G. M., Gibler, B., Gacono, C. B. & Hayes, G. (1994). Patient response to clozapine in a forensic psychiatric hospital. *Hospital and Community Psychiatry*, **45**(3), 271–273.

Eichelman, B. S. & Hartwig, A. C. (Eds) (1995). *Patient Violence and the Clinician.* Washington, DC: American Psychiatric Press.

Elie, R., Langlois, Y., Cooper, S. F., Gravel, G. & Albert, J. M. (1980). Comparison of SCH-12679 and thioridazine in agagressive mental retardates. *Canadian Journal of Psychiatry*, **25**, 484–491.

Eronen, M., Tiihonen, J. & Hakola, P. (1996). Schizophrenia and homicidal behaviour. *Schizophrenia Bulletin*, **22**(1). 83–89.

Fava, M., Rosenbaum, J. F., Pava, J. A., McCarthy, M. K., Steingard, R. J. & Bouffides, E. (1993). Anger attacks in unipolar depression. Part 1. Clinical correlates and response to fluoxetine treatment. *American Journal of Psychiatry*, **150**, 1158–1163.

Fisher, W. A. (1994). Restraint and seclusion: a review of the literature. *American Journal of Psychiatry*, **151**(11), 1584–1591.

Freeman, M. P. & Stoll, A. L. (1998). Mood stabilizer combinations: a review of safety and efficacy. *American Journal of Psychiatry*, **155**(1), 12–21.

Friedman, L. J., Tabb, S. E., Worthington, J. J., Sanchez, C. J. & Sved, M. (1991). Clozapine—a novel antipsychotic agent (letter). *New England Journal of Medicine*, **325**, 518.

Geller, M. P. (1980). Sociopathic adaptations in psychotic patients. *Hospital and Community Psychiatry*, **31**(2), 108–112.

Gertz, B. (1980). Training for prevention of assaultive behaviour in a psychiatric setting. *Hospital and Community Psychiatry*, **31**(9), 628–630.

Goldman, M. B. & Janecek, H. M. (1990). Adjunctive fluoxetine improves global function in chronic schizophrenia. *Journal of Neuropsychiatry and Clinical Neurosciences*, **2**, 429–431.

Greenblatt, D. J., Divoll, M., Harmatz, J. S. & Shader, R. I. (1982). Pharmacokinetic comparison of sublingual lorazepam with intravenous, intramuscular, and oral lorazepam. *Journal of Pharmaceutical Sciences*, **71**(2), 248–252.

Greenblatt, D. J., Shader, R. I., Franke, K., MacLaughlin, D. S., Harmatz, J. S., Allen, M. D., Werner, A. & Woo, E. (1979). Pharmaokinetics and bioavailability of intravenous, intramuscular, and oral lorazepam in humans. *Journal of Pharmaceutical Sciences*, **68**(1), 57–63.

Grinfeld, M. J. (1995). Jury finds Prozac did not cause violence. *Psychiatric Times*, February, p. 33.

Hacke, W. (1980). The pharmacological management of aggressive and autoaggressive behaviour in mentally retarded patients with melperone (author's translation from the German). *Pharmakopsychiatrie Nuero-Psychopharmakologie*, **13**, 20–24.

Hakola, H. P. & Laulumaa, V. A. (1982). Carbamazepine in treatment of violent schizophrenics (letter). *Lancet*, **1**, 1358.

Heilgenstein, J. H., Beasley, C. M. & Potvin, J. H. (1993). Fluoxetine not associated with increased aggression in controlled clinical trials. *International Clinical Psychopharmacology*, **8**, 277–280.

Herrera, J. N., Sramek, J. J., Costa, J. R., Roy, S., Heh, C. W. & Nguyen, B. N. (1988). High potency neuroleptics and violence in schizophrenics. *Journal of Nervous and Mental Disorders*, **176**, 558–561.

Husain, A., Anasseril, D. E. & Harris, P. W. (1983). A study of young-age and mid-life homicidal women admitted to a psychiatric hospital for pre-trial evaluation. *Canadian Journal of Psychiatry*, **28**(2), 109–113.

Kanofsky, J. D. & Lindenmayer, J. P. (1993). Relapse in a clozapine responder following lorazepam withdrawal (letter). *American Journal of Psychiatry*, **150**(2), 348–349.

Karson, C. N., Weinberger, D. R., Bigelow, L. & Wyatt, R. J. (1982). Clonazepam treatment of chronic schizophrenia: negative results in a double-blind, placebo-controlled trial. *American Journal of Psychiatry*, **139**(12), 1627–1628.

Keats, M. M. & Mukherjee, S. (1988). Antiaggressive effect of adjunctive clonazepam in schizophrenia associated with seizure disorder. *Journal of Clinical Psychiatry*, **49**(3), 117–118.

Keckich, W. A. (1978). Neuroleptics. Violence as a manifestation of akathisia. *Journal of the American Medical Association*, **240**, 2185.

Klimke, A. & Klieser, E. (1994). Sudden death after intravenous application of lorazepam in a patient treated with clozapine (letter). *American Journal of Psychiatry*, **151**(5), 780.

Koczapski, A. B., Ledwidge, B., Paredes, J., Kogan, C. & Higenbottam, J. (1990). Multisubstance intoxication among schizophrenic inpatients: reply to Hyde. *Schizophrenia Bulletin*, **16**(3), 373–375.

Koo, J. Y. M. & Chien, C.P. (1986). Coma following ECT and intravenous droperidol: case report. *Journal of Clinical Psychiatry*, **47**(2), 94–95.

Krakowski, M., Convit, A., Jaeger, J., Lin, S. & Volavka, J. (1989a). Inpatient violence: trait and state. *Journal of Psychiatric Research*, **23**(1), 57–64.

Krakowski, M., Convit, A., Jaeger, J., Lin, S. & Volavka, J. (1989b). Neurological impairment in violent schizophrenic inpatients. *American Journal of Psychiatry*, **146**, 849–853.

Lehmann, L. S., Padilla, M., Clark, S. & Loucks, S. (1983). Training personnel in the prevention and management of violent behaviour. *Hospital and Community Psychiatry*, **34**(1), 40–43.

Lindqvist, P. & Allebeck, P. (1990). Schizophrenia and assaultive behaviour: the role of alcohol and drug abuse. *Acta Psychiatrica Scandinavica*, **82**, 191–195.

Linnoila, M., Virkkunen, M., Scheinen, M., Nuutila, A., Rimon, R. & Goodwin, F. K. (1983). Low cerebrospinal fluid 5-hydroxyindole acetic acid concentration differentiates impulsive from non-impulsive violent behaviour. *Life Sciences*, **33**, 2609–2614.

Luchins, D. J. (1984). Carbamazepine in violent non-epileptic schizophrenics. *Psychopharmacology Bulletin*, **20**, 569–571.

Maier, G. J. (1992). The impact of clozapine on 25 forensic patients. *Bulletin of the American Academy of Psychiatry and the Law*, **20**(3), 297–307.

Mallya, A. R., Roos, P. D. & Roebuck-Colgan, K. (1992). Restraint, seclusion, and clozapine. *Journal of Clinical Psychiatry*, **53**(11), 395–397.

Marder, S. R. & Meibach, R. C. (1994).   Risperidone in the treatment of schizo-phrenia. *American Journal of Psychiatry*, **151**(6), 825–835.

McElroy, S. L., Keck, P. E., Pope, H. G. & Hudson, J. I. (1989).   Valproate in psychi-atric disorders: literature review and clinical guidelines. *Journal of Clinical Psychia-try*, **50**(3, suppl.). 23–29.

Mendez, M. F., Doss, R. C. & Taylor, J. L. (1993).   Interictal violence in epilepsy. *Journal of Nervous and Mental Disease*, **181**(9). 566–569.

Morinigo, A., Martin, J., Gonzalez, S. & Mateo, I. (1989).   Treatment of resistant schizophrenia with valproate and neuroleptic drugs. *Hillside Journal of Clinical Psychiatry*, **11**(2), 199–207.

Neppe, V. M. (1983).   Carbamazepine as adjunctive treatment in non-epileptic chronic inpatients with EEG temporal lobe abnormalities. *Journal of Clinical Psychi-atry*, **44**, 326–331.

Neppe, V. M. (1988).   Carbamazepine in non-responsive psychosis. *Journal of Clini-cal Psychiatry*, **49**(4, suppl.), 22–28.

Okuma, T., Yamashita, I., Takahashi, R., Itoh, H., Otsuki, S., Watanabe, S., Sarai, K., Hazama, H. & Inanaga, K. (1989).   A double-blind study of adjunctive car-bamazepine vs. placebo on excited states of schizophrenic and schizoaffective disorders. *Acta Psychiatrica Scandinavica*, **80**, 250–259.

Palmstierna, T., Huitfeldt, B. & Wistedt, B. (1991).   The relationship of crowding and aggressive behaviour on a psychiatric intensive care unit. *Hospital and Community Psychiatry*, **42**(12), 1237–1240.

Pope, H. G. & Lipinski, J. F. Jr (1978).   Diagnosis in schizophrenia and manic-depressive illness: a reassessment of the specificity of "schizophrenic" symptoms in the light of current research. *Archives of General Psychiatry*, **35**(7), 811–828.

Prakash, R. (1985).   Lithium-responsive schizophrenia: case reports. *Journal of Clini-cal Psychiatry*, **46**, 141–142.

Rao, N., Jellinek, H. M. & Woolston, D. C. (1985).   Agitation in closed head injury: haloperidol effects on rehabilitation outcome. *Archives of Physical Medicine and Rehabilitation*, **66**, 30–34.

Rasmussen, P. (1989).   Prescription of neuroleptics to mentally retarded patients is broadly criticized (in Swedish). *Lakartidningen*, **86**, 3977.

Ratey, J. J., Leveroni, C., Kilmer, D., Gutheil, C. & Swartz, B. (1993).   The effects of clozapine on severely aggressive psychiatric inpatients in a state hospital. *Journal of Clinical Psychiatry*, **54**, 219–223.

Ratey, J.J., Sorgi, P., O'Driscoll, G. A., Sands, S., Daehler, M. L., Fletcher, J. R., Kadish, W., Spruiell, G., Polakoff, S., Lindem, K. J., Bemporad, J. R., Richardson, L. & Rosenfeld, B. (1992).   Nadolol to treat aggression and psychiatric symptomatol-ogy in chronic psychiatric inpatients: a double-blind, placebo-controlled study. *Journal of Clinical Psychiatry*, **53**, 41–46.

Regier, D. A., Farmer, M. E., Rae, D. S., Locke, B. Z., Keith, S. J., Judd, L. L. & Goodwin, F. K. (1990).   Co-morbidity of mental disorders with alcohol and other drug abuse. Results from the Epidemiologic Catchment Area (ECA) Study. *Journal of the American Medical Association*, **264**, 2511–2518.

Robins, L. N., Tipp, J. & Przybeck, T. (1991).   Antisocial personality. In L. N. Robins & D. A. Regier (Eds), *Psychiatric Disorders in America. The Epidemiologic Catchment Area Study* (pp. 258–290). New York: Free Press.

Robins, L. N. (1966).   *Deviant Children Grown Up. A Sociological and Psychiatric Study of Sociopathic Personality* (p. 240). Baltimore, MD: Williams & Wilkins.

Rosenbaum, M. & Bennett, B. (1986).   Homicide and depression. *American Journal of Psychiatry*, **143**(3). 367–370.

Roy, A. & Linnoila, M. (1988).   Suicidal behaviour, impulsiveness and serotonin. *Acta Psychiatrica Scandinavica*, **78**, 529–535.

Salzman, C. (1988).   Use of benzodiazepines to control disruptive behaviour in inpatients. *Journal of Clinical Psychiatry*, **49** (12, suppl.). 13–15.

Schatzberg, A. F. & Cole, J. O. (1991).   *Manual of Clinical Psychopharmacology*, 2nd edn (p. 99). Washington, DC: American Psychiatric Press.

Shalev, H., Hermesh, H. & Munitz, H. (1987).   Severe akathisia causing neuroleptic failure: an indication for lithium therapy in schizophrenia? *Acta Psychiatrica Scandinavica*, **76**, 715–718.

Sheppard, G. P. (1979).   High-dose propranolol in schizophrenia. *British Journal of Psychiatry*, **134**, 470–476.

Simhandl, C. & Meszaros, K. (1992).   The use of carbamazepine in the treatment of schizophrenic and schizoaffective psychoses: a review. *Journal of Psychiatry and Neuroscience*, **17**(1), 1–14.

Siris, S. G. (1985).   Three cases of akathisia and "acting out". *Journal of Clinical Psychiatry*, **46**, 395–397.

Smith, J. & Hucker, S. (1994).   Schizophrenia and substance abuse. *British Journal of Psychiatry*, **165**, 13–21.

Sorgi, P. J., Ratey, J. J. & Polakoff, S. (1986).   Beta-adrenergic blockers for the control of aggressive behaviours in patients with chronic schizophrenia. *American Journal of Psychiatry*, **143**, 775–776.

Swanson, J. W. (1994).   Mental disorder, substance abuse, and community violence: an epidemiological approach. In J. Monahan & H.J. Steadman (Eds), *Violence and Mental Disorder. Developments in Risk Assessment* (pp. 101–136). Chicago: University of Chicago Press.

Swartz, M. S., Swanson, J. W., Hiday, V. A., Borum, R., Wagner, H. R. & Burns, B. J. (1998).   Violence and severe mental illness: the effects of substance abuse and non-adherence to medication. *American Journal of Psychiatry*, **155**(2), 226–231.

Tardiff, K. (1992).   The current state of psychiatry in the treatment of violent patients. *Archives of General Psychiatry*, **49**, 493–499.

Teicher, M. H., Glod, C. & Cole, J. O. (1990).   Emergence of intense suicidal preoccupation during fluoxetine treatment. *American Journal of Psychiatry*, **147**(2), 207–210.

Thackrey, M. (1987).   *Therapeutics for Aggression: Psychological/Physical Crisis Intervention*. New York: Human Science Press.

Thomas, H., Schwartz, E. & Petrilli, R. (1992).   Droperidol vs. haloperidol for chemical restraint of agitated and combative patients. *Annals of Emergency Medicine*, **21**(4), 407–413.

Tollefson, G. D., Rampey, A. H., Beasley, C. M., Enas, G. G. & Potvin, J. H. (1994).   Absence of a relationship between adverse events and suicidality during pharmacotherapy for depression. *Journal of Clinical Psychopharmacology*, **14**(3), 163–169.

Travin, S. & Protter, B. (1982).   Mad or bad? Some clinical considerations in the misdiagnosis of schizophrenia as antisocial personality disorder. *American Journal of Psychiatry*, **139**, 1335–1338.

Tupin, J. P. (1983).   The violent patient: a strategy for management and diagnosis. *Hospital and Community Psychiatry*, **34**(1), 37–40.

Vartiainen, H., Tiihonen, J., Putkonen, A., Virkkunen, M., Hakola, P. & Lehto, H. (1995). Citalopram, a selective serotonin reuptake inhibitor, in the treatment of aggression in schizophrenia. *Acta Psychiatrica Scandinavica*, **91**, 348–351.

Virkkunen, M., De Jong, J., Bartko, J. & Linnoila, M. (1989).   Psychobiological con-
comitants of history of suicide attempts among violent offenders and impulsive
fire setters. *Archives of General Psychiatry*, **46**, 604–606.
Virkkunen, M., Goldman, D., Nielsen, D. A. & Linnoila, M. (1995).   Low brain
serotonin turnover rate (low CSF 5-HIAA) and impulsive violence. *Journal of Psychiatry and Neuroscience*, **20**, 271–275.
Virkkunen, M. & Linnoila, M. (1990).   Serotonin in early onset, male alcoholics with
violent behaviour. *Annals of Medicine*, **22**, 327–331.
Volavka, J. & Krakowski, M. (1989).   Schizophrenia and violence. *Psychological Medi-
cine*, **19**, 559–562.
Volavka, J., Zito, J.M, Vitrai, J. & Czobor, P. (1993).   Clozapine effects on hostility
and aggression in schizophrenia. *Journal of Clinical Psychopharmacology*, **13**, 287–289.
Volavka, J. (1988).   Can aggressive behaviour in humans be modified by beta-
blockers? *Postgraduate Medicine* (a Special Report). February 29, 163–168.
Volavka, J. (1995).   *Neurobiology of Violence*. Washington, DC: American Psychiatric
Press.
Wassef, A., Watson, D.J., Morrison, P., Bryant, S. & Flack, J. (1989).   Neuroleptic–
valproic acid combination in treatment of psychotic symptoms: a three-case report.
Journal of Clinical Psychopharmacology, **9**, 45–48.
Wilcox, J. (1994).   Divalproex sodium in the treatment of aggressive behaviour.
Annals of Clinical Psychiatry, **6**(1), 17–20.
Wilson, W. H. & Claussen, A. M. (1995).   18-Month outcome of clozapine treatment
for 100 patients in a state psychiatric hospital. *Psychiatric Services*, **46**, 386–389.
Wilson, W. H. (1993).   Addition of lithium to haloperidol in non-affective, anti-
psychotic non-responsive schizophrenia: a double-blind, placebo-controlled paral-
lel design clinical trial. *Psychopharmacology*, **111**, 359–366.
Yesavage, J. A. (1983).   Bipolar illness: correlates of dangerous inpatient behaviour.
British Journal of Psychiatry, **143**, 554–557.
Young, J. L. & Hillbrand, M. (1994).   Carbamazepine lowers aggression: a review.
Bulletin of the American Academy of Psychiatry and the Law, **22**(1), 53–61.
Yudofsky, S., Williams, D. & Gorman, J. (1981).   Propranolol in the treatment of rage
and violent behaviour in patients with chronic brain syndrome. *American Journal of
Psychiatry*, **138**, 218–220.
Yudofsky, S. C., Silver, J. M. & Hales, R. E. (1990).   Pharmacologic management of
aggression in the elderly, *Journal of Clinical Psychiatry*, **51**:10 (suppl.), 22–28.
Yudofsky, S. C., Stevens, L., Silver, J. M., Barsa, J. & Williams, D. (1984).   Propranolol in the treatment of rage and violent behaviour associated with Kor-
sakoff's psychosis. *American Journal of Psychiatry*, **141**, 114–115.
Zapletalek, M., Hametova, M. & Rydlova, E. (1989) Isofloxythepin in restless
oligophrenic children. *Activatas Nervosa Superior*, **31**, 265.
Zemlan, F. P., Hirschowitz, J., Sautter, F. J. & Garver, D. L. (1984).   Impact of lithium
therapy on core psychotic symptoms of schizophrenia. *British Journal of Psychiatry*,
144, 64–69.

Chapter 8

PHARMACOLOGICAL TREATMENTS FOR PERSONALITY DISORDERED OFFENDERS

JARI TIIHONEN

Department of Forensic Psychiatry, University of Kuopio, Kuopio, Finland

INTRODUCTION

Epidemiological studies from the Nordic countries indicate that antisocial and borderline personality disorders and substance abuse are the most important mental disorders contributing to severe violent behaviour (Hodgins, 1992; Tiihonen, Eronen & Hakola, 1993a; Tiihonen & Hakola, 1994; Eronen, 1995; Eronen et al., 1995; Hodgins et al., 1996; Eronen, Hakola & Tiihonen, 1996a, b, c; Räsänen et al., 1998; Tiihonen et al., 1997a). Studies of Swedish and Danish birth cohorts have shown among both sexes higher odds ratios (OR) or relative risks (RR) for substance abuse (Hodgins, 1992), as well as for alcohol and drug use disorders and antisocial personality disorder (Hodgins et al., 1996), when compared with other psychiatric disorders. In a Finnish birth cohort study of major mental disorders and criminality, the highest OR for having at least one registered crime was obtained for males with alcohol-induced psychoses (Tiihonen et al., 1997a). Studies of homicide offenders using comprehensive nationwide cohorts have shown markedly higher OR

Violence, Crime and Mentally Disordered Offenders. Edited by S. Hodgins and R. Müller-Isberner.
© 2000 John Wiley & Sons, Ltd.

for antisocial personality disorder and alcoholism than for other mental disorders among both males and females (Tiihonen, Eronen & Hakola, 1993a; Eronen, 1995; Eronen, Hakola & Tiihonen, 1996a). None of the afore-mentioned studies separately investigated different personality disorders, except antisocial personality disorder. To date, the association between spe-cific personality disorders and severe violent (homicidal) behaviour in a large, comprehensive cohort has been investigated in only one published study (Eronen et al., 1995). The results showed that 57% of 510 homicide offenders (males and females) obtained personality disorder diagnosis in the forensic psychiatric examination. Among homicide offenders, the most com-mon personality disorders were mixed-type personality disorder (usually with antisocial features) (17%), antisocial personality disorder (15%) and borderline personality disorder (13%).

When the prevention of violent or criminal behaviour is considered, one has to focus efforts on those subjects who have shown previous habitual violent or criminal behaviour. However, there exist very few meth-odologically sound published data about the association between mental disorders and recidivistic violent behaviour. Three different studies from the Nordic countries suggest that about 70–80% of homicide recidivistic offend-ers have a personality disorder and most of those also a coexisting alcohol use disorder (Adler & Lidberg, 1995; Eronen, Hakola & Tiihonen, 1996c; Tiihonen & Hakola, 1994). Only in one study were the clinical data and diagnoses presented in detail (Tiihonen & Hakola, 1994). The results of this study showed that 77% of recidivistic homicide offenders fulfilled the diag-nostic criteria of DSM-III-R for antisocial personality disorder and alcohol dependence (type 2). While there are no comparable studies from outside Finland, Sweden and Denmark, it is apparent that early-onset alcohol de-pendence associated with antisocial personality disorder (type 2 alcoholism; Cloninger, 1987) is the most important factor in repetitive violent behaviour in the Nordic countries (Adler & Lidberg, 1995; Tiihonen & Hakola, 1994; Eronen, Hakola & Tiihonen, 1996c). In the USA, the use of illicit drugs— especially cocaine—is a relatively more important factor.

Recent studies suggest that the prevalence of antisocial personality disor-der is as high as 3% among men and about 1% among women in the USA (Perry & Vaillant, 1989). According to the DSM-III-R and DSM-IV diagnostic criteria, subjects with antisocial personality disorder have a conduct disor-der with onset before the age of 15, and a pattern or irresponsible and antisocial behaviour as adults. Antisocial personality disorder is quite resist-ant to treatment, and a rule of thumb is that, after 21 years of age, 2% of all antisocial personalities remit each year (Perry & Vaillant, 1989). However, only some of the antisocial personalities commit habitually criminal of-fences, and relatively little is known about the course of the psychopathol-ogy of these repetitive offenders. It is generally believed that criminality, and violent offending especially, decreases as a function of age. However, there are no published studies that have investigated the incidence of violent offending in different age groups and have taken into account the markedly higher mortality among habitual offenders. Data from Finnish offenders suggest that the incidence of committing homicides is highest between ages 27 and 30 years, and decreases by 75% during the next 20 years (to age 50) (M. Eronen, personal communication). However, since mortality is approximately five times higher among habitually violent offenders between ages 30 and 50 years compared with males of the same age group in the general population in Finland (Paanila, Hakola & Tiihonen, 1999), about 36% of habitually violent offenders die between ages 30 and 50 years. If we assume that the population of potential homicide offenders have a mortality of the same magnitude, the real decrease in the incidence of committing a homicide between ages 30 and 50 years is about 60%.

The prevalence of borderline personality disorder has been estimated to be approximately 2% and is twice as common among females as males (Perry & Vaillant, 1989). This suggests that it may be a more important factor contributing to violent behaviour among females than males. Studies with follow-up periods as long as five years suggest that borderline patients change little over time, but that this personality disorder is rarely first diagnosed in patients older than 40 years. This latter fact may be explained by maturation and, possibly, by increased rates of premature death.

While abnormalities in the monoaminergic activity of the brains of individuals with personality disorders, substance dependence and impulsive violent behaviour have been revealed in investigations of cerebrospinal fluid (CSF) (Virkkunen et al., 1989, 1994, 1996) and brain imaging studies (Tiihonen et al., 1995, 1997b), the aetiologies of these disorders remain unclear. There are very few controlled studies of the efficacy of pharmacological treatments in individuals with personality disorders, substance abuse and habitual violent or criminal behaviour. At present, there are no published controlled studies which have investigated the efficacy of pharmacological treatment in preventing crime and violence, using the incidence of offences (e.g. from police or prison registers) as an outcome measure. The obvious reason for this is that large placebo-controlled studies among populations prone to criminal behaviour are extremely difficult to conduct, mainly due to poor compliance and cooperation from the individuals involved.

The pharmacological treatment of violent and criminal behaviour can be achieved by treating the underlying mental disorder or by treating the violent behaviour *per se* as a symptom. At the moment, there is no specific treatment for personality disorders. Because a substantial proportion of the habitual criminal violence by subjects with personality disorders or substance abuse is thought to be explained by poor impulse control (Marzuk,

1996), treatment of the impulsive behaviour is the main target when preventing violence with pharmacological agents. Another approach is to treat substance abuse, which contributes to offending in several ways. Although relatively effective treatments have been obtained during the last few years for alcohol use disorders, treatments for drug use disorders are still in the developmental phase.

There are no published studies of the efficacy of pharmacological treatment in preventing criminal and violent behaviour in subjects with primary alcohol and drug abuse. Alcohol use disorders without coexisting personality disorder increases the risk of homicide by a factor of two, whereas alcohol dependence with a co-morbid personality disorder is associated with an over 10-fold increase in risk of committing a homicide (Tiihonen, Eronen & Hakola, 1993a). It is obvious that criminal behaviour can be influenced by alcohol and drug abuse in several different ways: (a) acute intake of ethanol, amphetamine and cocaine induce a rapid release of dopamine in the limbic system, causing euphoria and an increase in aggressive behaviour (Baggio & Ferrari, 1980; Thor & Ghiselli, 1975; Barros & Miczek, 1996; Rossetti et al., 1991; Sorensen et al., 1992; Spanagel et al., 1991); (b) chronic intake of alcohol (and possibly other drugs) leads to the suppression of cerebral blood flow and metabolism, especially in the frontal lobe, which may affect impulse control (Kuruoğlu et al., 1996); (c) long-term chronic intake of alcohol and drugs leads to cerebral atrophy and organic brain disorder, which affects impulse control (Charness, 1993); and (d) substance abusers commit crimes to finance their drug use. Therefore, it is obvious that effective treatment of alcohol and drug use disorder would be beneficial in preventing criminal behaviour, even among those individuals who do not present a coexisting personality disorder.

PHARMACOLOGICAL TREATMENT OF IMPULSIVE AND VIOLENT BEHAVIOUR IN PATIENTS WITH PERSONALITY DISORDERS

The efficacy of pharmacological treatment of impulsive and violent behaviour has been studied in a few open and controlled studies among subjects with personality disorders. The study designs and the key results of these studies are presented in Table 8.1.

Lithium

The study by Sheard and colleagues (1976) is the only double-blind placebo-controlled trial on the efficacy of pharmacological treatment of impulsive

Table 8.1 The effectiveness of pharmacological treatments on the impulsive and violent behaviour in subjects with personality disorders or impulse-control disorders

Study	Study design	Key findings
Lithium (Sheard et al., 1976)	Double-blind placebo-controlled trial of 66 impulsive violent prisoners with psychotic disorders	Lithium significantly reduced impulsive violent behaviour. The number of infractions of institutional rules committed by the subjects was reported by the institutional staff
Carbamazepine (Mattes, 1984)	Open uncontrolled study of 34 inpatients with rage outbursts (most patients had intermittent explosive disorder)	Carbamazepine reduced the severity of outbursts. Ratings (non-structured) by psychiatrist, patient and research assistant evaluated improvement
Metoprolol (Mattes, 1985)	Open study with two patients with intermittent explosive disorder	Metoprolol reduced aggression as evaluated by the patient and the psychiatrist
Valproic acid (Wilcox, 1994)	35 patients with borderline personality disorder ($n = 10$, bipolar disorder ($n = 11$), schizophrenia spectrum disorder ($n = 14$)	Valproic acid reduced the need for seclusion
Fluoxetine (Coccaro et al., 1990)	Open trial with three patients with personality disorders	Fluoxetine reduced impulsive aggression as assessed with the Overt Aggression Scale (OAS-M) (Yudofsky et al., 1986)
Fluoxetine (Markovitz et al., 1991)	Open 12-week trial with 22 patients with borderline or schizotypal personality disorder	Fluoxetine reduced self-mutilation, as evaluated with Hopkins Symptom Checklist and self-reports
Fluoxetine (Cornelius et al., 1991)	Open study in five patients with borderline personality disorder	Fluoxetine reduced impulsiveness as assessed with Ward Scale (Soloff et al., 1986)
Fluoxetine (Salzman et al., 1995)	Double-blind placebo-controlled trial with 22 patients with borderline personality disorder	Fluoxetine was significantly more effective in decreasing anger than placebo as assessed with OAS, Personality Disorder Rating Scale (PDRS) (Salzman et al., 1995) and Profile of Mood States (POMP) (McNair, Lorr & Droppleman, 1981).
Fluoxetine (Coccaro & Kavoussi, 1997)	Double-blind placebo-controlled trial with 40 subjects with DSM-III-R personality disorders	Fluoxetine significantly reduced irritability and aggression as assessed with the OAS-M

violent behaviour in subjects with personality disorders. The results of this study indicate that lithium is effective in reducing violent behaviour, even at relatively low plasma levels (< 1.0 mmol/l). Data obtained from an open (non-blind) study in violent prisoners with schizophrenia or organic mental syndromes (Tupin et al., 1973), suggest that lithium reduces aggressive behaviour in various mental disorders.

Lithium may induce severe side effects, especially in the long term. Also, acute side effects may have a substantial effect on treatment compliance: for example, in the study by Sheard et al. (1976) about one-third of the subjects stopped their medication due to adverse events such as hand tremor or shakiness, dryness of mouth, polyuria and nausea. In long-term treatment, the most important side effects are: electrocardiogram (ECG) and electroencephalogram (EEG) abnormalities; dysfunction of the kidneys, resulting in increased creatinine levels; and dysfunction (hypoactivity) of the thyroid gland, resulting in decreased thyroxin (T4) levels. Because of the narrow therapeutic range of serum concentration and the adverse effects—the lithium levels, as well the functioning of the kidneys, the thyroid gland and the heart—must be monitored by laboratory tests. During long-term treatment laboratory tests should be conducted at 2–6 month intervals.

Anticonvulsants

There are no controlled studies documenting the anti-aggressive effects of carbamazepine in subjects with personality disorders or substance abuse. The results of the open (non-blind) trial by Mattes (1984) suggest that carbamazepine may reduce the severity of rage outbursts in patients with intermittent explosive disorder or attention deficit disorder. An open trial by Wilcox (1994) indicated that valproic acid also may reduce impulsive behaviour in patients with borderline personality disorder.

SSRIs

Selective serotonin re-uptake inhibitors (SSRIs), such as fluoxetine, increase central serotonergic transmission. Since habitual impulsive violent behaviour is associated with dysfunction of the CNS serotonergic system (Virkkunen et al., 1989, 1994, 1996), it could be logically argued that these agents should enhance impulse control and suppress impulsive violent or criminal behaviour. At present, only two controlled trials have been published investigating the effect of SSRIs on impulsive and aggressive behaviour in subjects with personality disorder (Salzman et al., 1995; Coccaro & Kavoussi, 1997). The study by Salzman and colleagues (1995) demonstrated that fluoxetine significantly decreased anger among patients with borderline personality disorder. The results of the investigation conducted by Coccaro and Kavoussi (1997) showed that treatment with fluoxetine resulted in a sustained reduction of irritability and aggression during a three month trial. The daily dose of fluoxetine was 20–60 mg and the mean plasma levels of fluoxetine were 300–400 ng/ml during the last month of the trial. The results of open studies also indicate that fluoxetine reduces impulsive behaviour in patients with personality disorders (Cornelius et al., 1991; Markovitz et al., 1991). A meta-analysis of the results of placebo-controlled trials which included several thousands of patients with various medical conditions, such as alcohol dependence, obsessive-compulsive disorder and depression, showed that aggressive symptoms were significantly less frequent in patients receiving fluoxetine than in those receiving placebo (Heiligenstein, Beasley & Potvin, 1993).

β-Blockers

β-Adrenergic blockers have not been studied in the treatment of aggressive behaviour in subjects with personality disorder, with the exception of a case report of two patients with intermittent explosive disorder (Mattes, 1985). In addition, a beneficial effect has been attributed to propranolol in children and adolescents with organic brain dysfunction and uncontrolled rage outbursts (Williams et al., 1982).

Anxiolytics

Buspirone, a serotonergic anxiolytic, has proved to be effective in reducing aggressive behaviour among mentally retarded patients in a double-blind placebo-controlled study (Ratey et al., 1991), but no published studies exist on its efficacy in treating patients with other mental disorders. Benzodiazepines can be used to calm a patient with a personality disorder in the acute phase, but their long-term use in subjects with personality disorders, substance abuse and habitual violent behaviour is contraindicated due to their potential addictive properties.

Antipsychotics

The suppression of aggressive behaviour by neuroleptic treatment seen in psychotic patients is not fully explained by a reduction of their psychotic symptoms, such as hallucinations or delusions, or by sedation, and it seems clear that clozapine (Chiles, Davidson & McBride, 1994) and risperidone (Czobor, Volavka & Meibach, 1995) may have some selective effect on hostility and aggression. On the other hand, those drugs which provoke the most aggressive behaviour (ethanol, cocaine and amphetamine) also induce a rapid release of dopamine into the limbic system (Baggio & Ferrari, 1980; Thor & Ghiselli, 1975; Barros & Miczek, 1996; Rossetti et al., 1991; Sorensen et al., 1992; Spanagel et al., 1991). Therefore, it could be reasoned that dopamine blockers—such as neuroleptics—could be used to control violent behaviour among persons with personality disorders or substance abuse. The classical neuroleptics and clozapine suffer from many major adverse effects, which result in poor compliance, but the new atypical neuroleptics, such as risperidone and especially olanzapine and sertindole, are well tolerated. The efficacy of these agents in the treatment of violent behaviour among non-psychotic subjects should be studied in long-term placebo-controlled trials. Unfortunately, this is a tremendously difficult task.

Serenics

Eltoprazine is classified as belonging to the group of "serenics", which are 5-HT_1-receptor agonists. These agents have a selective anti-aggressive effect in animals (Rasmussen et al., 1990). The role of 5-HT_{1B}-agonism has been demonstrated recently in a knock-out gene study in which mice lacking serotonin 5-HT_{1B} receptors were shown to be very aggressive (Saudou et al., 1994).

The clinical efficacy of serenics in human aggression has been studied in mentally retarded subjects (Verhoeven et al., 1992; Kohen, 1993; Tiihonen et al., 1993b; de Koning et al., 1994) and schizophrenic patients (Tiihonen et al., 1993b). These studies have shown that eltoprazine may be effective in those patient groups, but in the lone double-blind study published, eltoprazine was statistically significantly more effective in the treatment of hetero-aggressive or auto-aggressive behaviour only in the most aggressive mentally retarded patients (de Koning et al., 1994). One could postulate that the most promising—and clinically significant—patient group for evaluating 5-HT_{1B}-agonist therapy would be those individuals with personality disorders and habitual impulsive aggressive behaviour. However, no such studies have been conducted in these populations.

Opiate antagonists

In mentally retarded patients, self-mutilation may be not an impulsive act but deliberate euphoria-seeking behaviour. By damaging body tissue, pain is induced and endorphins are released; endorphins suppress the pain but also induce a euphoric feeling, which reinforces auto-aggressive behaviour. Therefore, it is not surprising that opiate antagonists such as naltrexone have been reported to reduce self-mutilation and aggression among mentally retarded patients (Campbell et al., 1989; Osman & Loschen, 1992; Casner, Weinheimer & Gualtieri, 1996). It is quite possible that self-mutilation could be treated pharmacologically with opiate antagonists in subjects with personality disorders, but thus far no data, with the exception of a single case report (McGee, 1997), have been published. A recent case report suggests that naltrexone might be effective in the treatment of kleptomania (Kim, 1998).

PHARMACOLOGICAL TREATMENT OF PRIMARY ALCOHOL AND DRUG ABUSE DISORDERS

Until the present decade, pharmacological treatment of alcohol dependence had appeared to be quite ineffective. Disulfiram (Fuller & Roth, 1979; Fuller et al., 1986) and lithium (Dorus et al., 1989) have been studied in controlled clinical trials which failed to demonstrate any significant differences in outcome for patients receiving the active medication and patients receiving placebo. The results of controlled studies (Naranjo et al., 1987; Naranjo & Sellers, 1989) suggest that the SSRIs, citalopram and zimelidine, are effective in the treatment of the early-stages of problem drinking. The results from a recent study indicate that citalopram is significantly more effective than placebo, even in the treatment of severe, early onset alcohol dependence (Tiihonen et al., 1996). However, some recent studies indicate that SSRIs may not have any significant effect in reducing craving and alcohol use (Agosti, 1995).

In 1992, the results of two double-blind placebo-controlled studies with naltrexone were published which both demonstrated its substantial efficacy in the treatment of alcohol dependence (Volpicelli et al., 1992; O'Malley et al., 1992). The results showed that patients receiving placebo had approximately twice the rate of relapse as those receiving naltrexone. A recent large clinical trial showed that 43% of patients receiving acamprosate remained abstinent during a one year follow-up period, compared to 21% of patients receiving placebo (Sass et al., 1996). It can be concluded on the basis of evidence from large clinical trials that both naltrexone and acamprosate are safe and effective agents for treating alcohol-dependent patients.

Pharmacological treatment of drug abuse has focused mainly on patients with opioid dependence. Pharmacological treatment for subjects abusing cocaine, amphetamine and other synthetic drugs is still at a developmental stage, although some studies have shown lower rates of cocaine use in buprenorphine-maintained patients (Kosten, Kleber & Morgan, 1989a, b). Ibogaine, an N-methyl-D-aspartate (NMDA) antagonist, is regarded as a potential pharmacological treatment for cocaine and stimulant abuse (Popik et al., 1995). Studies on the treatment of opioid dependence have shown that although methadone maintenance (Schottenfeld & Kleber, 1995) and buprenorphine maintenance treatments (Schottenfeld et al., 1997) are quite successful, the use of illicit drugs, especially cocaine, persists in up to 40% of patients (Schottenfeld et al., 1997). Methadone treatment is more likely to be effective when higher doses, longer durations of treatment and more realistic goals are set (Wodak, 1994). L-α-acetylmethadol (LAAM) has similar properties to methadone but a longer half-life, which should result in clinical advantages. Naltrexone is used in the opiate relapse prevention of detoxified patients (Tennant et al., 1984), and clonidine has been used in opioid detoxification (Warner, Kosten & O'Connor, 1997). The clinical treatment of cannabis and hallucinogen abuse has not been adequately studied, but since these agents do not markedly induce euphoria, they are not markedly addictive.

In order to be effective, the pharmacological treatment of alcohol and drug abuse has to be integrated into a treatment programme which includes, for example, counselling and supportive or cognitive therapy. The results of the study of naltrexone treatment of alcohol dependence showed that the cumulative rate of abstinence was highest for patients treated with naltrexone and supportive therapy, and that among those patients who began drinking again, those who received both naltrexone and coping skills therapy were the least likely to relapse (O'Malley et al., 1992). Methadone maintenance treatment is an attractive treatment option for the majority of drug users and also cost-effective for the society (Wodak, 1994). Since many such patients are likely to use methadone and illicit drugs, they are not usually allowed to take doses with them to be used without supervision. Methadone is most successfully used in structured programmes which include other treatment components, such as social skills training and job training, and also strict monitoring of methadone and other drug use by urine analysis.

CONCLUDING REMARKS

Habitual violent behaviour has a remarkable impact on public health and the quality of life in many industrialized countries. In developed societies, a large proportion of violent and criminal behaviour is attributable to individuals with antisocial and borderline personality disorders, alcohol use disorders and cocaine and amphetamine abuse. Although it might be feasible to treat these conditions, which form the foundation for habitual violent and criminal behaviour—and possibly also the impulsive violent behaviour *per se*—no substantial effort has been invested in evaluating the effectiveness of pharmacological treatments in these populations using large double-blind placebo-controlled trials. The reason for this is not that there are no potentially effective pharmacological agents, but rather the practical difficulties which would be encountered in organizing a well-controlled trial. While the aggressive behaviour of psychotic inpatients can be observed by staff during relatively long treatment in hospital, and the intake of drugs can be reliably documented, it is much more difficult to quantify and assess violent and criminal behaviour and drug intake among offenders released back into the community. Their behaviour can only be observed when they are incarcerated in prisons or other institutions. They are unlikely to commit offences during imprisonment (except for a small subgroup of the most impulsive subjects) because of supervision by the staff and the limited access to alcohol and drugs which induce their violent behaviour. An even more important issue is that if there were drugs available which were proved to be well-tolerated and effective in the prevention of criminal and violent behaviour, how could the pharmacological treatment be achieved regularly and effectively in practice? There are at least three ways to guarantee appropriate intake and dosage of the drugs in research and clinical practice. One possibility would be to give the drug orally under supervision (such as is already done with methadone and buprenorphine treatment), but this requires two to seven visits per week, depending on the pharmacological properties of the drug. Another method would be to monitor plasma levels of the medication in order to confirm its appropriate use. Technically, a third possibility would be to make an intramuscular depot injection of, for example, SSRIs, although at present no such preparation is available. Since one cannot expect compliance and cooperation from habitual offenders, the only way to ensure such long-term treatment in the community would be to use legislation which compelled offenders being released to probation to comply with treatment. If the offender refused, the alternative option would be serving the entire sentence in a correctional facility without any possibility of release on parole.

The results of controlled clinical studies have shown that lithium, carbamazepine, SSRIs, β-blockers and buspirone decrease impulsive and aggressive behaviour in patients with various mental disorders. These trials have focused mainly on psychotic and mentally retarded patients and, therefore, there is less extensive evidence of their effectiveness in patients with personality disorders. In clinical practice, SSRIs can be regarded as suitable treatment for impulsive patients in an outpatient setting, since they do not cause any severe adverse effects, there is no need for laboratory tests, and they do not have narrow therapeutic windows like lithium and carbamazepine. Evidence from controlled clinical trials indicates that the first choice of treatment for impulsive and aggressive behaviour among patients with personality disorders is fluoxetine, starting with a dose of 20 mg/day which can be increased to 60 mg/day. Fluoxetine is well tolerated and the most common side effect, as with other SSRIs, is nausea. If fluoxetine is not effective, lithium (plasma levels 0.8–1.2 mmol/l) or carbamazepine (up to 1200 mg/day) can be used under supervision (e.g. in hospitals and prisons), so that appropriate dosage can be established, plasma concentrations measured and severe adverse effects, such as heart, kidneys and thyroid dysfunction, can be detected early. The key issue is to ensure that the patient uses the medication according to instructions. It remains to be seen whether the first possibly specific anti-aggressive agents, the serenics, will actually be effective in the treatment of violent behaviour in subjects with personality disorders, as one might predict on the basis of the results with the $5-HT_{1B}$-agonist, eltoprazine.

Naltrexone and acamprosate are the first really effective pharmacological treatments for alcohol use disorders. Acamprosate (with doses up to 2000 mg/day) has proved to be well tolerated in long-term use. The rate of adverse events did not differ much from those of placebo in a two year follow-up study (Sass et al., 1996). The most common side effects during acamprosate treatment are nausea and diarrhoea. Naltrexone has been used in a dose of 50 mg/day, and it is generally quite well tolerated. The most usual adverse effects are nausea and dizziness. Since naltrexone may affect liver functioning, it should be used with care among those with liver dysfunction. However, since naltrexone is effective because it prevents the subject from getting any euphoric feeling from ethanol intake, the patient must be cooperative and motivated or—as in the case of habitual offenders—he/she must be forced to take the drug under supervision, or otherwise compelled to use the medication according to the instructions. In all cases, patients should also receive counselling and, if possible, supportive or coping skills therapy. Opiate dependence can be treated relatively effectively with methadone or buprenorphine under supervision, but treatments for cocaine, amphetamine and other synthetic drugs are still in their infancy. Research is being done to find new approaches to the treatment of drug abuse, for example molecular biological research has pointed to new ways (Fox et al., 1996) and one could anticipate that a vaccine against cocaine will be available within the next decade.

REFERENCES

Adler, H. & Lidberg, H. (1995).   Characteristics of repeat killers in Sweden. *Criminal Behaviour and Mental Health*, **5**, 5–13.

Agosti, V. (1995).   The efficacy of treatments in reducing alcohol consumption: a meta-analysis. *International Journal of Addictions*, **30**, 1067–1077.

Baggio, G. & Ferrari, F. (1980).   Role of brain dopaminergic mechanisms in rodent aggressive behaviour: Influence of (+, −) N-n-propyl-norapomorphine on three experimental models. *Psychopharmacology*, **70**, 63–68.

Barros, H. M. T. & Miczek, K. A. (1996). Neurobiological and behavioral charac-teristics of alcohol-heightened aggression. In D. M. Stoff and R. B. Cairns (Eds), *Aggression and Violence. Genetic, Neurobiological, and Biosocial Perspectives* (pp. 237–264). Hillsdale, NJ: Erlbaum.

Campbell, M., Overall, J. E., Small, A. M., Sokol, M. S., Spencer, E. K., Adams, P., Poltz, R. L., Monti, K. M., Peny, R., Nobler, M. & Roberts, E. (1989). Naltrexone in autistic children: an acute open dose range tolerance trial. *Journal of Child and Adolescent Psychiatry*, **28**, 200–206.

Casner, J. A., Weinheimer, B. & Gualtieri, T. (1996). Naltrexone and self-injurious behavior: a retrospective population study. *Journal of Clinical Psychopharmacology*, **16**, 389–394.

Charness, M. E. (1993). Brain lesions in alcoholics. *Alcohol*, **17**, 2–11.

Chiles, J. A., Davidson, P. & McBride, D. (1994). Effects of clozapine on use of seclusion and restraint at a state hospital. *Hospital and Community Psychiatry*, **45**, 269–271.

Cloninger, C. R. (1987). Neurogenetic adaptive mechanisms in alcoholism. *Science*, **236**, 410–416.

Coccaro, E. F., Astill, J. L., Herbert, J. L. & Schut, A. G. (1990). Fluoxetine treatment of impulsive aggression in DSM-III-R personality disorder patients. *Journal of Clinical Psychopharmacology*, **10**, 373–375.

Coccaro, E. F. & Kavoussi, R. J. (1997). Fluoxetine and impulsive aggressive be-haviour in personality-disordered subjects. *Archives of General Psychiatry*, **54**, 1081–1088.

Cornelius, J. R., Soloff, P. H., Perel, J. M. & Ulrich, R. F. (1991). A preliminary trial of fluoxetine in refractory borderline patients. *Journal of Clinical Psychopharmacology*, **11**, 116–120.

Czobor, P., Volavka, J. & Meibach, R. C. (1995). Effect of risperidone on hostility in schizophrenia. *Journal of Clinical Psychopharmacology*, **15**, 243–249.

de Koning, P., Mak, M., de Vries, M. H., Allsopp, L. F., Stevens, R. B., Verbruggen, R., van den Borre, R., van Peteghem, P., Kohen, D., Arumainayagam, M. et al. (1994). Eltoprazine in aggressive mentally handicapped patients: a double-blind, placebo-controlled and baseline-controlled multi-centre study. The Eltoprazine Aggression Research Group. *International Clinical Psychopharmacology*, **9**, 187–194.

Dorus, W., Ostrow, D. G., Anton, R., Cushman, P., Collins, J. F., Schaefer, M., Charles, H. L., Desai, P., Hayashida, M., Malkerneker, U., Willenbring, O., Fiscella, R. & Sather, M. R. (1989). Lithium treatment of depressed and non-depressed alco-holics. *Journal of American Medical Association*, **262**, 1646–1652.

Eronen, M. (1995). Mental disorders and homicidal behavior in female subjects. *American Journal of Psychiatry*, **152**, 1216–1218.

Eronen, M., Tiihonen, J., Ylitapio, J. & Hakola, P. (1995). Uusimpia tutkimushavain-toja rikoksista syytettyjen henkilöiden oikeuspsykiatrisista mielentilatutkimuk-sista. *Lakimies*, **4**, 538–547 (in Finnish).

Eronen, M., Hakola, P. & Tiihonen, J. (1996a). Mental disorders and homicidal behavior in Finland. *Archives of General Pscychiatry*, **53**, 497–501.

Eronen, M., Tiihonen, J. & Hakola, P. (1996b). Schizophrenia and homicidal be-havior. *Schizophrenia Bulletin*, **22**, 83–89.

Eronen, M., Hakola, P. & Tiihonen, J. (1996c). Factors associated with homicide recidivism in a 13-year sample of homicide offenders in Finland. *Psychiatric Ser-vices*, **47**, 403–406.

Fox, B. S., Kantak, K. M., Edwards, M. A., Black, K. M., Bollinger, B. K., Botka, A. J., French, T. L., Thompson, T. L., Schad, V. C., Greenstein, J. L., Gefter, M. L., Exley, M. A., Swain, P. A. & Briner, T. L. (1996). Efficacy of a therapeutic cocaine vaccine in rodent models. *Nature Medicine*, **2**, 1122–1132.

Fuller, R. K. & Roth, H. P. (1979). Disulfiram for the treatment of alcoholism: an evaluation in 128 men. *Annals of Internal Medicine*, **90**, 901–904.

Fuller, R. K., Branchey, L., Brightwell, D. R., Derman, R. M., Emrick, C. D., Iber, F. L., James, K. E., Lacoursiere, R. B., Lee, K. K., Lowenstam, I., Manny, I., Neiderhiser, D., Nocks, S. & Show, J. J. (1986). Disulfiram treatment of alcoholism: a Veterans Administration cooperative study. *Journal of American Medical Association*, **256**, 1449–1455.

Heiligenstein, J. H., Beasley, C. M. & Potvin, J. H. (1993). Fluoxetine not associated with increased aggression in controlled clinical trials. *International Clinical Psychopharmacology*, **8**, 277–280.

Hodgins, S. (1992). Mental disorder, intellectual deficiency, and crime. *Archives of General Psychiatry*, **49**, 476–483.

Hodgins, S., Mednick, S. A., Brennan, P. A., Schulsinger, F. & Engberg, M. (1996). Mental disorder and crime: evidence from a Danish birth cohort. *Archives of General Psychiatry*, **53**, 489–496.

Kim, S. W. (1998). Opioid antagonists in the treatment of impulse-control disorders. *Journal of Clinical Psychiatry*, **59**, 159–164.

Kohen, D. (1993). Eltoprazine for aggression in mental handicap. *Lancet*, **341**, 628–629.

Kosten, T. R., Kleber, H. D. & Morgan, C. (1989a). Role of opioid antagonists in treating intravenous cocaine abuse. *Life Science*, **44**, 887–892.

Kosten, T. R., Kleber, H. D. & Morgan, C. (1989b). Treatment of cocaine abuse with buprenorphine. *Biological Psychiatry*, **26**, 637–639.

Kuruoğlu, A. Ç., Arikan, Z., Vural, G., Karatas, M., Araç, M. & Isik, E. (1996). Single photon emission computerized tomography in chronic alcoholism: antisocial personality disorder may be associated with decreased frontal perfusion. *British Journal of Psychiatry*, **169**, 348–354.

Markovitz, P. J., Calabrese, J. R., Schultz, S. C. & Meltzer, H. Y. (1991). Fluoxetine in the treatment of borderline and schizotypal personality disorders. *American Journal of Psychiatry*, **148**, 1064–1067.

Marzuk, P. M. (1996). Violence, crime, and mental illness. How strong a link? *Archives of General Psychiatry*, **53**, 481–486.

Mattes, J. A. (1984). Carbamazepine for uncontrolled rage outbursts. *Lancet*, **2**, 1164–1165.

Mattes, J. A. (1985). Metoprolol for intermittent explosive disorder. *American Journal of Psychiatry*, **142**, 1108–1109.

McGee, M. D. (1997). Cessation of self-mutilation in a patient with borderline personality disorder treated with naltrexone. *Journal of Clinical Psychiatry*, **58**, 32–33.

McNair, D. M., Lorr, M. & Droppleman, L. F. (1981). *Edits Manual for the Profile of Mood States (POMS)*. San Diego: Educational and Industrial Testing Service.

Naranjo, C. A., Sellers, E. M., Sullivan, J. T., Woodley, D. V., Kadlec, K. & Sykora, K. (1987). The serotonin uptake inhibitor citralopram attenuates ethanol intake. *Clinical Pharmacology and Therapeutics*, **41**, 266–274.

Naranjo, C. A. & Sellers, E. M. (1989). Serotonin uptake inhibitors attenuate ethanol intake in problem drinkers. *Recent Developments in Alcoholism*, **7**, 255–266.

O'Malley, S. S., Jaffe, A. J., Chang, G., Schottenfeld, R. S., Meyer, R. E. & Rounsaville, B. (1992). Naltrexone and coping skills therapy for alcohol dependence. *Archives of General Psychiatry*, **49**, 881–887.

Osman, O. T. & Loschen, E. L. (1992). Self-injuries behavior in the developmentally disabled: pharmacologic treatment. *Psychopharmacology Bulletin*, **28**, 439–449.

Paanila, J., Hakola, P. & Tiihonen, J. (1999). Mortality among habitually violent offenders. *Forensic Science International*, **100**, 187–191.

Perry, J. C. & Vaillant, G. E. (1989).   Personality disorders. In H. I. Kaplan & B. J. Sadock (Eds), *Comprehensive Textbook of Psychiatry, Vol. V* (pp. 1352–1387). Philadelphia, PA: Williams & Wilkins.

Popik, P., Layer, R. T., Fossom, L. H., Benveniste, M., Geter-Douglass, B., Witkin, J. M. & Skolnick, P. (1995).   NMDA antagonist properties of the putative anti-addictive drug, ibogaine. *Journal of Pharmacology and Experimental Therapeutics*, **275**, 753–760.

Rasmussen, D. L., Olivier, B., Raghoebar, M. & Mos, J. (1990).   Possible clinical application of serenics and some implications of their preclinical profile for their clinical use in psychiatric disorders. *Drug Metabolism Drug Interactions*, **8**, 159–186.

Ratey, J., Sovner, R., Parks, A. & Rogentine, K. (1991).   Buspirone treatment of aggression and anxiety in mentally retarded patients: a multiple-baseline, placebo lead-in study. *Journal of Clinical Psychiatry*, **52**, 159–162.

Rossetti, Z. L., D'Aquila, P. S., Hmaidan, Y., Gessa, G. L. & Serra, G. (1991).   Repeated treatment with imipramine potentiates cocaine-induced dopamine release and motor stimulation. *European Journal of Pharmacology*, **201**, 243–245.

Räsänen, P., Tiihonen, J., Isohanni, M., Rantakallio, P., Lehtonen, J. & Moring, J. (1998).   Schizophrenia, alcohol abuse and violent behavior: a 26-year follow-up study of an unselected birth cohort. *Schizophrenia Bulletin*, **24**, 437–441.

Saltzman, C., Wolfson, A. N., Schatzberg, A., Looper, J., Henke, R., Albanese, M., Schwartz, J. & Miyawaki, E. (1995).   Effect of fluoxetine on anger in symptomatic volunteers with borderline personality disorder. *Journal of Clinical Psychopharmacology*, **15**, 23–29.

Sass, H., Soyka, M., Mann, K. & Zieglgänsberger, W. (1996).   Relapse prevention by acamprosate. Results from a placebo-controlled study on alcohol dependence. *Archives of General Psychiatry*, **53**, 673–680.

Saudou, F., Amara, D. A., Dierich, A., LeMeur, M., Ramboz, S., Segu, L., Buhot, M. C. & Hen, R. (1994).   Enhanced aggressive behavior in mice lacking 5-HT$_{1B}$ receptor. *Science*, **265**, 1875–1878.

Schottenfeld, R. S. & Kleber, H. D. (1995).   Methadone maintenance. In H. I. Kaplan and B. J. Sadock (Eds), *Comprehensive Textbook of Psychiatry, Vol. VI* (pp. 2031–2038). Philadelphia, PA: Williams & Wilkins.

Schottenfeld, R. S., Pakes, J. R., Oliveto, A., Ziedonis, D. & Kosten, T. R. (1997). Buprenorphine vs. methadone maintenance treatment for concurrent opioid dependence and cocaine abuse. *Archives of General Psychiatry*, **54**, 713–720.

Sheard, M. H., Marini, J. L., Bridges, C. I. & Wagner, E. (1976).   The effect of lithium on impulsive aggressive behavior in man. *American Journal of Psychiatry*, **133**, 1409–1413.

Soloff, P. H., George, A., Nathan, R. S., Schulz, P. M., Ulrich, R. F. & Perel, J. M. (1986). Progress in the pharmacology of borderline disorders. *Archives of General Psychiatry*, **43**, 691–697.

Sorensen, S. M., Humphreys, T. M., Taylor, V. L. & Schmidt, C. J. (1992). 5-HT$_2$ receptor antagonists reverse amphetamine-induced slowing of dopaminergic neurons by interfering with stimulated dopamine synthesis. *Journal of Pharmacology and Experimental Therapeutics*, **260**, 872–878.

Spanagel, R., Herz, A., Bals-Kubik, R. & Shippenberg, T. S. (1991).   β-Endorphin-induced locomotor stimulation and reinforcement are associated with an increase in dopamine release in the nucleus accumbens. *Psychopharmacology (Berlin)*, **104**, 51–56.

Tennant, F. S. Jr, Rawson, R. A., Cohen, A. J. & Mann, A. (1984).   Clinical experience with naltrexone in suburban opioid addicts. *Journal of Clinical Psychiatry*, **45**, 42–45.

Thor, D. H. & Ghiselli, W. P. (1975).   Suppression of mouse killing and apomorphine-induced social aggression in rats by local anesthesia of the mystacial vibrissae. *Journal of Comparative and Physiological Psychology*, **88**, 40–46.

Tiihonen, J., Eronen, M. & Hakola, P. (1993a). Criminality associated with mental disorder and intellectual deficiency. *Archives of General Psychiatry*, **50**, 916–918.

Tiihonen, J., Hakola, P., Paanila, J. & Turtiainen, M. (1993b). Eltoprazine for aggression in schizophrenia and mental retardation. *Lancet*, **341**, 307.

Tiihonen, J. & Hakola, P. (1994). Psychiatric disorders and homicide recidivism. *American Journal of Psychiatry*, **151**, 436–438.

Tiihonen, J., Kuikka, J., Bergström, K., Hakola, P., Karhu, J., Ryynänen, O.-P. & Föhr, J. (1995). Altered striatal dopamine re-uptake site densities in habitually violent and non-violent alcoholics. *Nature Medicine*, **1**, 654–657.

Tiihonen, J., Ryynänen, O.-P., Kauhanen, J., Hakola, H. P. A. & Salaspuro, M. (1996). Citalopram in the treatment of alcoholism: a double-blind placebo-controlled study. *Pharmacopsychiatry*, **29**, 27–29.

Tiihonen, J., Isohanni, M., Räsänen, P., Koiranen, M. & Moring, J. (1997a). Specific major mental disorders and criminality: a 26-year prospective study of the 1966 Northern Finland birth cohort. *American Journal of Psychiatry*, **154**, 840–845.

Tiihonen, J., Kuikka, J. T., Bergström, K. A., Karhu, J., Viinamäki, H., Lehtonen, J., Hallikainen, T., Yang, J. & Hakola, P. (1997b). Single-photon emission tomography imaging of monoamine transporters in impulsive violent behaviour. *European Journal of Nuclear Medicine*, **24**, 1253–1260.

Tupin, J. P., Smith, D. B., Clanon, T. L., Kim, I., Nugent, A. & Groupe, A. I. (1973). The long-term use of lithium in aggressive prisoners. *Comprehensive Psychiatry*, **14**, 311–317.

Verhoeven, W. M. A., Tuinier, S., Sijben, N. A. S., van den Berg, Y. W. H. M. & de Witte-van der Schoot, E. P. P. M. (1992). Eltoprazine in mentally retarded self-injuring patients. *Lancet*, **340**, 1037–1038.

Virkkunen, M., DeJong, J., Bartko, J., Goodwin, F. K. & Linnoila, M. (1989). Relationship of psychobiological variables to recidivism in violent offenders and impulsive fire setters. A follow-up study. *Archives of General Psychiatry*, **46**, 600–603.

Virkkunen, M., Rawlings, R., Tokola, R., Poland, R. E., Guidotti, A., Nemeroff, C., Bissette, G., Kalogeras, K., Karonen, S.-L. & Linnoila, M. (1994). CSF biochemistries, glucose metabolism, and diurnal activity rhythms in alcoholic, violent offenders, fire setters, and healthy volunteers. *Archives of General Psychiatry*, **51**, 20–27.

Virkkunen, M., Eggert, M., Rawlings, R. & Linnoila, M. I. (1996). A prospective follow-up study of alcoholic violent offenders and fire setters. *Archives of General Psychiatry*, **53**, 523–529.

Volpicelli, J. R., Alterman, A. I., Hayashida, M. & O'Brien, C. P. (1992). Naltrexone in the treatment of alcohol dependence. *Archives of General Psychiatry*, **49**, 876–880.

Warner, E. A., Kosten, T. R. & O'Connor, P. G. (1997). Pharmacotherapy for opioid and cocaine abuse. *Medical Clinics of North America*, **8**, 909–925.

Wilcox, J. (1994). Divalproex sodium in the treatment of aggressive behavior. *Annals of Clinical Psychiatry*, **6**, 17–20.

Williams, D. T., Mehl, R., Yudofsky, S., Adams, D. & Roseman, B. (1982). The effect of propranolol on uncontrolled rage outbursts in children and adolescents with organic brain dysfunction. *Journal of American Academy of Child Psychiatry*, **21**, 129–135.

Wodak, A. (1994). Managing illicit drug use. A practical guide. *Drugs*, **47**, 446–457.

Yudofsky, S., Silver, J. M., Jackson, W., Endicott, J. & Williams, D. (1986). The overt aggression scale for the objective rating of verbal and physical aggression. *American Journal of Psychiatry*, **143**, 35–39.

Chapter 9

COMMUNITY-BASED TREATMENT PROGRAMMES

Kirk Heilbrun and Lori Peters*

Department of Clinical and Health Psychology, MCP Hahnemann University and
*Villanova School of Law, Philadelphia, PA, USA

INTRODUCTION

The community-based mental health treatment of mentally disordered offenders is discussed in this chapter, with the goal of determining the efficacy and effectiveness of various forms of treatment in preventing violence and other kinds of criminal behaviour. The major focus of this chapter will be on mentally disordered offenders in non-jail community settings, in one of two legal categories: "not guilty by reason of insanity" acquittees, or mentally disordered offenders on parole or probation. The relevant literature in this area can be divided into two types of study: (a) an experimental or quasi-experimental design, in which an intervention was delivered to one group of individuals and a control condition (consisting of either a different intervention or no intervention beyond the standard criminal justice conditions), with the conditions either randomly assigned or the control group matched; and (b) a design in which a group of individuals are measured in terms of independent/predictor and dependent/outcome variables, with a

Violence, Crime and Mentally Disordered Offenders. Edited by S. Hodgins and R. Müller-Isberner.
© 2000 John Wiley & Sons, Ltd.

"comparison" group (neither matched nor randomly assigned) measured on the same variables. The results from the literature in each of these areas are described, and the implications of these results for practice, policy and research are discussed.

Recent years have witnessed opposing trends in the treatment of mentally disordered offenders in the community in the USA. First, there has been a trend away from long-term involuntary treatment of mentally disordered offenders in maximum-security, geographically remote institutions, and toward treating such individuals in the community, roughly paralleling the deinstitutionalization movement for civilly committed patients in the USA over the past three decades. Second, however, there have been signs during the 1990s that US society is inclined again toward laws and policies involving longer-term incarceration, at least for certain groups within the criminal and juvenile justice systems (e.g. lower ages for juvenile transfer laws, the 1997 *Kansas v. Hendricks* decision by the US Supreme Court (*Kansas v. Hendricks*, 117 U.S. 2072, 1997) involving post-sentence commitment for sexual offenders). It is not clear how such trends will ultimately affect treatment of mentally disordered offenders in the community, but there is little doubt that such increasing concern regarding public safety will intensify the focus on crime and violence as outcome measures of the effectiveness of community-based mental health treatment with mentally disordered offenders.

A useful analysis of the respective roles in treatment research of effectiveness studies (focusing on the health and cost impacts of mental health treatments under "usual care" conditions) and efficacy studies (using controlled clinical trials to provide information on treatment outcomes under "best practice" conditions) has recently been provided (Wells, 1999). Even treatments such as medication, with which it is more customary to use controlled clinical trials to assess efficacy, must be considered in light of the potential loss of external validity that can accrue when internal validity influences are carefully controlled. In the current chapter, we will focus primarily on effectiveness research because efficacy research, in the form of controlled clinical trials, can be extremely difficult and at times impossible to conduct with individuals in the criminal justice system in the community, when a major goal is the prevention of crime and violence. The reasons for such difficulty, and the possible use of certain designs incorporating some elements of efficacy research, will be described in more detail later in this chapter.

As programmes and more isolated interventions for mentally disordered offenders increase in number, but undergo more intense scrutiny, it is important to assess their impact in delivering treatment services. Even more, it is crucial to make the best-informed, empirically-based judgments regarding what is known about how well they can prevent future violence and other crime committed by individuals receiving treatment services.

Issues of definition

The phrase "mentally disordered offender", when applied to populations that are in correctional or secure hospital settings, has been used to describe the following categories: (a) "incompetent to stand trial"; (b) "not guilty by reason of insanity" (NGRI); (c) "mentally disordered sex offender"; or (d) "mentally ill (jail or prison) inmate" (Steadman et al., 1982). In community settings, the most applicable of these categories are: (a) "parole" or "probation", or (b) NGRI (on conditional release from hospitalization) (Heilbrun & Griffin, 1993, 1998). Because of the absence of programmatic information or empirical data on the treatment of "incompetent to stand trial" individuals in non-jail community settings, this category will not be discussed in this chapter. We will also consider only adults, since the treatment of juvenile offenders presents substantially different issues than does the treatment of adults with mental disorder (see e.g. Gordon, Arbuthnot & Jurkovic, 1998). "Mental disorder" will include the various forms of severe mental illness and their frequently co-occurring disorders (e.g. substance abuse, personality disorder). However, we will not address the treatment of individuals who are substance abusers but are without other disorders.

The next definition concerns "community-based" programmes and services. Our focus in this chapter will include community-based facilities such as halfway houses, outpatient clinics, crisis stabilization units and inpatient psychiatric facilities that provide emergency or short-term psychiatric care in the community. Service delivery agents will include psychiatrists, psychologists, social workers and nurses, as well as case managers and parole and probation officers. The chapter will not include jails, however.

"Treatment services" will include the various mental health treatments commonly delivered to mental health consumers. Psychotropic medication, case management, assertive community treatment, psychosocial rehabilitation, therapy and counselling, vocational training and other forms of treatment will all be included. We will also consider interventions designed for specific deficits, such as anger or impulsivity.

Classification of studies

We reviewed the relevant literature on community-based treatment, with particular attention to the outcomes of crime and violence, by identifying studies and articles published between January 1976 and February 1999 through the computerized databases PSYCHINFO, PSYCHALERT, Criminal Justice Periodical Index, Sociological Abstracts, MEDLINE and EMBASE. First, we identified review articles and chapters addressing community-based treatment. Next, we categorized each article as having either: (a) an experimental or quasi-experimental design in which an intervention was delivered to one group of individuals and a control condition (consisting of either a different intervention or no intervention beyond the standard criminal justice conditions), with the conditions either randomly assigned or the control group matched; or (b) a design in which a group of individuals was measured in terms of independent/predictor and dependent/outcome variables, with a "comparison" group (neither matched nor randomly assigned) measured on the same variables. These two categories are comparable to efficacy and effectiveness designs, respectively, that have been used in other kinds of treatment outcome research. We originally considered including studies focusing on programme descriptions, without necessarily providing quantitative data, but decided against this because of the overall focus of the chapter.

The articles were classified in this way to identify some studies for which an "effect size" (a quantitative difference between an experimental and a control group resulting from the intervention being studied) could be calculated, and other studies that were mainly descriptive, providing little or no data. Other studies may have provided some data, but did not have a design that would allow comparison to a control group, so an effect size could not be calculated.

When an effect size can be calculated from a number of studies, a "meta-analysis" can be performed. By considering different studies, using somewhat different methods and variables, an overall "effect size" can be calculated that is more stable and has more power, since the overall number of participants across the different studies is larger in the meta-analysis. One original goal for this chapter was to conduct such a meta-analysis. However, our review of research in this area revealed that it was not possible to do so because there were few studies which had a design that allowed calculation of an effect size. The few studies of this kind provide valuable information about the effectiveness of certain kinds of programmes in preventing crime and violence, because they eliminate the influence of extraneous variables through use of a control group. Studies that provide quantitative data but are not controlled through their design can provide less valuable, but still useful, information about the impact of a programme or intervention.

REVIEW OF LITERATURE

Recent meta-analysis on the prediction of criminal and violent recidivism among mentally disordered offenders

The recent publication of a meta-analysis of studies published between 1959 and 1995 on the prediction of criminal and violent recidivism in mentally disordered offenders (Bonta, Law & Hanson, 1998) is somewhat relevant to the current chapter. It is only "somewhat" relevant because the studies included in this analysis allow the estimate of the predictive value of variables in several domains (demographic, criminal history, deviant life-style history, and clinical) on outcomes of "general recidivism" (an arrest or a return to a hospital for criminal behaviour) and "violent recidivism" (criminal re-offending of a violent nature). However, these studies do not attempt to address questions regarding the risk-reduction value of various interventions, particularly those delivered in the community. In this sense, the Bonta et al. (1998) article focuses on *predicting* recidivism, while the current chapter is more concerned with the efficacy and effectiveness of interventions in *reducing* the risk of crime and violence (see Heilbrun, 1997, for a fuller discussion).

Nonetheless, the meta-analysis of pooled data provides valuable information regarding the empirical relationship between a number of factors and the outcomes of crime and violence. Effect sizes were calculated for 35 predictors of general recidivism and 27 predictors of violent recidivism, drawn from a total of 68 non-overlapping samples. The major predictors of recidivism for mentally disordered offenders were similar to those for non-mentally disordered offenders, with criminal history variables (e.g. adult criminal history, juvenile delinquency, violent history) the strongest predictors and clinical variables the weakest. Among the other predictors showing positive relationships with both general and violent recidivism were objective risk assessment, antisocial personality disorder, institutional adjustment, hospital admissions, poor living arrangements, male gender, substance abuse, escape history, drug abuse, marital status (single) and weapon use. The average effect size for treatment history as a predictor of general recidivism was non-significant; the authors suggested that inconsistent "treatment targets" may be responsible for this finding. More specifically, they speculated that studies in which non-criminogenic needs were targeted for intervention would not show significant risk-reduction value, while the fewer studies that did focus on criminogenic interventions would show significance, but this overall pattern would not yield a significant effect size. In other words, Bonta et al. (1998) are strongly suggesting that programmes with the goal of reducing violent and criminal behaviour should target specific dynamic risk factors that show a positive relationship with recidivism risk. This conclusion seems reasonable and perhaps justified on theoretical grounds. It would be helpful to investigate it empirically.

Recent reviews of community-based treatment relevant to crime and violence

Several recent reviews of community-based forensic treatment (CBFT) in this area are available. These reviews have focused on describing programmes and interventions for NGRI acquittees in the community

(Heilbrun & Griffin, 1993), NGRI acquittees plus individuals with mental disorder on parole or probation (Heilbrun & Griffin, 1998) and a broad overview of forensic treatment (Heilbrun & Griffin, 1999). While none of these reviews focused exclusively on the outcomes of violence and crime, these outcomes were considered.

Several conclusions can be drawn from these reviews. First, much of the available information about CBFT is reported by a relatively small number of sites, making it difficult to generalize from the published literature to the many programmes and sites that do not publish. Second, the great majority of published accounts are primarily descriptive; few involve using experimental or quasi-experimental designs, or inferential statistical analysis. For the studies that do use inferential statistics, the majority have regression-based designs (which may use only a single group) which identify variables that predict a designated, quantitatively-measured outcome variable, rather than experimental or quasi-experimental designs (using an experimental group and a control group) that would allow an efficacy or effectiveness measure of a given programme or intervention. These studies reflect the reality that CBFT programmes, which treat clients under the jurisdiction of courts or departments of parole/probation, cannot easily meet the conditions for experimental study of interventions.[1] This problem makes it more difficult to obtain good information about the specific impact of an intervention.

Third, it is possible to identify principles that are derived from published accounts and professional experience with CBFT, although such principles are not empirically based. These principles will be discussed in more detail later in this chapter.

Experimental or quasi-experimental (Type 1) studies

The first category of studies includes those having: (a) an experimental or quasi-experimental design in which an intervention was delivered to one

---

[1] There are several reasons for this. The first involves the role of research in populations for which public safety is explicitly a consideration. "Experiments" may not be supported by the necessary agencies, or by society more generally, when it is likely that some who are in the experimental condition will, nonetheless, commit a further offence. Support for continuing such a study may be weak in the event of such an outcome, particularly if it is serious and widely publicized. The second reason, related to the first, is that support for treatment and rehabilitative interventions with those who are involved in the criminal justice system must compete with a strong societal orientation toward punishment, particularly in contemporary US society. Third, it may be difficult to obtain public funding for enhanced or different procedures within the criminal justice system, and grant funding may not apply because of the conditions for subject selection and confidentiality imposed by many granting agencies. Finally, it is difficult to obtain truly informed consent to participate in such research using individuals who are involved in the criminal justice system, given the explicit coercion that is already present for such individuals and the potential for this to be applied as well as part of such research.

group of individuals; and (b) a control condition (consisting of either a different intervention or no intervention beyond the standard criminal justice conditions), with the conditions either randomly assigned or the control group matched. We found two studies meeting these criteria.[2]

In one such study from California (Wiederanders, 1992), a total of 235 NGRI acquittees were studied. The first group were on conditional release in the community, and therefore were required to satisfy requirements involving treatment compliance and other conditions. The second group were in the community following NGRI hospitalization and release, but were not on conditional release. Re-arrest and rehospitalization were used as outcome measures for the study. Individuals in the conditional release group had a significantly lower arrest rate than those who were not on conditional release. The proportion who were rehospitalized was higher in the conditional release group, but this difference was not statistically significant.

One other study was located in this category, although it involved a combination of hospital intervention and community follow-up. This study (described in two articles; see Cohen et al., 1988; Silver, Cohen & Spodak, 1989) included a total of 389 participants in three groups: (a) NGRI acquittees ($n = 127$); (b) individuals convicted of felonies (more serious offences) ($n = 127$), matched on the basis of age, race, length of incarceration and type of offence; and (c) mentally disordered offenders transferred from prison to hospital for treatment ($n = 135$). All NGRI individuals had been charged with felonies, released on a 5-year conditional release programme, and had been living in the community for 7–17 years (mean = 10.5 years). Outcome measures included arrest, arrest severity, hospitalization, employment and global functioning, and were assessed at three stages: after 2.5 years, after 5 years, and over the entire follow-up period (up to 17 years). After 5 years, a total of 54.3% of NGRI acquittees had been re-arrested, while 65.4% of the convicted felon control group and 73.3% of the hospitalized mentally disordered offenders had been re-arrested. By the end of the follow-up period, the proportion of each group that had been re-arrested increased somewhat (NGRI acquittees, 65.8%; control felony group; 75.4%; hospitalized mentally disordered offenders, 78.4%). Discriminant function analysis[3] between arrested and not arrested groups showed certain differences. For the felon control group, the variables discriminating between arrested and not-

---

[2] A third study (Swartz et al., in press) involved a randomized controlled trial of the effectiveness of involuntary outpatient commitment in reducing rehospitalizations among individuals with severe mental illnesses. It included variables involving violence and arrest; when these variables are analysed, the results of this study will be relevant to the current chapter. However, as this chapter is being completed, the Swartz et al. data on violence and arrest have not yet been fully analysed as they relate to intensity of services and outpatient commitment.

[3] Discriminant function analysis is a statistical technique that measures the extent to which quantitative variables discriminate between two or more separate groups, and the accuracy of this discrimination.

arrested individuals included age, race, prior employment, prior arrests as a juvenile and as an adult, and poor school adjustment. For the hospitalized mentally disordered offender group, these variables also discriminated between those arrested and those not arrested, but there were other variables which also discriminated: trauma as a child, alcoholism, type of offence, global functioning score and hospital adjustment. Finally, for those in the NGRI group, re-arrest was predicted by prior arrests, alcoholism, unemployment and type of offence, but also by prior hospitalization for mental illness, hospital adjustment and clinical assessment of hospital adjustment. Because there were only two studies which met the criteria for both experimental design and intervention in the community, it was not possible to perform a meta-analysis addressing the effect size of intervention.

Comparison and single-group (Type 2) studies

We found more studies using a design in which one group is measured in terms of independent/predictor and dependent/outcome variables, with a "comparison" group (neither matched nor randomly assigned) measured on the same variables, or a single group in which predictor and outcome variables were analysed in a regression-based design. In this section, we will describe studies which address the importance of: (a) differences between jurisdictions; (b) diagnosis; (c) treatment/commitment; (d) type of release; and (e) type of case management, as well as several studies that are particularly important in identifying risk factors for crime and violence in the community.

A study of insanity acquittees in three US states (California, New York and Oregon) provided data on the rates of client contact, revocation of conditional release, re-offence, and rehospitalization for individuals over different periods of time (Oregon, 1978–1986, $n = 366$; New York, 1980–1987, $n = 331$; California, 1986–1993, $n = 888$) (Wiederanders, Bromley & Choate, 1997). An interesting relationship was seen among these variables. California had the most frequent outpatient service contacts monthly, with Oregon reporting an intermediate number and New York apparently the lowest. California also had the lowest "estimated annualized arrest rate" (3.4%), with Oregon's rate at an intermediate level (5.8%) and New York's the highest (7.8%). This relationship between more service contacts and fewer arrests was clearest for less serious offences. This study suggested that the frequency of contacts during the conditional release period may be inversely related to risk of re-arrest. Given the frequency and intensity of California's conditional release monitoring, it also raised the question of whether some relatively minor acts that might result in an arrest in another state were being handled differently in California.

An important series of studies have been conducted in Oregon, involving the impact of conditional release for individuals hospitalized as NGRI and subsequently returned from hospitalization into the community and the oversight of the Oregon Psychiatric Review Board (PSRB) (Bigelow, Bloom & Williams, 1990; Bloom, Bradford & Koford, 1988; Bloom, Rogers & Manson, 1988; Bloom et al., 1986a, 1986b; Bloom, Wiliams & Bigelow, 1991, 1992; Bloom & Bloom, 1981). These studies have used a "naturally occurring experiment"—the implementation of the PSRB and conditional release as system-level changes in the decision-making regarding insanity acquittees—to assess the impact of conditional release and a review panel. The overall project from which these studies are derived tracked a total of 971 NGRI acquittees between 1978 and 1986 (Bloom, Williams & Bigelow, 1992). Findings from several of these studies suggest that conditional release, with associated community monitoring and formal compliance demands, is associated with a lower rate of criminal offending while the individual is under review board jurisdiction in the community. In one study, focusing on the period 1978–1982, a total of 13% of PSRB clients were re-arrested while under conditional release in the community, but much higher percentages were rehospitalized: 78% (1980), 62% (1981), 31% (1982) and 20% 1983). In another study (Bloom et al., 1986a), the lifetime police contacts (including arrests and subarrest encounters) were compared for patients prior to, during and following PSRB jurisdiction. The rate of police contacts per patient per year was 0.78 prior to conditional release, 0.20 while on conditional release under PSRB jurisdiction, and 0.54 following release from PSRB jurisdiction. When only patients with schizophrenia were considered (Bloom, Williams & Bigelow, 1992), a similar pattern was observed. Of the 381 individuals studied, only 57 had criminal justice contacts while under PSRB jurisdiction. Following discharge from PSRB jurisdiction, subjects had significantly fewer criminal justice contacts (0.41 contacts per year) than they had before PSRB jurisdiction (0.69 per year), a statistically significant difference. These Oregon studies underscore the value of conditional release, careful monitoring, centralized and rapid decision-making, and treatment programming designed to address needs associated with symptoms, life skills, housing and work in reducing the risk of criminal arrest. It is noteworthy that the rate of such arrests dropped quite sharply while individuals were under PSRB jurisdiction, but remained under pre-PSRB rates even after they were discharged from conditional release.

The type of release from secure hospitalization into the community for NGRI acquittees has been considered. Two types of release were studied: (a) conditional release directly from the programme into the community; and (b) conditional release from the programme to a regional facility, and then to the community (Tellefsen et al., 1992; see Silver, Cohen & Spodak, 1989, for other findings from this study). Four outcomes were considered over 5 years after release: (a) re-arrest; (b) overall functioning in the community; (c) re-hospitalization for mental illness; and (d) successful completion (nonrevocation) of the conditional release. Discriminant analysis (see footnote 3) predicted these four outcomes with an overall accuracy rate of 69–83% for the directly-released patients and 88–96% for the regionally released individuals. Although there was no cross-validation,[4] the findings did suggest that these groups can be distinguished at better than chance levels. Variables predicting community functioning included severity of instant offence, Global Assessment Score (GAS) at release, functioning before the offence, hospital adjustment, clinical assessment of patient's improvement, and marital status. Variables predicting re-arrest included birth order, adjustment in hospital, clinical assessment of patient's improvement, GAS at release, functioning before instant offence, and heroin addiction. The regionally released group was arrested more frequently (63% vs. 47%) and committed more serious offences than the directly-released group, and were also re-arrested sooner. No difference in the rate of rehospitalization was seen, but the regionally released group was rehospitalized for a longer time. There is no random assignment to release type, so we cannot conclude that the "regional release" process in itself is responsible for poorer outcomes. Indeed, it is likely that NGRI acquittees perceived by staff or the committing court as being at higher risk would tend to go through the more gradual regional release process.

A more detailed examination of the conditional release process for NGRI acquittees in New York State communities (McGreevy et al., 1991) considered data on all NGRI clients placed on conditional release in New York State between 1980 and 1987 ($n = 331$). The average outcome period for the study was 3.8 years. A total of 22% of clients were arrested and 5% had their commitments re-instated. The great majority of the re-arrests and recommitments occurred during the first year in the community. The authors suggested that the "key features" of a successful conditional release programme include centralized responsibility, a uniform system of treatment and supervision and a network of community services.

We found three studies focusing on the characteristics of case management. First the impact of "assertive case management" versus a standard case management condition[5] was studied by following individuals with

---

[4] Cross-validation allows a check on the accuracy of predictive weights developed in a regression-based analysis of one sample by applying these weights in a second sample. It is expected that the weights will yield less accurate overall prediction when applied in this second sample, because some of the predictive accuracy in the original sample is attributable to chance. When chance influences are reduced by applying the weights to a second sample, then the researcher can better estimate the "true" relationship between predictors and outcome.

[5] Standard case management involves linking the client to existing community resources in important areas such as housing, vocational or public assistance, transportation, substance abuse, mental health and others as needed. Intensive case management involves having a smaller caseload, allowing the case manager to see the client more frequently and possibly to provide additional services.

chronic mental disorders ($n = 26$) who received case management services over a 36-month period. They were compared with similar individuals ($n = 33$) who did not receive case management services (Wilson, Tien & Eaves, 1995). Criminal justice contacts for both groups were recorded at three times before incarceration (6, 12 and 18 months) and again at three times after release (6, 12 and 18 months). No significant differences between these groups were found in the average number of days spent in jail before incarceration. After release, however, the group receiving case management services spent fewer days in correctional institutions and more days in the community before coming into contact with the criminal justice system ($M = 270.0$ days vs. $M = 119.6$ days, respectively).

The small numbers of participants limit the conclusions that can be drawn from this study, but the findings are consistent with the assertions of others (e.g. Dvoskin & Steadman, 1994) that intensive case management can reduce the risk of violence and criminality by mentally disordered offenders in the community. The third study involved a comparison between the styles of case management delivered as part of a randomized clinical trial for seriously mentally ill people who were also homeless and leaving a large urban jail system (Solomon, Draine & Meyerson, 1994; Solomon & Draine, 1995). A total of 60 individuals were assigned to the Assertive Community Treatment (ACT) team of case managers, 60 to individual case managers at community mental health centres and 80 to the usual aftercare referral from community mental health centres. A total of 32% of the study clients had returned to jail at least once during the first 6 months of follow-up (Solomon, Draine & Meyerson, 1994) and a total of 46% had returned to jail at least once during the first year of follow-up (Solomon & Draine, 1995). Differences in re-incarceration rates were reported at 6 months between clients served by the Assertive Community Treatment team (60%), those assigned to individual case managers (35%) and those referred to mental health centres (40%) (Solomon, Draine & Meyerson, 1994) and again at 1 year (Assertive Community Treatment, 60%; individual case managers, 40%; and mental health centres, 36%; Solomon & Draine, 1995). These differences were not statistically significant, however; the only variable that was significantly associated with re-incarceration, when these data were analysed using discriminant function analysis, was "identified service needs not met" (Solomon, Draine & Meyerson, 1994).

A Swedish study (Belfrage, 1991) provides some information regarding the impact of mandatory psychiatric hospital treatment, compared with prison, on two groups. The first group was composed of offenders judged (in forensic psychiatric examination) to have "equivalent" treatment needs to insanity acquittees ($n = 298$), while the second group consisted of those during the same period and from the same area (Stockholm) who did not have equivalent treatment needs ($n = 256$). The two groups were similar in some important respects (e.g. age, gender, having previous criminal arrests, and the types of crime of which they were convicted). They were not, however, equivalent in the distribution of mental health diagnoses, with diagnoses of "borderline", "psychosis", "mental retardation" and "brain damage" observed in the first group but not in the second. Considering that neither the treatment needs nor the observed interventions (mandatory psychiatric treatment vs. prison, respectively) for these groups were equivalent, the impact of each intervention is difficult to judge. However, one intriguing finding was reported: individuals in the first group (psychiatric treatment) released to the community who had been violent offenders were recorded for committing new offences during the 3-year outcome period at a lower rate than those who had been imprisoned for violent offences. However, property offenders from both groups re-offended at comparable rates, suggesting that community interventions for individuals with mental disorders might be more effective in reducing the risk of violent behaviour than property offending.

Another study considered the influence of specialized forensic community treatment of mentally disordered offenders in Germany who were sentenced to a hospital as an alternative to prison, meeting the criteria for (a) diminished or absent criminal responsibility, and (b) high risk for future serious offending (Müller-Isberner, 1996). Following conditional release from hospitalization, one group of individuals ($n = 56$) was treated in the community through a specialized forensic psychiatric clinic, while another group ($n = 67$) did not receive that specific aftercare. In the latter group, about one-third had no aftercare at all, and the remainder received services through non-forensic outpatient institutions (e.g. homes for the mentally ill, rehabilitation centres and psychiatrists in private practice). A higher proportion of the patients assigned to the clinic had initial offences involving a violent crime or arson (89%) than did those not receiving services from the clinic (76%), perhaps reflecting a tendency to assign "higher-risk" patients to receive clinic services following release into the community. Even so, the percentage of clinic patients who were detected for another violent offence, or arson, was lower than the percentage of non-clinic patients (5% vs. 12%, respectively, over outcome periods of 32 and 31 months, respectively). While the absence of random assignment or matching to these groups makes it impossible to draw firm conclusions about the impact of the specialized clinic, the reported results of a lower recidivism rate with a possibly higher-risk group is consistent with other findings discussed in this section on the risk-reducing impact of specialized forensic community intervention.

Several studies have examined the influence of various kinds of psychopathology on criminal recidivism. The diagnosis of schizophrenia was considered in one study involving individuals diagnosed with schizophrenia who had been treated in a maximum security facility and subsequently released (n = 96). They were compared with a matched sample of individuals who did not meet the criteria for schizophrenia and who had been evaluated but not treated at this facility (n = 96). They were also compared with all subjects evaluated or admitted between 1975 and 1981 (Rice & Harris, 1992). Over an outcome period that ranged from initial contact (between 1975 and 1981) to final rating (in 1988), individuals with schizophrenia showed a significantly lower rate of criminal recidivism than comparison subjects (35% vs. 53%) and a somewhat lower rate of violent recidivism (16% vs. 24%), although the offences did appear less severe. This difference in the rate of violent recidivism between these two groups was not statistically significant, however.

The nature of the comparison group is important in determining how a certain factor relates to an outcome such as crime or violence. In the Rice and Harris (1992) study, individuals with schizophrenia were compared with another group that contained individuals at relatively high risk for reoffending (such as psychopaths), so it appeared that schizophrenia was associated with a lower risk for offending. However, if individuals with schizophrenia or other forms of severe mental disorder were compared with those in the general population without mental disorder, these mental disorders might be associated with higher rates of violent behaviour.[6]

In another study, the importance of mental illness as a risk factor for criminal behaviour was considered (Feder, 1991). Offenders who required psychiatric hospitalization as part of prison incarceration (n = 147) were compared with those who did not (n = 400) over an 18-month period following hospital release. No significant differences were found between these two groups in the rates or types of re-arrest, except in drug offences (12% of the non-mentally ill group were arrested for drug offences, while 5% of the mentally ill group were arrested for such offences). Age and prior criminal record were associated with re-arrest risk for both groups in this study.

Diagnosis as a risk factor for reoffending has also been considered (Hodgins & Gaston, 1989). Five groups of individuals (total n = 181) who had been found "incompetent to stand trial" or NGRI in Quebec during 1973–1975 were distinguished, using discriminant function analysis (DFA) (see footnote 3 for a brief explanation of DFA): (a) career criminals; (b) chronic schizophrenics; (c) violent psychotics; (d) violent middle-class

---

[6] For example, a re-analysis of the data collected in the Epidemiologic Catchment Area study, a large-scale, multi-site project conducted during the early 1980s in the USA, found that the presence of obsessive-compulsive disorder, panic disorder, major depression, major depression with grief, mania or bipolar disorder, or schizophrenia or schizophreniform disorder raised the frequency of self-reported violent behaviour during the last year from 2% (without these disorders) to 10–12%. Drug abuse was a stronger risk factor, raising the self-reported violence rate to 19% (cannabis), 25% (alcohol) and 35% (other drugs) (Swanson et al., 1990). This study is not included among those formally reviewed in this chapter because the participants were not in the groups on which we have focused in the present discussion.

individuals; and (e) intellectually handicapped individuals (for a fuller description of this cohort, see Hodgins, 1983). These groups differed in the severity of their offending and the length of their sentences when followed for an average of 6.1 years in the community following hospital discharge. However, they did not differ in the frequency of their rehospitalization. "Career criminals" committed the least number of violent crimes, and intellectually handicapped individuals committed the most.[7] The authors cautioned that the latter finding particularly needed replication.

The association between (a) diagnostic and demographic characteristics, and (b) future criminal behaviour was investigated in a sample of 611 young adult patients who received public inpatient, outpatient and community residential care in Missouri (Holcomb & Ahr, 1988). Substance abuse and "organic brain syndrome" (now usually called "organic mental disorder") were associated with higher rates of offending during the 1 year outcome period, while schizophrenia, major affective disorder and personality disorder were associated with lower overall rates of offending. These five groups did not differ in their rates of re-offending for *violent* offences, however. Demographic characteristics associated with re-offending included younger age and minority group membership. A higher number of life-time felony arrests and a younger age at which public mental health services were first received were also associated with higher overall re-offence risk.

The role of psychopathy as a risk factor for mentally disordered offenders (n = 169) released from maximum security psychiatric hospitalization in Canada and followed over an average outcome period of 10 years has been described (Harris, Rice & Cormier, 1991). Psychopathy was measured by the Psychopathy Checklist (completed on a "file only" basis). Psychopathy was a strong risk factor for violent re-offending, with 77% of psychopaths but only 40% of the total sample committing a violent offence during the outcome period. These differences in violent re-offending were seen even for individuals over 40 years old (which is inconsistent with the clinical wisdom that psychopaths "burn out" after 40). It is also important that the predictive power of psychopathy alone was not improved by adding historical, demographic or clinical variables.

A study of three groups of NGRI acquittees (n = 61) in Oklahoma—those released at an initial court review, those who completed the NGRI treatment programme, and those who escaped from secure hospitalization—revealed that those who had escaped during hospitalization had significantly more previous and subsequent arrests than those who had been discharged from treatment (Nicholson, Norwood & Enyart, 1991). The follow-up period in this study averaged more than 2.5 years. During this time, 16.6% of patients were re-arrested, 16.6% were rehospitalized, and 16.6% were both re-arrested and rehospitalized.

---

[7] For a fuller discussion of patterns of criminal behaviour among mentally retarded persons, when compared with those without mental retardation, see e.g. Crocker & Hodgins (1997).

Finally, there are several studies that are important because they identify risk factors for violence and crime in the community. In a study conducted by the MacArthur Research Network on Mental Health and Law (Steadman et al., 1998), a total of 1136 male and female patients aged 18–40 with mental disorders were monitored for violence towards others every 10 weeks during the first year following discharge from psychiatric hospitalization, and these results were compared with violence toward others by a comparison group (n = 519) that was randomly sampled from the same census tracts as the discharged patient group. Outcome behaviour was divided into two categories of seriousness: violence (battery resulting in physical injury, sexual assaults, and threats with a weapon) and other aggressive acts (battery that did not result in a physical injury). Information sources included self-report (every 10 weeks), collateral report (every 10 weeks) and agency records (arrest, hospitalization). Major findings included: (a) the co-occurrence of a substance abuse diagnosis with major mental disorders in 40–50% of cases; (b) the significant addition of self-report and collateral report to the identified frequency of violence and other aggressive acts beyond the frequency reflected in official records, raising this rate from 4.5% to 27.5% for violence and from 8.8% to 56.1% for other aggressive acts during index period; (c) substance abuse was associated with increased frequency of both serious violence and other aggressive acts; (d) the patient group without substance abuse did not differ from the community control group without substance abuse in the frequency of either violence or other aggressive acts; (e) patients had symptoms of substance abuse more often than community controls; and (f) the patient group showed a greater risk of violence and other aggressive acts than community controls when both experienced symptoms of substance abuse, particularly during the period immediately following hospital discharge. This study did not address a particular intervention or programme, but strongly suggested that patients with co-occurring psychotic and substance abuse disorders should be considered at higher risk (a finding consistent with other recent European studies; see e.g. Modestin & Ammann, 1995; Raesaenen et al., 1998; Tiihonen et al., 1997). It also underscored the importance of the use of collateral information in estimating most accurately the frequency with which violence occurs.

WHAT DO WE KNOW ABOUT THE EFFICACY AND EFFECTIVENESS OF COMMUNITY TREATMENT PROGRAMMES IN PREVENTING CRIME AND VIOLENCE?

The literature does not provide much good empirical research about the impact of specific programmes or particular interventions in reducing the risk of future non-violent crime or violent behaviour in mentally disordered offenders. As may be seen from the studies reviewed in this chapter, most of the relevant research has used either single groups or two groups in a non-experimental design. It would take a significant change in research approaches in this area to allow a meta-analysis estimating effect sizes for intervention studies. However, it is just such information that would be most useful to programme planners, treatment agents and policy-makers involved with issues of public safety and rehabilitation for mentally disordered offenders in hospital and community settings.

Despite this caution, however, it is possible to summarize several considerations that are empirically supported in designing community programmes and delivering interventions to reduce violence and criminality. The first sounds simplistic, but cannot be ignored: the programme must prioritize the prevention of violence and criminality among its most important goals and communicate this priority to staff, clients and others. Several influences may be incorporated toward this end: conditional release; increased intensity of outpatient case management; specialized programming designed for skills-based training among the severely mentally ill and delivered by those experienced with forensic populations; the delivery of a range of services, including housing support and vocational assistance as well as clinical treatment; and a particular focus on rehabilitating and preventing substance abuse (whether it occurs as a primary diagnosis or co-occurs with a major mental disorder)—these can all help to reduce the risk of violence. It may be possible to reduce the risk of violent behaviour more than that of property offending, so violence may be more treatable as well as being clearly more problematic when it occurs. When programmes incorporate these services and conditions to the greatest extent possible, they are guided by the best empirical literature that is currently available.

Another important step is a good individualized assessment. A plan designed to minimize the risk for crime and violence in the community would consider relevant risk factors and determine which apply to the individual. Relevant risk factors may be divided into static variables (those that do not change through planned intervention, such as age, gender and criminal history) and dynamic variables (with the potential to change through intervention, such as substance abuse and medication non-compliance). The two-stage process of assessing risk that may be seen in some of the recent risk assessment tools, such as the HCR-20 (Webster et al., 1995a) and the Violence Prediction Scheme (Webster et al., 1995b) allows both *a priori* classification of risk, based primarily on static risk factors combined actuarially, and a section on dynamic risk factors that are relevant to risk reduction intervention planning. When both stages are administered to an individual in a community programme, there are resulting implications for the intensity of the interventions and monitoring (presumably higher for higher-risk individuals) and the nature of the interventions (delivered to address the individuals' relevant risk factors). This kind of approach is designed to focus planning and service delivery in areas that are "criminogenic" (risk reducing), and function to divert individuals from further criminal behaviour, and help them build the skills that would allow them to lead responsible lives.

The second way in which community programmes can function to prevent crime and violence is to function effectively, broadly speaking. Certain principles of effective community-based forensic treatment programmes have been described previously (Heilbrun & Griffin, 1998; Griffin, Steadman & Heilbrun, 1991) and others can be added, based on the current review:

1. Use conditional release, parole or probation as a mechanism for designing and implementing treatment and monitoring compliance.
2. Communication encompassing both criminal justice and mental health personnel is essential for success.
3. Clarify the legal requirements in areas such as confidentiality and duty to protect, specific reporting demands (e.g. child abuse) and malpractice.
4. There must be an explicit balance between individual rights, the need for treatment and public safety.
5. Set, practise and monitor sound "risk management" procedures, including risk assessment and intervention planning, obtaining records, questioning clients regarding violent thoughts and acts, and communicating such information as indicated.
6. It is important to know the range of supervision and treatment needs of clients who will be served in the community, particularly "criminogenic" factors such as anger control, vocational skills, co-occurring disorders and housing support.
7. Treat and monitor high-risk clients more intensely.
8. Allow clients to demonstrate increasing degrees of responsibility through progressively less intense levels of monitoring and greater levels of privilege.
9. Practise principles promoting health care compliance, including specification of the conditions and expectations for treatment and the consequences for violating these conditions.
10. Develop a uniform system of treatment and supervision, to be applied within a network of community services.

IMPLICATIONS

Practice

The implications for practice in delivering community services to mentally disordered offenders that will effectively reduce their risk for further crime and violence are limited by the absence of evidence on "empirically validated treatments" for this outcome. Nonetheless, it is possible to identify implications for practice from the present review of the literature.

1. *Risk assessment should be done in two steps, involving actuarial risk classification and individualized assessment of dynamic risk factors relevant to intervention.* Several risk tools have been developed within the last 5 years that would apply to mentally disordered offenders generally (see e.g. the HCR-20, Webster et al., 1995a; and the Violence Prediction Scheme, Webster et al., 1995b). Others have been developed with more specialized populations such as the domestically violent [see e.g. Spousal Assault Risk Assessment (SARA), Kropp et al., 1994] and sexual offenders [see e.g. the Violence Risk Appraisal Guide (VRAG), Rice & Harris, 1997, as applied to sexual offenders]. Not all such tools provide both steps, and it may be necessary for the evaluators to individualize the assessment when using an actuarial tool such as the VRAG. If both steps are taken, then useful information for planning treatment and monitoring is available from the beginning. It is also useful to assess protective factors— influences that would incline the client away from crime and violence— and allow the building of strength in these areas in addition to attempting to improve risk-relevant deficits.

2. *Overall programme planning should include the delivery of intervention for empirically common risk factors for mentally disordered offenders.* Such interventions would include treatment and monitoring for substance abuse, anger/impulse control, medication compliance, job skills, living circumstances, problem-solving skills, social support and related behavioural and attitudinal risk factors for crime and violence. Planning should also seek to identify protective factors that are not only the converse of deficits, but that may have some unique capacity to help the individual live responsibly.

3. *Behavioural contracting is useful in both fully informing the client of the conditions of treatment, in a way that is both clear and understandable, and enhancing the likelihood of compliance with these conditions.* Most clients whose community treatment is discussed in this chapter will have some form of legal oversight. Formal coercion is used, and there are consequences for non-compliance. However, less formal coercion can also be effective in enhancing compliance, and such a contract can incorporate the role of family, employers or other important individuals who may contribute to the effectiveness of treatment.

4. *Intensive case management/assertive community treatment/intensive parole should be employed for high-risk clients.* If such clients are accepted into a treatment programme, the staff should be clear about their needs and the indicated intensity of services to be delivered. Particularly dedicated and

specialized case managers with reasonable caseloads can make an important difference to the effectiveness of a programme in dealing with individuals who have a range of deficits, few protective factors, or particularly severe deficits inclining them towards offending.

5. *Careful monitoring should provide information that is used for multiple purposes.* The needs and status of each client being served should be prominent. However, information like this could also be used to address such questions as "what works" in the community. Programme evaluation and modifications in programme goals and services can be facilitated through the collection of such data and the maintenance of an aggregated data base.

Policy

1. *The development of policy on treating mentally disordered offenders in the community should be informed by successful programmes in other jurisdictions.* There are a number of examples of programmes that provide treatment to certain kinds of mentally disordered offenders in a way that strikes a reasonable balance between public safety, treatment needs and individual rights. Unfortunately, such programmes often do not publish or otherwise appear prominently in the literature, so that an effective search for model programmes often must rely more on a professional network than the published literature.

2. *Law and policy stemming from a single highly-publicized case are not likely to be effective.* Legislative changes made in the face of public outrage and fear, stemming from a small number of cases, may not only adversely affect the capacity of community programmes to offer sufficient flexibility to make treatment meaningful, but may also (on balance) fail to protect the public.

3. *Changes in policy should be made in light of the results of pilot testing and careful planning for implementation in a way that is well supported.* Some of the most adverse effects of hastily conceived legislation and policy include the failure to anticipate how it will be implemented, the insufficient amount of time available for pilot testing, and the failure to fund it adequately.

Research

1. *More controlled study of treatment interventions, specifically designed to address criminogenic deficits and strengthen protective factors, is needed.* This could be accomplished in the community through the introduction of

small pilot treatment programmes that could be contrasted with the outcomes obtained using the conditions of standard parole or conditional release. Since such programmes would be small, it might be possible to select participants on a random basis and obtain a clearer view of the impact of the programme itself.

2. *Increased collaboration between external researchers and programmes, or research by programme staff, would help to facilitate such research.* Some examples of community treatment programmes for mentally disordered offenders have been developed as part of a collaboration between an agency or board and external researchers from a nearby university. This allows researchers to examine a process and participants that cannot be replicated with other populations or in other settings; it allows programmes to obtain better data, possibly more external funding, and a better capacity for disseminating findings than would otherwise be the case.

3. *Research in this area can also be facilitated through the use of naturally occurring "experiments".* Changes in law or policy, or policy that mandates that some participants will be under jurisdiction for only a limited period of time, provide useful opportunities to examine the influence of important considerations, such as the intensity of treatment and monitoring, the form of coercion (formal vs. informal), the durability of reduction in offending across changes in legal circumstances, and the "survival times" for outcomes such as substance abuse relapse, medication non-compliance and other risk factors relevant to offending.

ACKNOWLEDGEMENTS

We are grateful to Joseph Bloom, Sheilagh Hodgins, Kim Mueser, Rudolph Müller-Isberner and Hank Steadman for their helpful comments on earlier versions of this chapter.

REFERENCES

Belfrage, H. (1991). The crime preventive effect of psychiatric treatment on mentally disordered offenders in Sweden. *International Journal of Law and Psychiatry*, **14**, 237–243.

Bigelow, D. A., Bloom, J. D. & Williams, M. H. (1990). Costs of managing insanity acquittees under a psychiatric security review board system. *Hospital and Community Psychiatry*, **41**, 613–614.

Bloom, J. D., Bradford, J. M. & Kofoed, L. (1988). An overview of psychiatric treatment approaches to three offender groups. *Hospital and Community Psychiatry*, **39**, 151–158.

Bloom, J. D., Rogers, J. & Manson, S. (1982). After Oregon's insanity defense: a comparison of conditional release and hospitalization. *International Journal of Law and Psychiatry*, **5**, 391–402.

Bloom, J. D., Rogers, J., Manson, S. & Williams, M. (1986a). Lifetime police contacts of discharged Psychiatric Security Review Board clients. *International Journal of Law and Psychiatry*, **8**, 189–202.

Bloom, J. D., Williams, M., Rogers, J. & Barbur, P. (1986b). Evaluation and treatment of insanity acquittees in the community. *Bulletin of the American Academy of Psychiatry and the Law*, **14**, 231–244.

Bloom, J. D., Williams, M. H. & Bigelow, D. A. (1991). Monitored conditional release of persons found Not Guilty by Reason of Insanity. *American Journal of Psychiatry*, **148**, 444–448.

Bloom, J. D., Williams, M. H. & Bigelow, D. (1992). The involvement of schizophrenic insanity acquittees in the mental health and criminal justice systems. *Psychiatric Clinics of North America*, **15**, 591–604.

Bloom, J. L. & Bloom, J. D. (1981). Disposition of insanity defenses in Oregon. *Bulletin of the American Academy of Psychiatry & the Law*, **9**, 93–100.

Bonta, J., Law, M. & Hanson, K. (1998). The prediction of criminal and violent recidivism among mentally disordered offenders: a meta-analysis. *Psychological Bulletin*, **123**, 123–142.

Cohen, M. I., Spodak, M. K., Silver, S. B. & Williams, K. (1988). Predicting outcome of insanity acquittees released to the community. *Behavioral Sciences and the Law*, **6**, 515–530.

Conditional Release Program for the Judicially Committed (1985). Sacramento, CA: Department of Mental Health.

Crocker, A. G. & Hodgins, S. (1997). The criminality of non-institutionalized mentally retarded persons: evidence from a birth cohort followed to age 30. *Criminal Justice and Behavior*, **24**, 432–454.

Feder, L. (1991). A comparison of the community adjustment of mentally ill offenders with those from the general prison population. *Law and Human Behavior*, **15**, 477–493.

Gordon, D., Arbuthnot, J. & Jurkovic, G. (1998). Treatment of the juvenile offender. In R. M. Wettstein (Ed.), *Treatment of Offenders with Mental Disorder* (pp. 365–428). New York: Guilford.

Griffin, P. A., Steadman, H. J. & Heilbrun, K. (1991). Designing conditional release systems for insanity acquittees. *Journal of Mental Health Administration*, **18**, 231–241.

Harris, G. T., Rice, M. E. & Cormier, C. A. (1991). Psychotherapy and violent recidivism. *Law and Human Behavior*, **15**, 625–637.

Heilbrun, K. (1997). Prediction vs. management models relevant to risk assessment: the importance of legal decision-making cohort. *Law and Human Behavior*, **21**, 347–359.

Heilbrun, K. & Griffin, P. (1993). Community-based forensic treatment of insanity acquittees. *International Journal of Law and Psychiatry*, **16**, 133–150.

Heilbrun, K. & Griffin, P. (1998). Community-based forensic treatment. In R. Wettstein (Ed.), *Treatment of Offenders with Mental Disorders* (pp. 168–210). New York: Guilford.

Heilbrun, K. & Griffin, P. (1999). Forensic treatment: the state of the discipline. In R. Roesch, S. Hart & J. Ogloff (Eds), *Law and Psychology: The State of the Discipline* (pp. 242–274). New York: Kluwer Academic/Plenum.

Hodgins, S. (1983). A follow-up study of persons found incompetent to stand trial and/or not guilty by reason of insanity in Quebec. *International Journal of Law and Psychiatry*, **6**, 399–411.

Hodgins, S. & Gaston, L. (1989). Patterns of recidivism and relapse among groups of mentally disordered offenders. *Behavioral Sciences and the Law*, **7**, 551–558.

Holcomb, W. R. & Ahr, P. R. (1988). Arrest rates among young adult psychiatric patients treated in inpatient and outpatient settings. *Hospital and Community Psychiatry*, **39**, 52–27.

Kropp, P. R., Hart, S. D., Webster, C. D. & Eaves, D. (1994). *Manual for the Spousal Assault Risk Assessment Guide*. Vancouver: British Columbia Institute on Family Violence.

McGreevy, M. A., Steadman, H. J., Dvoskin, J. A. & Dollard, N. (1991). New York State's system of managing insanity acquittees in the community. *Hospital and Community Psychiatry*, **42**, 512–517.

Modestin, J. & Ammann, R. (1995). Mental disorders and criminal behaviour. *British Journal of Psychiatry*, **166**, 667–675.

Müller-Isberner, J. R. (1996). Forensic psychiatric aftercare following hospital order treatment. *International Journal of Law and Psychiatry*, **19**, 81–86.

Nicholson, R. A., Norwood, S. & Enyart, C. (1991). Characteristics and outcomes of insanity acquittees in Oklahoma. *Behavioral Sciences and the Law*, **9**, 487–500.

Raesaenen, P., Tiihonen, J., Isohanni, M., Rantakallio, P., Lehtonen, J. & Moring, J. (1998). Schizophrenia, alcohol abuse, and violent behavior: a 26-year follow-up study of an unselected birth cohort. *Schizophrenia Bulletin*, **24**, 437–441.

Rice, M. E. & Harris, G. T. (1992). A comparison of criminal recidivism among schizophrenic and non-schizophrenic offenders. *International Journal of Law and Psychiatry*, **15**, 397–408.

Rice, M. E. & Harris, G. T. (1997). Cross-validation and extension of the violence risk appraisal guide for child molesters and rapists. *Law and Human Behavior*, **21**, 231–241.

Silver, S. B., Cohen, M. & Spodak, M. (1989). Follow-up after release of insanity acquittees, mentally disordered offenders, and convicted felons. *Bulletin of the American Academy of Psychiatry and Law*, **17**, 387–400.

Solomon, P. & Draine, J. (1995). One-year outcomes of a randomized trial of ease management with seriously mentally ill clients leaving jail. *Evaluation Reviews*, **19**, 256–273.

Solomon, P., Draine, J. & Meyerson, A. (1994). Jail recidivism and receipt of community mental health services. *Hospital and Community Psychiatry*, **45**, 793–797.

Steadman, H. J., Monahan, J., Hartstone, E., Davis, S. & Robbins, P. C. (1982). Mentally disordered offenders: a national survey of patients and facilities. *Laws and Human Behavior*, **6**, 31–38.

Steadman, H. J., Mulvey, E., Monahan, J., Robbins, P., Appelbaum, P., Grisso, T., Roth, L. & Silver, E. (1998). Violence by people discharged from acute psychiatric inpatient facilities and by others in the same neighborhoods. *Archives of General Psychiatry*, **55**, 1–9.

Swanson, J., Holzer, C., Ganju, V. & Jono, R. (1990). Violence and psychiatric disorder in the community: evidence from the Epidemiologic Catchment Area Surveys. *Hospital and Community Psychiatry*, **41**, 761–770.

Swartz, H., Swanson, J., Wagner, H. R., Burns, B., Hiday, V. & Borum, R. (in press). Can outpatient commitment reduce hospital recidivism? Findings from a randomized trial in severely mentally ill individuals. *American Journal of Psychiatry*.

Tarasoff vs. Regents of University of California, 529 P.2d 553 (CA., 1974).

Tellefsen, C., Cohen, M. I., Silver, S. B. & Dougherty, C. (1992). Predicting success on conditional release for insanity acquittees: regionalized versus non-regionalized hospital patients. *Bulletin of the American Academy of Psychiatry and Law*, **20**, 87–100.

Tiihonen, J., Isohanni, M., Raesaenen, P., Koiranen, M. & Moring, J. (1997). Specific major mental disorders and criminality: a 26-year prospective study of the 1996 Northern Finland Birth Cohort. *American Journal of Psychiatry*, **154**, 840–845.

Webster, C. D., Eaves, D., Douglas, K. & Wintrup, A. (1995a). *The HCR-20 Scheme: The Assessment of Dangerousness and Risk*. Burnaby, BC: Simon Fraser University.

Webster, C. D., Harris, G., Rice, M., Cormier, V. & Quinsey, V. (1995b). *The Violence Prediction Scheme: Assessing Dangerousness in High Risk Men*. Toronto, Ontario: University of Toronto Centre of Criminology.

Wells, K. (1999). Treatment research at the crossroads: the scientific interface of clinical trials and effectiveness research. *American Journal of Psychiatry*, **156**, 5–10.

Wiederanders, M. (1992). Recidivism of disordered offenders who were conditionally vs. unconditionally released. *Behavioral Sciences and the Law*, **10**, 141–148.

Wiederanders, M. R., Bromley, D. L. & Choate, P. A. (1997). Forensic conditional release programs and outcomes in three states. *International Journal of Law and Psychiatry*, **20**, 249–257.

Wilson, D., Tien, G. & Eaves, D. (1995). Increasing the community tenure of mentally disordered offenders: an assertive case management program. *International Journal of Law and Psychiatry*, **18**, 61–69.

Chapter 10

CONCLUSION

SHEILAGH HODGINS

University of Montreal, Quebec, Canada, and The Karolinska Institute, Stockholm, Sweden

CONCLUSION

As the preceding chapters in this volume demonstrate, the development of an empirical foundation for the treatment of mentally disordered offenders is in its infancy. However, basing treatment on proof of efficacy is required in order to respect professionals' codes of ethics and to be accountable to the public for the use of their taxes. Building an empirical foundation involves importing components of treatment that have been shown to be effective elsewhere or with other populations and modifying, implementing and evaluating their impact on various types of mentally disordered offenders.

WHY BASE TREATMENT ON EMPIRICAL FINDINGS?

Basing treatment on demonstrated effectiveness has numerous. positive consequences. First, it is the only way to improve the efficacy and cost-effectiveness of treatment. Second, it provides feedback and encouragement to staff and allows them to be proud of what they accomplish. This is critical because often they are judged negatively, both by the public and by

Violence, Crime and Mentally Disordered Offenders. Edited by S. Hodgins and R. Müller-Isberner.
© 2000 John Wiley & Sons, Ltd.

themselves, on the basis of a small number of sensational incidents of re-offending. Generally, the failures get a lot of attention and the successes go largely unnoticed. The third positive consequence of basing treatment on empirical findings is that it makes the jobs of both professional and non-professional staff more interesting. Staff are motivated to read books and journals and to participate in presentations in order to learn about the implementation and evaluations of treatments similar to those they are conducting and, in time, they can present evidence of the effectiveness of their treatments. Fourth, such an approach provides clinical staff and administrators with hard evidence that can be used to defend the treatment of mentally disordered offenders. Such data are necessary for ensuring appropriate long-term stable funding. They are also very useful for convincing journalists and politicians of the positive impact of treatment and for putting into perspective particularly lurid occurrences of recidivism. Another positive consequence of basing treatment on proof of efficacy and of evaluating components of treatment and the overall programme is that, in so doing, clinicians and administrators begin to collaborate with researchers. This lessens the isolation and marginalization of mental health professionals who work with forensic patients. As staff collect data on the efficacy of their treatment, they can venture out of their own work milieu and present their findings to other professionals. Giving talks to other clinicians and administrators not only provides them with feedback about their own work, but fosters and facilitates learning about what goes on in similar settings elsewhere and about new treatments that may be modified and adapted for use with mentally disordered offenders.

HOW TO BASE TREATMENT ON EMPIRICAL FINDINGS?

Modifying interventions for use with mentally disordered offenders

As the chapters in this book have demonstrated, the initial step in developing an empirical foundation for the treatment of mentally disordered offenders is to import components of treatment that have been shown to be effective with other types of patients and to modify them for use with a particular group of mentally disordered offenders. Whether the authors were describing treatments for brain-damaged patients, offenders with personality disorders, or offenders with major mental disorders, they all identified interventions that have been used successfully with other populations and proposed adapting them for a particular group of mentally disordered offenders. The authors were able to do this, in large part, because they were not preoccupied with the diagnosis of the patient. Rather they focused on precise cognitive, emotional and/or behavioural patterns as targets of treatment. The consensus among the authors on this point is important to note. It marks a significant departure from traditional psychiatric treatment, which facilitates the development of treatment based on proof of efficacy.

As was discussed in Chapter 1, and demonstrated in the subsequent chapters, modifying specific treatment components for use with mentally disordered offenders is not easy. One of the difficulties involves adapting the treatment to the patient's legal status. For example, many of the interventions that have been identified as effective were developed for use in the community. Using them inside security hospitals and prisons involves, among other things, ensuring that patients have opportunities to practise new skills that they are learning. The effectiveness of learning-based interventions is increased if, during the course of the intervention, the patient can practise newly-learned skills, consult staff about difficulties and problems experienced in trying to use these newly-learned skills in the real world, and use the support of the treatment programme to help organize a life in the community that does not include situations which increase the risk of re-offending. Importing treatments used with other clienteles for use with mentally disordered offenders also involves deciding when the treatment will be most beneficial. For example, it may be more beneficial to offer specific interventions involving learning how to function in the community only in the months preceding discharge. Otherwise, depending on the length of detention, there may be too long a delay between the treatment and discharge. Adapting interventions for use with mentally disordered offenders also means modifying them to take account of the fact that those who conduct the treatment cannot make decisions about discharge. This limits the positive reinforcers that they control and can offer to the patients. This is often the most powerful reinforcer, the one the patients want most.

Evaluation studies have shown that one of the essential ingredients of many effective interventions relates to staff characteristics and staff's relationship with the patients. Given the different relationship that forensic clinicians have with their patients as compared to that of mental health professionals generally, adapting interventions means adjusting to the fact that in many situations forensic clinicians cannot guarantee their patients confidentiality, as well as not being able to provide patients with the rewards that they value most highly. For example, when a patient is learning a new skill or learning not to engage in an illegal behaviour, it is not unusual that he/she will make a mistake. Ideally, the mistake will be discussed with treatment staff and ways of avoiding further mistakes identified. Learning proceeds quickly and efficiently when appropriate behaviours are positively reinforced and inappropriate behaviours are sanctioned. The more often this occurs, the more rapidly the appropriate response is learned. Allowing inappropriate behaviours to go unsanctioned seriously hinders learning. Yet, if patients cannot trust staff to keep information confidential, they probably will not tell them about inappropriate behaviours, and consequently the behaviour will not be sanctioned. This seriously limits learning. However, if clinicians are required by law to report offences, patients must be informed at the beginning of treatment. This will likely lower the effectiveness of treatment. Because staff are required to behave as agents of social control, and because they cannot make the most important decisions about patients, their relationships with patients may be less open and trusting than those between staff and non-offender patients, and they may consequently have less influence on patients.

In order to be effective, all interventions have to be adapted to the characteristics of the patient. In adapting interventions shown to be effective with other clienteles to mentally disordered offenders, it is necessary to match the requirements of the specific intervention and the characteristics of the patient. The relevant characteristics are determined by the requirements of the intervention. For example, certain physical characteristics must be present in order to use certain pharmacological agents. An ability to think abstractly and concentrate must be present in order to participate in a cognitive training programme. Reading skills are required for many job-training programmes. When patients do not have the ability or skill necessary for a particular intervention, either the skill can be taught (patients learn to read and then go to job training) or the intervention can be modified to take account of the patient's characteristics. This has to be done, for example, in adapting learning-based interventions for patients with low intelligence. In addition, however, forensic patients often present specific characteristics that limit their compliance and participation in any form of treatment. For example, patients who are very impulsive have great difficulty participating in an intervention which requires them to cooperate with other patients and confront unknown and/or frustrating situations. They may have to be take medications which lessen impulsivity or learn to control their behaviour before beginning specific training programmes. Patients who react to even minor problems in an emotional rather than an instrumental way need to learn how to analyse and solve problems before beginning more specific training programmes. Psychotic patients have to be treated with medication so that their delusions and hallucinations are at a minimum before participating in learning-based programmes. In other words, it is necessary to make a hierarchy of patient characteristics that may interfere with compliance and success in specific interventions, and then to decide on the order in which they will be treated.

Regardless of their primary diagnosis, many mentally disordered offenders present a history of antisocial behaviour that goes back to childhood. This characteristic limits their compliance with any form of treatment. In adapting interventions that have been shown to be effective with other clienteles to mentally disordered offenders, it is also necessary to identify strategies that increase the likelihood of compliance. This is a major challenge that will only be successfully met by evaluating and refining different strategies. It is necessary to identify a strategy for ensuring compliance for each type of patient with each component of treatment. In many cases, it may be necessary to use the law. Patients can be legally required to complete a particular treatment programme in lieu of incarceration. Short-term involuntary hospitalizations can be used to stabilize patients with major mental disorders. Legal powers are a clinical tool often necessary to ensure compliance of mentally disordered offenders, especially those who have a life-long history of antisocial behaviour. As noted in Chapter 9, and elsewhere (Hodgins, Lapalme & Toupin, 1999; Hodgins, in press), such legal powers appear to be one of the clinical tools necessary to prevent criminality and/or violence among persons with mental disorders.

One way to increase compliance may be to organize the sequence of interventions so that the characteristics which appear to be most important in limiting compliance and for successful participation are addressed first. However, there are no data available on how to do this. For example, is it better to use the programmes designed to limit antisocial thinking before, during or after treatment for alcohol abuse? To ensure compliance in the alcohol abuse programme, the modification of antisocial ideas is probably necessary. On the other hand, compliance in modifying antisocial ideas cannot be assured if the patient is drinking. Such questions can only be answered empirically.

The more complete and accurate the information gathered during the assessment, the better able the clinicians will be to design an individualized treatment plan likely to be effective. This information (if readable, accessible, precise, complete and objective) is used to distinguish between those who benefit from the intervention and those who do not. The matching of patient characteristics and needs to interventions has major implications for the organization of treatment services for mentally disordered offenders. Given the heterogeneity of mentally disordered offenders, and the heterogeneity even within diagnostic categories, the necessity of matching needs to services implies the availability of many different types of services. Specialized treatment programmes are required, both in institutions and in the community. The cost-effectiveness of treatment will be increased by locating these programmes in the same institution or same community, as some of the components of treatment will be included in programmes designed for several different types of patient. This argues in favour of large centralized security hospitals and correctional facilities which offer a wide array of different treatment programmes. It also argues for community programmes that are diverse. Not only do community programmes have to include multiple components of treatment to address the many problems presented by mentally disordered offenders, they also have to include a variety of housing arrangements with differing levels of care and a variety of levels of supervision and surveillance.

Evaluation and improvement of treatment programmes

In order to develop an empirical base for the treatment of mentally disordered offenders, it is necessary to embark upon a continual process of evaluation. In so doing, the lack of knowledge about effective treatments for this population is acknowledged and the procedure to remedy the situation is put in place. Evaluation has to become part of the clinical routine and daily clinical functioning. It is not something imposed from the outside by strangers, neither is it something that threatens staff or imposes extra work on them. It is an integral part of their work, undertaken to provide them with feedback so that they can modify their interventions and increase their effectiveness. Such thinking represents a radical departure from the traditional attitudes and training of most mental health professionals and administrators. However, it is required by professional ethics and public accountability, and the advantages in the medium and long term are numerous. This is true even though most hospitals and services for mentally disordered offenders are overcrowded, understaffed and have no control over admissions and discharges. Consequently, setting-up an evaluation programme requires motivation, enthusiasm and leadership on the part of senior staff and, probably, extra work.

Clinical evaluations conducted to identify effective treatments involve measuring how the patient changes as a result of the intervention. In order to be useful, the measures have to be appropriate, given the nature of the intervention (symptom scales to measure the effects of medication, a measure of social skills to measure the effect of a social skills training programme), in order to take account of any untoward effects of the intervention (side effects of medications, use of social skills to better manipulate the mentally retarded patients) and be easy to use (not take too long, not be difficult for either the patients or the staff). Researchers are experts in measurement. Collaboration with them can greatly enhance the quality of the evaluation and provide clinical staff and administrators with additional resources. In addition, researchers are knowledgeable about the measures that have been used elsewhere and that are described in scientific and professional journals. The psychometric properties of such instruments have been examined, and they are standardized and validated. Using them allows clinical staff to compare their patients with those described in the scientific literature. Not only does this serve to demarginalize forensic treatment staff, it also provides valuable information. For example, it may be that a particular intervention has been shown to be effective with a group of men with schizophrenia who have killed. But, when tried in another setting, there are few positive effects. One of the reasons for the difference in the effectiveness of the programme may be the characteristics of the patients. For example, the group who responded well to the intervention were those with a history of only one or two violent offences in the presence of systematic paranoid delusions, while those who did not respond to the intervention had a history of many non-violent as well as violent offences in the absence of delusions. Using standardized and validated measures before and after the intervention not only provides information on what has changed but also on why the change occurred or did not occur.

Step I—collecting information

A clinical programme of evaluation includes four steps. The first step is undertaken at admission and simply involves systematizing the information that is gathered at this time. As discussed in Chapter 1, the development of individualized treatment programmes is based on a thorough assessment which includes all aspects of the patient's functioning and a great deal of historical information. This information is essential for evaluating the effectiveness of the treatment which will follow, and especially for identifying which type of patient will comply with and benefit from a particular intervention. To be useful, the information has to be: *readable* (hand-written notes illegible to all but a few dedicated nurses are not readable); *accessible* (information is either easily extracted from files or computerized); *precise* to the extent possible (not "He always was aggressive", but rather descriptions of incidents and the consequences: "During the first year of school he was sent home numerous times for fighting, and in Grade 3 he was expelled for severely injuring another boy"); *complete* (the complete criminal record including infractions during adolescence, the complete history of psychiatric treatment, the history of conduct problems and substance abuse); must tap *multiple sources* (criminal files, hospital files, military records, employment records, school records, interview with family, interviews with the patient); and include as much *objective* information as is possible (records, intelligence test, neuropsychological tests, measures of personality traits, measures of aggressive behaviour). This information provides precise descriptions of the characteristics of the patients who complete a particular intervention.

Step II—measuring treatment targets

The second step in the evaluation involves measuring the target of the intervention before, during and after the intervention. The measure must be sensitive to all aspects of functioning that may reasonably be expected to change as a result of the intervention. The appropriate measures can often be identified in the studies that have reported on the effectiveness of the intervention and in manuals that describe the intervention. Home-made measures are not necessarily inadequate. The objective is simple: measure the target (symptom, behaviour, cognition, emotion) before, during and after the intervention in a feasible manner. Sometimes a home-made question-naire that the patients can complete themselves is sufficient and provides all the necessary information.

This second step also involves using the information collected at assessment to identify the type of patient that benefits from the intervention, those that do not benefit, and those that get worse. Subsequently, the intervention is only offered to patients resembling those who have benefited. For the others, it is necessary to find another intervention or to produce a modified version better adapted to their needs.

The second step in an evaluation programme also involves describing the profile of patients who comply with a particular intervention and the conditions under which they comply (threat of incarceration or rehospitalization, for example) and those who do not comply. An intervention cannot be effective if patients will not comply with it. Therefore, part of the clinical challenge is to identify strategies for increasing compliance. For many types of patients and interventions this is done regularly. For example, given the necessity for persons with major mental disorders to take medications on a long-term basis, strategies have been identified to increase compliance. These involve: education of the patient and family about the importance of medication; training programmes designed to teach patients how to identify the onset of an acute episode, to identify side-effects of medications, etc.; patient support groups; and, when nothing else has worked, injectable, long-acting medications that require patient compliance every two weeks rather than several times a day. As noted above, compliance can be accomplished by legal means, but formal compliance does not necessarily imply active compliance. That is, patients can comply to fulfil legal requirements without actually participating in the programme. This is what is often seen with offenders with antisocial personality disorder, and with psychopaths. In other words, clinical compliance signifies a lot more than simply complying with an order from a court or legal tribunal. It implies that the patient is motivated and wants to complete the treatment programme and that he/she acknowledges the need for it.

Step III—identifying an effective organization of treatment components

The third step in evaluation is determining the most effective order for the various interventions. Given the multiple problems of mentally disordered offenders that must each be addressed by different treatment components, it is essential to determine how to organize all these interventions in order to ensure effectiveness. Certain interventions may potentiate each other and are thereby more effective if undertaken at the same time. Some interventions necessarily precede others. For example, the psychotic symptoms of patients with major mental disorders have to be reduced before they can participate in a life skills training programme.

Step IV—measuring relapse and recidivism

The fourth step in evaluating a treatment programme involves documenting long-term outcome. This means setting up a system of feedback to the treatment programme which includes information on relapse and recidivism. In countries with centralized health and criminal records this can be accomplished relatively easily, but of course involves obtaining the appropriate permissions for access to this information. In other countries, a specific tracking programme has to be established by the treatment programme. This work can often be facilitated by involving those who fund the treatment because information collected will provide them with a precise measure of the cost-effectiveness of the programme.

IMPORTANT MISSING KNOWLEDGE

In attempting to develop an empirical base for the treatment of mentally disordered offenders, four important issues warrant immediate attention. The first is the treatment of mentally retarded offenders. As noted in the introduction, there is almost no scientific literature on this subject, and what there is describes interventions designed to limit the aggressive behaviour of patients who live in institutions. Mentally retarded persons who offend are poorly assessed, simply because forensic experts have little or no training and experience with this clientele. They are often physically abused when sent to prison and are not capable of participating in the limited number of rehabilitation programmes that are offered. When sent to security hospitals or to community treatment programmes, there are often few components of the programmes adapted to their needs. This is probably a clientele that would respond well to behavioural interventions that are specifically adapted for them. There is an urgent need to identify mentally retarded offenders and to set up, conduct and evaluate treatment programmes aimed at preventing offending that are designed specifically for them. Such programmes will necessarily be long-term and include treatment components designed to teach how to resolve disagreements and conflicts without resorting to aggressive behaviour, how to budget and manage money, life skills, some social and sexual skills and, in certain milieux, job skills. They will involve matching the level of community supervision and care to the individual's need, and keeping mentally retarded offenders apart from offenders who can easily manipulate and abuse them.

A second aspect of the treatment of mentally disordered offenders that has been neglected are the special needs of female mentally disordered offenders. Mentally disordered women who offend are less numerous than males, but no less in need of treatment. Despite the low prevalence of offending among women, female offenders have a disproportionately nega-tive impact on society, as compared with males, because of their role as mothers. As can be noted in the descriptions of treatment for all the various sub-types of mentally disordered offenders, no attention is paid to sex dif-ferences. Mental health professionals, as well as jurists and policemen, do not expect women to behave violently. This positive discrimination, even when there is evidence of a history of aggressive behaviour, often leads to tragic situations.

The third aspect of the treatment of mentally disordered offenders that requires immediate attention is the development of interventions, adapted to the various types of mentally disordered offenders, that are designed to end substance abuse. Abuse of alcohol and other drugs is rampant in this popu-lation. It limits, if not nullifies, the positive effects of all other treatments, and significantly increases the risk of offending and of aggressive behaviour. This is not an easy task. Programmes that are adapted to the needs of the various categories of mentally disordered offenders have to be developed, tried, eval-uated, modified on the basis of the evaluation, tried again and again and modified again and again until they are shown to be effective.

An additional aspect of this problem needs attention. That is the use (as opposed to abuse) of alcohol by mentally disordered offenders. Because drugs are illegal, it is easy to identify drug use as a problem necessitating treatment. Alcohol, however, is a legal substance, but it increases the likeli-hood of aggressive behaviour and other types of illegal behaviour and limits the effectiveness of other forms of treatment. Whether or not certain types of mentally disordered offenders are especially sensitive to the effects of alco-hol in increasing aggression is still unknown. While clinicians generally identify incidents of serious abuse, binge drinking, and daily use of large amounts of alcohol as requiring treatment, there is no clinical consensus and no data on the consequences of more moderate alcohol use by mentally disordered offenders. Clinicians, especially front line staff, are often am-bivalent about prohibiting the use of alcohol for patients living in the com-munity. In many countries, alcohol use is normative behaviour. For example, in some cultures drinking a beer before dinner or wine with meals is usual. In such a culture, when a patient with schizophrenia and a history of offending describes having dinner with his/her family, which included a glass of beer or wine, he/she is praised for appropriate behaviour. However, we have no knowledge about the effects of the alcohol on the aggressive behaviour of someone with schizophrenia who is taking a particular com-bination of medications. Similarly, when an offender with an antisocial per-sonality disorder and a long history of substance abuse and non-violent offending, describes going to a bar with his brother for a beer, is this to be considered inappropriate behaviour? What happens if he and his brother drink three beers and then he goes home to find that his girlfriend is furious with him because he forgot that they had a date and he did not pay the rent? They get into a terrible argument and he hits her several times. Did the alcohol increase the likelihood of aggressive behaviour? Currently, alcohol use is often tolerated as it represents "normative behaviour". Yet, clinicians need more information about the consequences of social drinking by various types of mentally disordered offenders.

The fourth issue regarding the treatment of mentally disordered offenders which requires immediate attention is that of the effect of particular living environments on the risk of offending and/or violent behaviour. In other words, empirical data are required indicating how various living situations increase or decrease the risk of offending and violence for each type of offender. Little research has been conducted to assess the role of this factor in offending. Yet there are many hints in the literature that the living environment has a powerful effect on offending and aggressive behaviour. For example, since mental health services have been deinstitutionalized, there is an increase in offending among those with major mental disorders (Hodgins, 1998; Hodgins & Lalonde, 1999) and among the mentally retarded (Crocker & Hodgins, 1997). It has been shown that patients with schizophrenia who live with their families of origin are often the object of hostility and abuse which provokes aggressive behaviour (Estroff et al., 1998). Another study showed that patients with major mental disorders who were discharged to supervised apartments were witnesses to, victims of, and perpetrators of aggressive behaviour, and the longer they lived there the more symptomatic they became (Cyr et al., 1990). Given the policy that is in place in most countries, of allowing mentally disordered offenders to live in the community as much as possible, what are the living conditions which contribute to limiting offending? The available evidence, although sparse, suggests that a wide array of diverse living situations are necessary in order to take account of patient needs. These situations must be diverse with respect to the level of care and supervision they provide, the level of exposure to risk situations that they involve (a crowded downtown neighbourhood, a neighbourhood full of bars, petty criminals and drug dealers), and the skills that they require to cope. Some types of mentally disordered offenders, particularly some of the brain-damaged and mentally ill, may not have the capacity to develop the skills which allow them to live in the community without re-offending. On the other hand, they may function well in an environment that is less stressful than, for example, the centre of a large city, where they can work, be valued for the work that they accomplish and enjoy a level of autonomy that is not possible elsewhere. Programmes run in small rural communities and on farms may present effective alternatives for certain types of patients. This hypothesis needs testing. We need information about what living situations contribute to limiting offending for each type of mentally disordered offender.

THE NEXT STEP

An empirical foundation for the treatment of mentally disordered offenders is required, to fulfil both professional ethical requirements and public demands for accountability. There are many positive consequences to embarking on a project of constructing this knowledge base, including improved efficacy, ensuring continuous and stable funding, increased staff motivation and enthusiasm, and ending the isolation of forensic clinicians. Such a project involves adapting and modifying interventions that have proved effective with other clienteles to mentally disordered offenders, and integrating on-going evaluations of each intervention and of the overall programme into the clinical routine. It also involves developing specific programmes for the mentally retarded, assessing to what extent mentally disordered females require different treatments than their male counterparts, developing treatment programmes for substance abuse which are effective with the various types of mentally disordered offenders, and arranging living situations adapted to the capacities and needs of each type of mentally disordered offender.

REFERENCES

Crocker, A. G. & Hodgins, S. (1997). The criminality of non-institutionalized mentally retarded persons: evidence from a birth cohort followed to age 30. *Criminal Justice and Behavior*, **24**, 432–454.

Cyr, M., Hodgins, S., Gaston, L. & Viens, L. (1990). La vie au sein d'appartements surveillés pour patients psychiatriques chroniques. *Revue Canadienne de Santé Mentale Communautaire*, **9**, 23–38.

Estroff, S. E., Swanson, J. W., Lachicotte, W. S., Swartz, M. & Bolduc, M. (1998). Risk reconsidered: targets of violence in the social networks of people with serious psychiatric disorders. *Social Psychiatry and Epidemiology*, **33**(1), 95–101.

Hodgins, S. (1998). Epidemiological investigations of the associations between major mental disorders and crime: methodological limitations and validity of the conclusions. *Social Psychiatry and Epidemiology*, **33**(1), 29–37.

Hodgins, S. (in press). Major mental disorders and crime: stop debating and start treating and preventing. *International Journal of Law and Psychiatry*.

Hodgins, S. & Lalonde, N. (1999). Major mental disorders and crime: changes over time? In P. Cohen, C. Slomkowski & L. N. Robins (Eds), *Historical and Geographical Influences on Psychopathology* (pp. 57–83). Mahwah, NJ: Erlbaum.

Hodgins, S., Lapalme, M. & Toupin, J. (1999). Criminal activities and substance use of patients with major affective disorders and schizophrenia: a two year follow-up. *Journal of Affective Disorders*, **55**, 187–202.

INDEX